Integrated
Direct
Marketing

Integrated Direct Marketing

Techniques and Strategies for Success

Ernan Roman

Forewords by:

Bob Stone
Chairman Emeritus, Stone & Adler, Inc.

Jim Kobs
Chairman, Kobs & Brady Advertising, Inc.

McGraw-Hill Book Company

New York   St. Louis   San Francisco   Auckland
Bogotá   Hamburg   London   Madrid   Mexico
Milan   Montreal   New Delhi   Panama
Paris   São Paulo   Singapore
Sydney   Tokyo   Toronto

Library of Congress Cataloging-in-Publication Data

Roman, Ernan.
   Integrated direct marketing.

   Bibliography: p.
   Includes index.
   1. Direct marketing.   I. Title.
HF5415.126.R65   1988   658.8'4   87-37869
ISBN 0-07-053599-X

1234567890   DOC/DOC   893210987

ISBN 0-07-053599-X

*The editors for this book were William Sabin and Georgia Kornbluth, the
designer was Naomi Auerbach, and the production supervisor was Richard
A. Ausburn. It was set in Baskerville by the McGraw-Hill Book Company
Professional & Reference Division composition unit.*

Printed and bound by R. R. Donnelley & Sons Company.

IDM is a service mark of Ernan Roman Direct Marketing
Corporation.

The excerpt on page 3 was used by permission from *Webster's
Ninth New Collegiate Dictionary* © 1987 by Merriam-Webster, Inc.,
publisher of the Merriam-Webster® dictionaries.

For my wife Sheri,
the noblest Roman of us all,
whose support, insights, and understanding
made this book happen.

Contents

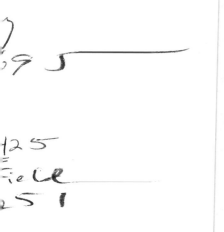

Foreword
by Bob Stone

been regarded by most people as a stand-
only a relative handful of visionaries have
rated direct marketing.

Ernan Roman is one of the visionaries who has identified IDM as the ultimate evolution of direct marketing and all that it has to offer. *Integrated Direct Marketing: Techniques and Strategies for Success* is the embodiment of the evolution, the next giant step forward.

As the author rightly acknowledges, the tools for IDM have long been available. And, for the most part, these tools and their refinements have been developed by stand-alone direct marketers.

During the explosive 1950s, 1960s, and 1970s, and into the equally explosive 1980s the stand-alones were in the forefront, developing break-through after breakthrough: multimedia synergisms, lifetime value (LTV), database management and marketing, recency-frequency-mon-etary (R-F-M) market overlays, regression analysis, strategic planning—all the tools we use now, with ever-increasing sophistication.

But the focus was stringently restricted to direct marketing as a sep-arate channel of distribution, as a separate profit center.

Other channels of distribution were viewed as *competitive*. Direct mar-keters cast themselves as mice trying to swallow elephants. Even the creative treatment was "different," attempting to establish a separate image, completely ignoring the value of millions of dollars already in-vested in highly successful image-building campaigns.

Integrated Direct Marketing eliminates the tunnel vision of the past. This book shows: How to identify "heavy users," utilizing direct marketing tools. How to integrate media and distribution channels. How to apply the two touchstones of direct marketing—measurability and accountability—to all marketing.

Ernan Roman's book could simply be regarded as a fascinating dissertation about a hypothesis, except for one thing: he documents his hypothesis with real-life case histories, backed by facts and figures.

A remarkable book. Well worth reading and applying!

BOB STONE, *Chairman Emeritus*
Stone & Adler, Inc.

Foreword

by Jim Kobs

This is probably the first book written by a second-generation direct marketer. And that in itself makes it rather special.

Some kids are born with silver spoons in their mouths. For Ernan Roman, it was more like a silver telephone. His father, the late Murray Roman, is also considered the father of telemarketing. He wrote books and articles, made many speeches, and established CCI, the telemarketing service bureau that provided Ernan's first taste of the business.

The direct marketing business has its roots in mail order and direct mail. But it wasn't until the late sixties that the term "direct marketing" came into use. We all owe a lot to the first generation of leaders in direct marketing: Bob Stone, Pete Hoke, Dick Hodgson, Bob DeLay, and the many others who helped us to make the transition to a multimedia environment, and to think of what we do as a database-driven marketing concept.

This first generation deserves all the credit for the tremendous growth direct marketing has had. Today, direct marketing is embraced by all types and sizes of organizations, from giant corporations to small stores on Main Street, because it's producing measurable, bottom-line results for them.

Sir Isaac Newton once said, "If I have seen further, it is by standing upon the shoulders of giants." My interpretation is that succeeding generations grow by standing on the shoulders of those who have gone before them. It's sort of like putting a kid on your shoulders at a crowded parade. He's got a better view of what has gone before—and what's ahead.

So it is with the second generation of direct marketers. The bright ones, like Ernan Roman, know what went before. Ernan was there when telemarketing was refined into what he calls a "fast, interactive link with our direct-response customers." But he was also smart enough to strike out on his own—to widen his horizons—to get experience with other media—and to learn the role that awareness advertising can play in a skillfully melded marketing program.

As a consultant, he and his firm have been fortunate to work with respected organizations like AT&T and Citicorp to help develop successful programs in both consumer and business direct marketing. At the same time, he helped develop and refine the concepts that are the cornerstone of this book.

There's a lot I like about this book. First and foremost, IDM is an idea whose time has come. It represents the next generation of this constantly evolving business.

Most important are the new thoughts and ideas you'll find in these pages: new segmentation techniques, like pattern recognition; new insights, like the linkage between market research and database development; new concepts, like the dramatic effect of response compression; even new buzzwords, like "positional proxies."

But this isn't just a book of theories. It's filled with useful information, like a media scorecard to help you understand the roles each major medium can play in five key areas. There are checklists to help you make wise decisions on important questions, like whether to develop in-house capabilities or use outside vendors. And Chapter 4 tells precisely what you, as a manager, must do to establish an integrated direct marketing program.

Besides Ernan's own wisdom, this volume also includes valuable experience from others. For example, there's "expert-witness" testimony from pros like Stan Fenvessey and John Groman. In my teaching and seminars, I've found there's nothing like a relevant case history to make the points and principles come alive. Ernan uses them here as a trained chef uses seasonings—sprinkling them around his chapters and varying their length to leave the reader with a taste for more.

All these things together make *Integrated Direct Marketing* a book that's unusually useful. It's a book you can read quickly for right-now ideas, but it's also designed to be a valuable reference in the months and years ahead.

When you finish the last checklist in the last chapter, I hope you will pause for a moment and reflect on your journey. For this is really a guidebook covering the transition from one era of direct marketing to the next. And it's a guidebook that a second-generation direct marketer like Ernan Roman was uniquely suited to write.

JIM KOBS, *Chairman*
Kobs & Brady Advertising, Inc.

Preface

The oil crisis of the 1970s fueled the birth of integrated direct marketing in the 1980s. The realities of limited resources, flimsy economies, shrinking profit margins, and evaporating budgets forced American industry to shake off its complacency and reevaluate time-honored methods of doing business. In this period of reassessment, traditional channels of distribution were clearly an item for examination, since they represented such a significant expense in the product development and distribution cycle.

It became obvious that relying on a single traditional channel of distribution, whether sales force or retail outlets, was too expensive and inflexible to meet the needs of a new reality created by technological change, intensified competition on an international scale, and increasingly demanding, educated consumers.

All the direct marketing media had been around long before the mid-1970s. Modern direct marketing began in 1872 when Aaron Montgomery Ward distributed his first mail-order catalog. But only during the decade of the seventies, with economic pressure and the consequent reevaluation, did direct marketing truly begin to flourish.

In this challenging environment, direct marketing flourished, propelled by the following forces:

Technological:

- Development of mass mailing capabilities.
- Construction and refinement of computerized databases for targeted marketing.

- Development of WATS and other low-cost nationwide outbound telephone calling systems.

- Institution of a nationwide 800-number toll-free system.

Cultural:

- Increase in per capita disposable income.

- Widespread entry of women into the workplace (accounting for 43 percent of the national work force in 1986).

- Change in leisure-time values, from shopping to more active forms of recreation.

The technological changes produced the capability to reach mass audiences economically and the precision to pinpoint individuals likely to be responsive to specific offers.

The cultural changes gave rise to a consumer marketplace with more money to spend but less time to spend it. Mom ceased to be the "designated shopper" of the family—she started earning a paycheck too. Convenience became ever more important, helping to drive direct-response purchases.

At the same time, the increasing size of American corporations and the diversification of their business activities has helped fund the development of direct marketing expertise. Companies with the capital to undertake major campaigns contributed directly to the growth of sophisticated database resources, market-research techniques, and telemarketing capabilities. A network of sophisticated service bureaus, experts, and consultants evolved to handle the knowledge base and implementation of the increasingly complex direct marketing undertaking.

Today direct marketing is an accepted way of doing business, both from the perspective of the corporate boardroom and from the viewpoint of the consumer or businessperson doing the purchasing. Direct-response techniques are being used to market a wider range of goods and services, including more sophisticated and higher-ticket offers. According to Maxwell Sroge of Chicago, mail-order sales totaled more than $50 billion in 1987.

But this is not the end of the story. The 1980s have brought increasing pressures for direct marketers. The performance benchmarks established in a less stringent era no longer apply. Nothing less than maximum profitability is acceptable today. And achieving this goal requires a fresh approach to the direct marketing process as a whole.

The early years of my career brought me into contact with hundreds of marketing specialists, many from Fortune 500 companies and many with disturbingly similar concerns. Their direct-response mailings, sales-force operations, and broadcast campaigns weren't producing the response they needed. They turned to telemarketing to lift their sagging performance. Sometimes it worked—sometimes it didn't. The power of telemarketing was beyond dispute. Still, the results fell short of the optimal response rates which were possible.

Over time, a pattern began to be discernible. Those companies that were deploying multiple media in planned, carefully structured campaigns generally achieved success. Those that did not use this methodology (the overwhelming majority) experienced only marginal response rates overall. And telemarketing, while producing a dramatic lift, was not able to generate the magnitude of incremental response it should have.

The fault did not lie in the telemarketing effort. The underlying problem was that companies able to employ the finest resources of direct marketing were not getting the most from any of them because they were not using all of them according to an integrated, coordinated strategy.

Creating more profitable direct marketing programs in the 1980s and beyond will require adopting a new perspective on the resources at our disposal, as the following anecdote (discussed also in the text) illustrates:

A lumberjack has been cutting down trees for 30 years with his trusty handsaw. He can only cut down 3 trees a day that way, though, and times are tough in the logging business. He needs to be more productive, to cut down more trees faster, if he's going to make a living. He goes to the local tool dealer for help.

The dealer has just the answer—the new gas-powered turbo-charged Mark V chain saw. It's a beautiful, state-of-the-art tool. The lumberjack will be able to cut down 30 trees a day! The dealer makes the sale.

The lumberjack works with the new saw for a month, but no matter how hard he tries, he can't cut more than 5 trees a day. An improvement, certainly, but not nearly enough to justify all that money he spent on the saw. He angrily brings his purchase back to the tool dealer and complains. "Only 5 trees a day?" the dealer asks, honestly puzzled. "Something's not right here. Let me try it out." He primes the engine, pulls the starter cord, and the saw roars into life.

"Wait a minute!" the lumberjack cries in amazement. "What's that sound?"

Those of us who are direct marketers sometimes fail to see the forest for the trees. Blessed with an incredible array of powerful marketing tools—capabilities that would astound the pioneers of our industry—we all too often fall short of our productivity and profitability goals.

One response to this shortfall would be to embark upon a quest for newer tools. Another is to reconfigure and refine the sophisticated tools that are presently at our disposal. The latter is the major focus of this book.

Integrated Direct Marketing presents in-depth case histories of successful campaigns conducted by some of the most astute corporations in America, and it explores the elements that made them work.

Integrated Direct Marketing provides a set of practical, actionable guidelines for making the most of modern direct marketing resources, with the ultimate purpose of helping you

> Unify and coordinate your marketing message across all media and thus heighten your persuasive powers.

> Gather the customer information coming in through multiple channels of distribution and use it to create more potent means of target marketing.

> Bring together the talents of specialists in discrete direct marketing disciplines to focus on a common purpose.

This book demonstrates the elegance of IDM—and there is something quite elegant about the precision and power of a synchronized marketing effort. Response rates regularly exceed historical performance by individual media. In fact, double-digit response rates are not uncommon!

On the agency side, a heightened sensitivity to the interconnected nature of direct-response disciplines, both across various media and in relation to the company's in-house systems, can only enhance the bottom-line results achieved on behalf of clients.

On the client side, IDM programs encourage and facilitate ongoing customer relationships that pay dividends far beyond any single marketing effort.

The aim of this book is to offer you a framework for implementing integrated direct marketing—a structure of ideas and recommendations which will spark a creative appraisal of opportunities for programs to meet *your* company's distinctive marketing needs.

The underlying challenge of IDM is the adoption of a new vision—a wholistic view of marketing which transcends traditional barriers of bureaucracy and specialization and repays this new sensibility with greater profits and increased job satisfaction. This book provides the insights needed to make these tools more powerful than ever before.

Ernan Roman

Acknowledgments

This book was shaped by the confluence of three forces.

The first force is those clients whose willingness to test the concepts of integrated direct marketing provided the vital empirical proof for this new methodology. Their courage in testing many of these previously untried strategies has been very gratifying. The book is the sum of what I have learned from every client. Unfortunately, I cannot list each of you by name; however, my debt to you is great.

I would like to single out and thank the following individuals for their commitment to testing the methodology and helping quantify the effects of media interaction and synergy: J. E. Gray and R. J. Crawford, AT&T; Melinda Beauvais, Christie's; Michael Carbone, Richard Srednicki, Gary Grosso, Jonathan McGrain, John Hunter, Joan Cox, Navroze Mody (in memoriam), Carol Knight, Gerald Rhodes, Mitchell Fried, and David Frankel, Citicorp; Robert J. Blair, formerly IBM; and Anthony Mazzeo, Anthony Mazzeo Associates.

The second force responsible for shaping this book is the group of contributors. They were selected because of their vision and innovation in their fields. They invested time and creative energy, working long hours during nights and weekends to structure their materials. Thanks to them, we have solid, empirical data.

These experts include Steven Landberg, The Michael Allen Company; J. E. Gray, AT&T; John Hunter, Citicorp; John Stevenson, Experts in Direct Marketing; Richard Orr and Web Thompson, Faultless Starch/ Bon Ami; Stanley Fenvessy, Fenvessy & Silbert; Scott Hornstein, Hornstein Associates; Robert J. Blair, formerly IBM; John Wilczak, consultant; Eric Langbaum, Eric Langbaum Associates; Steven Morgenstern, Morningstar Communications; Raymond Greenhill and Clifford Brundage, Oxxford Information Technologies; Hoyt Walbridge, Walbridge Research Associates; Kurt Medina, National Liberty Marketing.

Bob Stone and Jim Kobs were especially generous with their time and advice. Many thanks for their incisive and beautifully written forewords.

The third contributing force is the direct marketing industry. It is a youthful, energetic, open-minded group of innovative professionals. Representative of the diversity and expertise of this industry are the following people who have provided valuable counsel and perspectives: Scott Hornstein, Stanley Fenvessy, Lee Epstein, Richard Kuehn, Devin Scott, and Hoyt Walbridge.

Thanks are also due to the marketing experts, representing many disciplines, who made the time to review this book.

Special thanks to Donald Whipple for his thoughtful observations and guidance during these many years.

These acknowledgments would be incomplete without an expression of thanks to my parents, Murray and Eva, who first introduced me to this industry during my (and the industry's) formative years.

A final note of appreciation to Steven Morgenstern for his insight, creativity, patience, and sheer stamina in working with me to create this book.

1
A New Marketing Philosophy

As direct-marketing capabilities have grown, direct-marketing practitioners have increasingly become a collection of specialists.

Once upon a time everyone could be considered a specialist because there was only one specialty available. For generations, knowing direct mail in depth *was* knowing direct marketing; the universe was encompassed in a series of envelopes. This outlook is dead, though the burial has been slow in coming. In fact, not until 1984 did the major industry trade association change its name from *Direct Mail Marketing Association* to *Direct Marketing Association* (DMA), finally reflecting the true nature of its membership's widening sphere of interests.

Direct marketing has expanded into other media, particularly broadcast, print, and telemarketing. It has become more scientific and computerized, more finely tuned and measured. As the knowledge base involved in practicing the direct-marketing discipline has expanded, so has the need for specialists. We depend on experts in print production, media buying, database regression analysis, legal requirements, and the thousand and one other narrowly defined areas which make up the richness of information and experience available in modern direct marketing.

In the process, though, we have all too frequently put on blinders, losing sight of the overall process as we focus on improving the parts.

The phenomenon is all too common in all fields of human endeavor. We have folk sayings that refer to it, as when we say that certain people "can't see past the ends of their noses." We have plays and movies in abundance chronicling the sad stories of scientists, businesspeople, academics, and sports stars who concentrate all their efforts on perfecting their own narrowly defined abilities, and pay a bitter price.

In direct marketing the effect of hyperspecialization is not so dramatic that we can imagine someone writing a play about it. A book, on the other hand, is very much in order—this book.

A Consumer-Oriented Perspective

In the age of diverse media resources, we need a more wholistic approach to direct marketing. We must adopt a broader perspective on the way we are spending our money and doing our jobs. In a simplistic sense, we need to sit in the consumer's chair and view our own output.

As an individual, you frequently receive a variety of marketing messages from the same company across a range of media. You may open your morning paper and see an ad from your local bank, hear the same bank's radio commercial as you drive to the office, open your checking-account statement when you get home after work and glance at the enclosed brochure, read the few lines of promotional copy that flash across your computer monitor when you log on to do your home banking, and then watch a 60-second commercial promoting the same financial institution when you turn on your television set later in the evening.

Without devoting particular thought to the process, you add up all those messages and create an information base and an attitude toward the bank. Ideally, you don't experience the output of the direct-mail agency on some separate plane from the newspaper ad created by a different specialist, or the radio commercial produced by yet another agency. Rather, they all come together in a marketing gestalt.

If all the diverse media take supportive, interconnecting roles, you retain a healthy amount of the specific information conveyed, acquire the facts you need to make an informed decision about the products or services being promoted, and develop or maintain a positive attitude about the marketer.

More often, though, there is not enough cohesiveness in the marketing messages delivered to you throughout the day to make you focus on any offer being made, or even what company made them. Of the wealth of information delivered to you, at no small expense per impression, the vast majority is lost in the clutter.

The Alternative

There is a way to combat this epidemic of unproductive marketing. It entails peering beyond the walls of specialization we have erected, to create cohesive marketing programs which take the best of what modern direct marketing has to offer and use it in complementary ways to create a synergistic response.

The word *synergy* has unfortunately found its place in the cavalcade of buzzwords for the 1980s, and inevitably has had its meaning diluted. In fact, even the dictionary can be misleading in this regard. Look up *synergy* in *Webster's Ninth New Collegiate Dictionary* and you find the following definition: "combined action or operation." Combined action or operation is all well and good, but the heart of the matter is found on the same page under *synergism*: "interaction of discrete agencies (as industrial firms) or agents (as drugs) such that the total effect is greater than the sum of the individual effects."

There's the magic, such as it is, of integrated direct marketing (IDM)—that one plus one yields more than two. When a mailing piece which might generate a 2 percent response on its own is supplemented by a tollfree 800-number ordering channel, we regularly see response rise by 50 percent. A skillfully integrated outbound telemarketing effort can add another 500 percent lift in response. Suddenly our 2 percent response has grown to 13 percent or more by adding interactive marketing channels to a "business as usual" mailing.

The dollars and cents involved in adding media to the integrated media mix is normally marginal on a cost-per-order basis because of the high level of responses generated. In this instance, money is already being spent on direct mail. A message is being conveyed, but only a minimal level of action is generated. The additional media we bring to the mix add new ways for prospects to respond to the information already provided and new interactive channels of communication for delivering additional information. The existing investment in direct mail becomes more productive, and the investment in telemarketing is far more profitable than it would be in a vacuum, because it uses the direct-mail message as a keystone in building response.

The Logical Underpinnings of Multiple Media

Adding media to a marketing program will raise total response rather than simply increasing the level of activity in a single medium, because different people are inclined to respond to different stimuli.

Some of us prefer to fill out a coupon and drop it in the mail. Others thrive on the instant gratification of an 800-number response. One individual may pore over every line of a long-copy mail piece before making a purchase decision; others will get all the information they need from a 30-second broadcast ad. By employing multiple media, we open up more potential avenues of communication between our prospects and ourselves. It only makes sense that this will produce more orders—but at what cost?

Adding media to the marketing plan always entails start-up costs for management time, creative services, and production. In addition, some of the most potent forms of media communication (including teleconferencing and outbound telemarketing) are simply more expensive per prospect contact than the traditional mass-produced direct mailing. This does not make them intrinsically less desirable than direct mail, because they succeed in producing response from a larger section of our prospect universe—individuals who would otherwise not order at all. Using multiple media will produce maximum possible response from a limited prospect universe, by offering each prospect his or her preferred medium of communication and response. In fact, *not* using multiple media is passing up the opportunity to make a sale to a large percentage of your eligible prospects. However, the economics of a multimedia campaign demand higher overall levels of response than we have traditionally achieved.

The 2 Percent Solution

The belief that a 2 percent response rate represents heartening success may still be valid if the target market is enormous and undifferentiated. If the expenses involved in producing the solicitation are low enough, a direct-response campaign that generates magazine subscriptions from 2 percent of all households will probably be just fine; there is such a tremendous number of potential purchasers that the supply of prospects is virtually inexhaustible.

As the characteristics of the prospective purchaser become more restrictive, though, each name on the list grows in value, and our expectations should grow accordingly. The prospect for an insurance product, for example, must be qualified based on both need and financial resources. Virtually any business-to-business offer is targeted to a highly select industry segment, and even within that segment only a small group will represent true prospects. Thanks to modern market-research and database-analysis techniques, we can pinpoint prospects meeting these more tightly defined criteria with increasing precision. Having done so, though, the old guideline of 2 percent response represents a horrendous level of waste. Should we congratulate ourselves when 98 percent of a highly qualified and carefully selected target universe refuse our offer?

Even a mediocre professional baseball player is supposed to get a hit every four or five times at bat and maintain a better than .200 batting average. In direct marketing, we see a batting average of .020 and pat ourselves on the back. No wonder there is so much mediocre marketing going on; even minor-league talent can look good when a 2 percent response rate is considered a home run.

We *can* attain double-digit response rates to our direct-response campaigns, but some nontraditional thinking is required. The first step is recognizing the power of each medium at our disposal. The second, and far more thought-provoking, step is learning how to master the subtle, powerful interrelationships between marketing media. Only such mastery allows us to maximize response to an offer—and the demanding economics of modern direct marketing require nothing less than maximum response.

Integrated Direct Marketing Defined

The professionals who make the next major leap in direct marketing will embrace a different view of the marketing world. Instead of dealing with individual media, or even individual product promotions as separate and distinct undertakings, they will take a broader perspective. Tomorrow's winners will have a wholistic perspective on their company's marketing efforts, crossing product and media lines to understand the implications of their actions for the continuing health of their businesses. This big-picture management of resources amounts to a new marketing philosophy, predicated on the instinctively apparent idea that multimedia marketing communication deployed with a unified goal and message will be more effective than less organized, scattershot promotions. We call this new marketing perspective *integrated direct marketing*, or IDM. Here is a capsule definition:

Integrated direct marketing is the art and science of managing diverse marketing media as a cohesive whole. These interrelationships are catalysts for response. The resulting media synergy generates response rates higher than could ever be achieved by individual media efforts.

The economic advantages of integrated direct marketing arise from the use of sophisticated database methodologies to identify high-potential prospects, and the concentration of marketing resources on these select list segments. Of course, targeting media is a well-known direct-marketing concept. In contrast to a traditional single-medium effort, though, an IDM campaign selects prospects with a higher degree of precision from the outset, and increases the investment per prospect contacted. This may in fact result in higher up-front expenditures for media and creative costs than a single-medium campaign, though the relative lack of waste and higher response rates make up for much of the difference.

More significant than the initial investment per prospect is the higher total response level from the prospect universe created by the concentration of marketing impressions. Often the actual cost per order is the same as or less than in a traditional single-medium campaign. In addition, a successful IDM campaign produces far more orders per thousand contacts than traditional direct marketing. When we stop to consider the profit contribution of each purchaser over the life of the customer (a concept explained further in later chapters), then the economic advantages of maximizing list penetration become overwhelming.

The synergistic effect of integrated direct marketing does not arise automatically from the mixing of media. It takes talent, skill, understanding, and effort to manage marketing resources in such a way that a synergistic reaction takes place. In this sense, integrated direct marketing is both a philosophy and a methodology, defining strict requirements for success.

Integrated Direct Marketing Implemented

We have mentioned the financial industry as an example of an area which can benefit from IDM because of the diverse media employed. Now we turn to a real-world example of a truly integrated direct-marketing campaign that scientifically explored the interrelationships of direct-response media. The program was undertaken by Citicorp, a financial institution which regularly employs the entire array of state-of-the-art direct-marketing media and support services. In this instance, the decision was made to devote additional testing and analysis to quantifying the supportive role these media can play when they are coordinated in an IDM effort.

John Hunter, the Citicorp vice president who spearheaded the IDM effort, has generously provided this detailed case history. We think you will agree that the results of this experiment are significant far beyond the bounds of financial marketing.

A Case in Point
IDM Opens New Territory for Citicorp

John Hunter, *Vice President, Citicorp*

The 1980s have been a period of rapid and dramatic change in the financial-services industry. Where once banks were limited by law to operating within a single state, or even to maintaining a single branch, deregulation has begun to allow individual financial institutions to develop a customer base that spans the nation. Citicorp has been a leader in this territorial expansion.

One key aspect of the Citicorp strategy in this period of expansion has been direct marketing. In areas where the bank was not chartered to open bricks and mortar branch offices, direct marketing has provided the channel for creating remote banking customers who conduct transactions by mail or telephone. And even in the era of deregulation, when branch offices can legally be established subject to approval by individual states, the costs involved in establishing a physical presence can be prohibitive. Direct marketing offers an alternative channel of distribution for financial products without the lengthy start-up and capital investment required to establish a traditional branch structure.

An Exhaustive Test

During the early 80s Citicorp decided to enter the mortgage lending market in the mid-Atlantic states, an area where the Citicorp name had little brand recognition. There was, however, an existing business relationship with customers in Maryland and Virginia through the Citicorp subsidiary's Choice credit card, providing a promising market segment for further development.

As experienced direct marketers, Citicorp chose this occasion to test the effect of integrated direct marketing in a controlled environment. The corporation's annual investment in direct marketing is substantial, and its ongoing operations were profitable. However, the opportunity to maximize the profitability of direct-marketing activities without significantly increasing expenditures was compelling.

The product to be launched was a home equity loan—a second mortgage. This type of product had been direct-marketed successfully by Citicorp in other regions before this campaign, using newspaper, direct mail, and some account executives on the telephone. However, there were certain key elements that made the current program distinctive:

- Lack of local recognition of the Citicorp name.
- Legal and regulatory restraints imposed by Citicorp's not being a Maryland bank.
- Strong competition from local banks in pricing. The interest rate required by Citicorp was 2.5 percentage points higher than the lowest-priced competitor in the market.

In addition, the desire to conduct a test of the effects of a coordinated multimedia campaign imposed stringent list-segmentation, operational, and analytical requirements on the effort.

Developing the Program

Citicorp built a project team composed of representatives from several internal divisions that were needed to launch the product. The legal, systems,operations, and marketing departments were represented, as well as the advertising agency and a direct-marketing consultant.

The team members were responsible for input regarding the capabilities and requirements of their departments during the market planning and strategic design phases of the program, as well as supervising the implementation of the plan within their areas once the program was underway.

The direct-marketing consulting firm played an interesting role. As direct-marketing generalists, the firm served as the coordinating point for the diverse media used in the campaign. This role held true both during the planning stages and during the actual implementation of the campaign.

Citicorp tried to leverage existing research from other Citicorp programs within the United States to help determine the product positioning and target market. However, what was found helpful was doing market research within the region in which the product launch was being done, to determine whether there were some unique characteristics in the marketplace, such as

- Demographics of the customer
- Psychographics of the customer
- Oversaturation of the market for the product
- Special niches in the marketplace that were not being tapped sufficiently
- Special niches in the marketplace that promised higher levels of profitability

Part of the research included customer surveys to determine how customers felt about interest rates, administrative fees, and the whole process of applying for a loan. Citicorp learned that some customers did not have a problem with high interest rates for second mortgages provided they were using the loan for investment purposes. However, they also learned that customers had a significant objection to high administrative fees, commonly called *points*, and they had an even stronger objection to the long, tedious application process. Given the relatively high interest rate for the Citicorp loan, this research finding became the key to the strategic marketing and creative presentation of the product: a "hasslefree" loan could succeed even with higher interest rates.

The Media Mix

Examination of past direct-marketing efforts supporting second-mortgage products revealed an important problem. In the past both direct mail and newspaper had been used in conjunction with a telephone number that was tied to the local branch sales office. The newspaper and direct mail generated quite a number of inquiries to the sales offices. However, only a very small percentage of applications were taken as a result of the inquiries. This was primarily because the sales force was occupied with a variety of other functions that took them out of the sales office. However, it was not possible to eliminate the live person from the sales loop and rely on direct marketing exclusively. Because of the complexity and the length of the second-mortgage applications there was a general consensus that human intervention was required to help coach the customer through the application. In addition, various regulatory and legal parameters required that customers actually receive their loan checks in person.

Citicorp opted for an integrated approach utilizing mail, telephone, coupons, and newspaper advertising to generate leads and qualified applications, and field sales force to consummate the final sale. The key issue was how to get the prime prospects to a face-to-face closing with an account executive.

Newspaper Advertising. *Newspaper advertising* was used to generate inquiries in a general geographic area. While newspaper ads generated inquiries, they also produced exposure for the product. The strategy was to use newspaper advertising to create awareness before sending out the direct mailing. The synergy that was created between the print advertising and direct mail was planned to give consumers a greater comfort level and a better understanding of the product once they received the direct-mail piece.

Direct Mail. *Direct mail* was sent to a highly targeted base of consumers who were presumed to have a high equity value in their home. The mailing also went to existing customers (Choice credit-card holders) who met criteria for second-mortgage usage.

Telemarketing. *Telemarketing* was utilized inbound via an 800-number response to the newspaper and direct mail, and outbound to generate a highly personalized, highly efficient follow-up to prospect inquiries.

The outbound telemarketers were trained on the home equity program. A very detailed script was developed to allow the telemarketer to actually complete the application over the telephone for the consumer. The script also included answers to common consumer questions.

Outbound telemarketing was a two-step process. Step 1 was to respond to the customer inquiry, offering information about the home equity product and the rates. Step 2 was to set up an appointment for a further telephone call to actually fill out the application over the telephone. The consumer was told what information would be needed for the application and asked to have it ready for the second call. The application process initially took 45 minutes, but after the telemarketers became more proficient at handling the program and scripting techniques were developed to shorten the application, the time was reduced to 25 minutes.

Field Sales Force. The *field sales force* received the application completed by the telemarketer and handled credit approval and credit processing. To help facilitate the cooperation between telemarketing and the field sales groups, incentive contests and sales teams were set up between telemarketing and the field sales group. The telemarketers were rewarded for generating complete and qualified applications, and the field sales group were rewarded for closing the applications. In this manner, both units had to work together as a team to avail themselves of the incentives. Each group had to be concerned about quality and timeliness in order to assure that a completed sale was made and the customer satisfied.

Citicorp allocated approximately 40 percent of the budget to direct mail and newspaper, to generate the leads. Historically, approximately 70 percentof the budget was allocated to mail and newspaper, but in this case 30 percent was reassigned to the telemarketing operations. The remaining 30 percent was allocated to the field sales organization.

Political Ramifications

One major hurdle that had to be overcome is a common problem in establishing an integrated direct-marketing program within an existing organization—the belief that new techniques threaten existing structures.

Citicorp had a field sales organization that traditionally went after the second-mortgage market and the first-mortgage market. They had to understand the impact on the sales organization of implementing a major direct-marketing campaign. The direct-marketing effort enabled the field sales force to concentrate more heavily on the lucrative first-mortgage market. However, it was very important that this strategic direction be clearly communicated to the field salespeople, or they would simply feel as if they were being replaced rather than supported. Because initial opposition from the field sales force had been encountered, there was general agreement that branch managers were to receive credit for the sales generated from direct marketing, as long as they agreed to close and service the accounts.

Still, some problems arose. Once the sales force was told that it would no longer handle the second-mortgage product, its members began to feel that some of their function was slowly being taken away. They began to develop the suspicion that other functions would soon be taken away as well. The sales force began to slow down the processing time of the loans for applications that were generated through direct marketing. The time lag between the appointments for an appraiser to look at the customer's home and the actual credit approval of the loan was extended 2 weeks beyond the projected time frame as a result of these slowdowns.

In addition, many of the salespeople continued to call upon second-mortgage accounts, which was often a duplication of effort. We found sales-force members talking to the same customers that were generated from the direct-marketing newspaper or mail effort. We found salespeople claiming ownership of certain accounts that were also claimed by direct marketing.

Fortunately, all these issues were resolved within the first week or two of the direct-marketing effort. However, had these issues not been resolved, there would have been no clear way of measuring the actual direct-marketing effort. Citicorp found it absolutely essential to deal with the impact of direct marketing on the field sales force as an urgent and important issue.

Test Structure

Four test strategies were executed and tracked for accurate analysis of the effect of integrated direct marketing. These were:

- The control package, consisting of a direct-mail piece with a lengthy application (over 70 pieces of financial information required) to be filled in and returned by mail to the bank (Figure 1.1).

- An 800-number tollfree response option added to the basic mail package, providing an opportunity for consumers to ask questions and, if they chose, complete the application by telephone (Figure 1.2).

APPLICANT INFORMATION SHEET

NOTE: When a request for credit is made we may not discourage on a prohibited basis a reasonable person from making or pursuing an application.

| DATE 4/15/85 | OFF. NO. 365 | ☐ BY PHONE ☐ IN PERSON | INFORMATION TAKEN BY A. Davis | PERS NO 2375 | SOURCE GF Realty | SRC NO 52 |

| AMOUNT REQUESTED 20,000 | ☑ SECURED ☐ UNSECURED | PURPOSE Debt Consolidation | PROD 30 | APPLICATION NO. 101 |

If this is an INDIVIDUAL application, complete SECTION (A). If this is a JOINT application, complete both SECTIONS (A) and (B). "✓" box marked | ☑ to indicate who provided the information. **NOTE:** If married, the spouse cannot be required to be the JOINT applicant.

(A) PRIMARY APPLICANT INFORMATION * ✓	**(B) JOINT APPLICANT INFORMATION** *
NAME _Guard_ _Pam_ _M._	NAME _Guard_ _Sam_ _J_
DATE OF BIRTH 2/26/35 AGE 50 S.S. # (Optional for applicant) 215-20-1993	DATE OF BIRTH 4/3/33 AGE 52 SS # (Optional for applicant) 215-29-1662
LIST THE AGES OF ALL PERSONS DEPENDENT UPON YOURSELF FOR FINANCIAL SUPPORT 21, 16 NO. OF DEP INC. APPL 4	LIST THE AGES OF ALL PERSONS DEPENDENT UPON YOURSELF FOR FINANCIAL SUPPORT 21, 16 NO. OF DEP INC. APPL 4
STREET ADDRESS 917 Elm Rd.	STREET ADDRESS 917 Elm Rd.
CITY Baltimore STATE Md. ZIP CODE 21227	CITY Baltimore STATE Md. ZIP CODE 21227
HOW LONG AT ADDRESS? 13 YRS 0 MOS HOME PHONE (301) 242-7639	HOW LONG AT ADDRESS? 13 YRS 0 MOS HOME PHONE (301) 242-7639
PREV. (If less than 2 years at present address) ADD N/A	PREV. (If less than 2 years at present address) ADD N/A
Declared Bankruptcy in the Past 10 Yrs? ☐ YES ☑ NO	Any Garnishments, Judgements, Repos, or Other Legal Actions Filed in Past 7 Yrs? ☐ YES ☑ NO	Declared Bankruptcy in the Past 10 Yrs? ☐ YES ☑ NO	Any Garnishments, Judgements, Repos, or Other Legal Actions Filed in Past 7 Yrs? ☐ YES ☑ NO
EMPLOYER'S NAME I.B.M. SELF EMPLOYED? ☑ NO ☐ YES	EMPLOYER'S NAME G.E. SELF EMPLOYED? ☑ NO ☐ YES
EMPLOYER'S ADDRESS 16 Washington St.	EMPLOYER'S ADDRESS 102 Knecht Ave.
JOB TITLE OR OCCUPATION System Analyst OCC 3 HOW LONG 10 YRS 0 MOS	JOB TITLE OR OCCUPATION Supervisor OCC 3 HOW LONG 8 YRS 0 MOS
NATURE OF EMPLOYER'S BUSINESS Service (If union, what is name and no. of local?) EMP 10 PAYDAYS Fri	NATURE OF EMPLOYER'S BUSINESS Mfg. (If union, what is name and no. of local?) EMP 11 PAYDAYS Fri
WORK PHONE (301) 275-1000 X 301 GROSS MO. SALARY $ 1400	WORK PHONE ( ) GROSS MO. SALARY $ 1,000
PREV. (If less than 2 years with present employer) EMP N/A — YRS — MOS	PREV. (If less than 2 years with present employer) EMP N/A — YRS — MOS
PREV. EMP. ADDRESS N/A	PREV. EMP. ADDRESS N/A

OTHER INCOME NOTE: ADVISE ALL APPLICANTS THAT ALIMONY, CHILD SUPPORT OR SEPARATE MAINTENANCE INCOMES DO NOT HAVE TO BE REVEALED UNLESS THE APPLICANT WISHES TO HAVE SUCH SOURCES CONSIDERED AS A BASIS FOR REPAYMENT OF THE REQUESTED CREDIT

SOURCE(S) OF OTHER INCOME N/A AMT. OF OTH. INC. —	SOURCE(S) OF OTHER INCOME N/A AMT. OF OTH. INC. —
Is any income listed above likely to be reduced before the requested credit is paid off? ☑ NO ☐ YES (Explain on separate sheet)	Is any income listed above likely to be reduced before the requested credit is paid off? ☑ NO ☐ YES (Explain on separate sheet)
ADD TOTAL INCOME OF APPLICANT (A) AND (B) ▷ Total Gross Mo. Inc. To Be Considered $ 2400	JOINT APPLICANT'S RELATIONSHIP TO APPLICANT (A) Husband
MARITAL STATUS Note: Do not ask, if this is an application for individual unsecured credit in a non-community property state. ☑ MARRIED ☐ UNMARRIED ☐ SEPARATED ☐ NOT APPLICABLE	MARITAL STATUS Note: May ask ONLY if this is a joint application OR is an application for secured credit OR if the applicant resides in a community property state. ☑ MARRIED ☐ UNMARRIED ☐ SEPARATED ☐ NOT APPLICABLE
RESIDENTIAL STATUS. ☑ H.OWNER ☐ CONDO ☐ DUPL ☐ MIL BASE ☐ OWN/OCC MFDU ☐ RENT ☐ PAR./REL. ☐ MOHO/LD ☐ MOHO/PK
OTHER (Describe)	PURCH PRICE 20,000 DOWN PMT 5,000 EST VALUE 67,500

TYPE CREDIT	CREDITOR NAME / LOCATION / ACCT. NO. **	C/ BAL $	M / PMT $	ABJ	PO	COMMENTS
LIEN HOLDER OR LANDLORD	Baltimore Fed. St. Paul St. 21829	10,500	525	J		P.I.
82 VEH 1 Make/Model Toyota Supra	Saving Bk of Baltimore	7,000	217	A	✓	
VEH 2 Make/Model						
OTHER R/E						
	Md. Nat'l m/c Baltimore St. #10567	600	45	J	✓	
	Equitable Visa Light St. #49023	450	35	J	✓	
	HFC York Rd. #42510	2,500	100	J	✓	
	Sears Security Blvd. #533108	1,200	100	J	✓	
	Hechts Security Blvd # 71016	325	25	J	✓	
PREV EXP ☑						
BANK REF ☐ check ☐ ovrdf ☐ save ☐ share	Md. Nat'l Baltimore St.		T/PMTS $			
BANK REF ☐ check ☐ ovrdf ☐ save ☐ share			1047			

: LIST ALL OPEN OBLIGATIONS INCLUDING THE LIABILITY FOR PAYMENT OF ALIMONY, CHILD SUPPORT OR SEPARATE MAINTENANCE. ATTACH A SEPARATE SHEET IF NECESSARY
: INDICATE ACCOUNTS OR OWNERSHIP BY ENTERING THE APPROPRIATE LETTER "A"—PRIMARY APPLICANT, "B"—JOINT APPLICANT, OR "J"—JOINT ACCOUNTS

A-1 REV. 2/81

Figure 1.1. The applicant information sheet—a daunting document for applicants to complete without assistance.

RESULTS OF INITIAL INTERVIEW	COMMENTS	FINAL
AMOUNT _50,000_		
TERM		
RATE _8.95 OE-HE "Intio."_		
PAYMENT		
SECURITY		
INSURANCE ☐ Life ☐ A & H ☐ None ☐ Not discussed		
(A) APPLICANT When is best time for call-back?	Call-back at (location)	
(B) JOINT APPLICANT When is best time for call-back?	Call-back at (location)	

FINANCIAL CAPACITY ANALYSIS NOTE: IF THIS IS A JOINT APPLICATION USE COMBINED FIGURES FOR APPLICANT (A) AND (B)

SECTION 1: MONTHLY COST-OF-LIVING (C.O.L.) ALLOWANCE FACTOR

- $ _185_ per dependent × _4_ total number of dependents = $ _740_ (A)
- Plus $ _100_ (B) for overall family expenses = $ _840_ (sum of A + B)

TOTAL MONTHLY C.O.L. FACTOR

SECTION 2: MONTHLY DEBT STRUCTURE

- Total of all present monthly payments (including rent/mortgage) before consideration of the proposed obligation $ _1765_ (C)
- Subtract the total of monthly payment amounts to be removed by pay-off in the consideration of the proposed obligation   − $ _∅_ (D)
- Add the projected monthly payment amount for the proposed obligation   + $ _____ (E)
- Revised Monthly Debt Structure (C minus D plus E)   = $ _____ (F)

SECTION 3: MONTHLY LEEWAY ANALYSIS

- TOTAL Gross Monthly Income $ _____ (G)
- Subtract Tax Factor   − $ _____ (H)
- Net Monthly Income (G minus H)   = $ _____ (I)
- Sbtrct. Rvsd. Mo. Debt Struct (F)   − $ _____ (F)
- Mthly. Finan. Margin (I minus F)   = $ _____ (J)*

* Amount shown in (J) should be equal to or greater than the TOTAL MONTHLY C.O.L. FACTOR computed in SECTION 1

SECURITY LEGAL DESCRIPTION		INSURANCE	
R / E	☐ applicant ☐ title co	COMPANY NAME	
		POLICY NUMBER	
		EXP DATE	COVERAGE $
		INSURANCE AGENT	
		MAILING ADDRESS	
OTHER		AGENT'S TELEPHONE	
		HOW VERIFIED? ☐ phone ☐ in file ☐ policy ☐ not verified, see comments	

VERBAL APPRAISAL APPRAISER	DATE REQ	DATE REC	VERBAL TITLE INFO TITLE COMPANY	
FAIR MKT. VALUE $ _____ Q.S. VALUE $ _____ ✕ EQUITY FACTOR _____ =			DATE REQ	DATE REC
			LIEN HOLDER NAME	
BASE VALUE $ _____ − ENCUM $ _____ = LENDABLE EQUITY $ _____			LIEN INCEPTION OR FILING DATE	AMOUNT $
CONDITION:			LEGAL DESCRIPTION · may be sight-checked against applicant information or recorded above if not previously obtained	

DECISION:
1. MAKE: ☐ YES ☐ NO ; BY _____ AE Name & Pers. No. ACCEPTED BY _____ Applicant(s) DATE _____

IF "NO" SPECIFY REASON & CODE _____

_____ CODE _____

2. COUNTER OFFER: $ _____ _____ Terms. Conditions ; BY _____ AE Name & Pers. Number

ACCEPTED ☐ YES ☐ NO; BY _____ Applicant(s) ; DATE _____

3. WITHDRAWAL · BY _____ Applicant(s) ; RECEIVED BY _____ AE Name & Pers. No. DATE _____

PERSONAL REFERENCE 1 NAME/ADDRESS/PHONE

PERSONAL REFERENCE 2 NAME/ADDRESS/PHONE

(A) APPLICANT Driver's License No. or explain how I.D.'d	(B) JOINT APPLICANT Driver's License No. or explain how I.D.'d

COMMENTS:

Figure 1 . *(Continued)*

A Division of Citicorp

**What could you do right now with $5,000 to
$50,000 or more? If you know the answer, I urge
you to accept my invitation today!**

Dear CHOICE Cardmember:

As a homeowning cardmember, you enjoy special status.

The reason, frankly, is the equity in your home. . .which very likely qualifies you for $5,000
to as much as $50,000 or more. . .to use virtually any way you want.

In fact, I invite you to call our toll-free HOTLINE number today

1-800-552-2747 EXT. 20

to learn just how much money you might be able to get through a
CITICORP HOME EQUITY LOAN. There's no cost, no obligation.

A CITICORP HOME EQUITY LOAN could be the perfect solution to financial plans you may be
mulling over right now. Such as how to add on that extra bedroom to make your home more
livable and more valuable. How to buy a second home for investment purposes. Afford a college
education for your children. Or consolidate present obligations to improve your cash flow.

You can call our HOTLINE number anytime between 8:30 a.m. and 7:00 p.m., Monday
through Friday. A Citicorp Account Executive will be happy to answer your questions and
give you an idea of just how much money you qualify for right now.

I'm confident you'll feel comfortable working with us. We're part of Citicorp, one of the
world's largest financial institutions. We understand the financial needs of today's consumer
and have built a reputation for professionalism.

If you prefer, just detach and mail the reply coupon above. Either way, accept our invitation
now. As a homeowning CHOICE cardmember, you'll be pleasantly surprised at just how much
money you can get and at how convenient a CITICORP HOME EQUITY LOAN really is.

Sincerely,

Stephen Echols

Stephen Echols
Program Director

P.S. Our CITICORP HOME EQUITY LOAN rate is extremely competitive. Combine that with
Citicorp's flexible terms and you may find the CITICORP HOME EQUITY LOAN from
CHOICE to be one of the most affordable ways to turn your plans into reality. Why not
call our HOTLINE today!

Choice   P.O. Box 8236 ■ Richmond, VA 23226

Figure 1.2. A tollfree number—prominently displayed—gives customers the option of responding by telephone.

- Another package, including the letter and application form plus a business-reply card allowing consumers to request further information (Figure 1.3). Individuals who responded via business-reply card were contacted by outbound telemarketing.
- In selected test regions, newspaper ads featuring a tollfree 800-number response mechanism (Figure 1.4). These inquiries also received outbound telemarketing follow-up.

Significantly, the products offered via these different media were not identical. The basic offer across all media was a fixed-rate, fixed-amount home equity loan. However, an additional product, an open-ended line-of-credit account secured by the homeowner's equity, was also available and was included only in the telemarketing offer. Because of the complexity of these financial products, it was impractical to offer both in the same direct-mail package. However, once telephone contact had been established, a more flexible offering was possible. If prospects were hesitant about the fixed-rate home equity loan, or wanted a product with a lower interest rate, the telephone communicator was able to offer an alternative by introducing the revolving-credit-line option. Of course, this degree of flexibility required an intensive training program along with a detailed and lengthy script for telephone communicators.

Results

Citicorp established three criteria for judging the effectiveness of the program:

- The number of accounts generated
- The revenue per account
- The cost per amount loaned

The selection of these criteria is appropriate, given the nature of the product. The size of the loan generated was highly flexible, ranging anywhere from

---

| *An invitation to call our* CITICORP HOME EQUITY LOAN HOTLINE. 1-800-552-2747 EXT. 20 | This is a no cost, no obligation opportunity to learn how you may be able to get $5,000 to $50,000 or more from CHOICE . . . to use any way you want . . . with payments that fit your budget. Call anytime between 8:30 a.m. and 7:00 p.m., Monday through Friday. If you prefer, detach and mail this coupon in the postage-paid reply envelope enclosed. A Citicorp Account Executive will call you promptly. ☐ **YES** . . . I accept your invitation. Please call me. Approximate amount desired $_____ Phone Number_____ (Day) (Evening) Best time to call_____ **CHOICE®** A Division of Citicorp |

Figure 1.3. The business-reply card, a tool for outbound telemarketing.

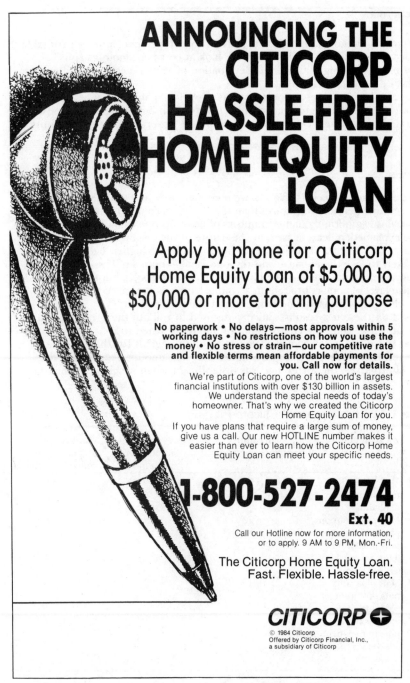

Figure 1.4. The newspaper ad featuring the Citicorp tollfree number.

$5000 to $50,000 or more. Clearly, a larger loan represents a more profitable transaction for the bank. Therefore, we look at cost per amount loaned as a means of establishing a meaningful evaluation of expense compared against a standard unit of measurement.

The results of the test panels were as shown in Table 1.1. The percentages included in this table represent a comparison between the response generated in each test cell versus the response generated in the mail-only control group.

Analysis

In assessing the results in Table 1.1, we note that test 2 and test 3 each produced lower revenue-per-account figures than test 1. This is counterbalanced in both cases against significantly higher numbers of accounts opened. The difference can be explained, at least in part, by the nature of the respondents. Those prospects with a relatively high level of need, and hence higher loan amounts, were likely to take the initiative and respond via 800 number. The outbound telemarketing contact also reached highly qualified prospects, but this more intensive level of contact brought in accounts from a wider market, including those whose level of need, and hence size of loan, were lower.

Based on these test results, Citicorp decided to roll out the program to a wider universe using the combination of all media tested (test 3). Gaining market share was a key consideration in setting the goals for this program. While test 3 represented a slightly higher cost per amount loaned than the other alternatives, the difference was insignificant when weighed against the

Table 1.1. Effectiveness of Citicorp Program

Test segment	Accounts opened, percent	Revenue per account, percent	Cost decreases per $1000 loaned, percent
Test 1: Mail plus 800 number versus mail alone	+ 7	+ 30	− 63
Test 2: Mail plus coupon plus 800 number plus outbound telemarketing versus mail alone	+ 13	+ 19	− 72
Test 3: Mail plus coupon plus 800 number plus outbound telemarketing plus newspaper ads versus mail alone	+ 15	+ 23	− 71

increased market share it produced—a 15 percent improvement for only 1 percent extra cost.

An interesting lesson about the timing of media presentation was demonstrated in the course of the program. Newspaper advertising was particularly effective before consumers received the direct mail. People always assume this to be true, but we generated hard statistical proof in the course of our test. In one market, one cell of the direct mail was dropped before the appearance of the newspaper ad. The response was 10 percent lower than that of a direct mailing which was dropped after the ad appeared, even though the demographics of the two cells were identical. The reason for the difference became apparent thanks to the telemarketing effort. In the course of follow-up calls to direct-mail responders, a large number of the customers volunteered the information that they had seen our newspaper ad. This, plus the 10 percent higher mail response, reaffirmed the industry wisdom that print ads should run before mail. This enabled us not only to capture the response rate produced from the newspaper ad itself but to leverage the general awareness that the advertising created into increased response rates for mail and presumably for telemarketing.

By combining media in an integrated, mutually supportive effort, Citicorp became a powerful presence in the consciousness of the target audience, and reaped the rewards of this strong level of awareness. Citicorp is well known in its home territory of New York, but was far less familiar in Maryland. However, the results of the marketing efforts for Home Equity were so successful that they contributed to establishing Citicorp as one of the leaders in the mortgage business in the mid-Atlantic region. Carrying the success a step further, the program produced new customer relationships in this geographical region, opening the door to additional sales of financial products at a future date. And by providing quantitative evidence of the effect of integrated direct marketing, the bank has laid the groundwork for similar programs in other market areas.

The Elements of IDM

Thanks to its extensive segmentation and analysis, this Citicorp case history provides a clear, quantifiable demonstration of the power of integrated direct marketing.

First and foremost, we must realize that it does *not* mean that using the greatest possible variety of media is necessarily desirable. Integrated direct marketing can involve as few as two media channels, or as many as your imagination can conjure up. The point is not the number of media in the mix, but the coordination of media resources and the concerted search for the most productive and profitable media mix available. Citicorp did not arbitrarily decide that more was better. Instead, they scientifically tested a number of media combinations in limited tests, analyzed the results based on appropriate units of measurement, and proceeded accordingly.

Many of the difficulties and the opportunities encountered in IDM are evident in the Citicorp experience. The problems encountered in integrating the field sales force in the direct-marketing operation were overcome through strong management intervention and ongoing communication. At the same time, the decision to devote substantial time and expense to market research, strategy development, program implementation, and analysis were amply rewarded.

The key element in overcoming difficulties and exploiting opportunities, in this case history and throughout the IDM experience, is the role of management. In fact, integrated direct marketing is first and foremost a management technique. It is designed to accomplish the primary task of management—to make the most of available resources—within the direct-marketing discipline.

In the course of this book we will dwell on each of the decision-making areas which can make or break the synergistic effect of integrated direct marketing. These include:

Media Selection and Implementation.   We must analyze the prospect's buying process in terms of consecutive steps taken along a purchase path, and match these stages with media whose strengths are appropriate to the needs of the moment.

Particularly exciting results have been achieved in integrated direct-marketing campaigns using a technique we call *response compression*, which produces high response rates by creating a "pressure-cooker" effect in which media impressions are concentrated in a tight time frame. A typical IDM schedule would deliver direct mail within 2 to 5 days of the appearance of print advertising, employ outbound telemarketing within 2 days of mail receipt, and fulfill orders (or send written confirmation) within 24 hours of the consumer's purchase decision. The optimal sequence of and interval between contacts will vary from program to program, of course, but there is always a strict time-frame requirement to create the immediacy and excitement that produces optimal response.

In Chapter 2 we will examine the theory and practice of response compression, and will also discuss the concept of "cannibalization" within the context of response compression.

Strategic Planning.   IDM cannot be implemented as a scattershot marketing tool using a vague strategy to achieve fuzzy goals. Instead, a comprehensive analysis of resources, responsibilities, and desired results must guide the deployment of direct-marketing media.

Making continued, self-reinforcing contact with each individual prospect does not necessarily increase the total marketing investment, but it does increase the investment per prospect. Therefore we need sophisticated market research and database analysis in order to preselect our target market with great precision.

In addition, we must apply appropriate qualifying standards to determine which medium will be used to contact selected individuals within our target universe. The Citicorp case history presented above offers an example of strategic thinking in its use of outbound telemarketing. It would have been possible to call everyone on the mailing list—but it would not have been economical. Instead, individuals identified themselves as highly qualified prospects by responding to mail or newspaper contact. Limiting outbound telemarketing contact to this select segment put this powerful medium to use in a profitable manner.

By designing programs that separate the wheat from the chaff early in the process, we can minimize our expenditure on nonprospects and concentrate our efforts on people who need our products and services and who have the authority to make a purchase decision. Chapter 3 will present specific guidelines for crystalizing the strategic considerations involved in your integrated direct marketing effort.

Ongoing Project Management. Coordinating diverse in-house and outside resources with precise timing and top-of-the-line quality execution is no easy task, yet that is precisely what IDM demands.

Management within an IDM environment involves distinctive challenges. Political questions inevitably arise as we break down established divisions of responsibility in order to create a system in which each medium and each function within the purchasing process combines with the others in a mutually reinforcing way to produce the most satisfying result for the consumer. This new, intensified level of interdependency extends beyond creating the required interrelationships between media. The legal and financial departments, customer service, and fulfillment must all be brought into the loop to achieve success.

This intensified involvement has an impact upon senior management as well. Take the analysis of results as an example. Simple mathematics tells us that testing in an integrated direct-marketing environment will be more demanding than testing using isolated media, because with each new medium added, the number of potential combinations grows. Testing different media groupings adds one level of complexity; testing different market-segmentation criteria across these multiple combinations adds still more possibilities to be assessed. And the challenge goes beyond simple mathematics, since a new perspective must be brought to bear in analyzing results as part of a synergistic whole. It is possible, for instance, that direct-mail response will be lower in a given cell because of the introduction of outbound telemarketing. This must not be construed off the cuff as a failing on the part of direct mail, but must be considered within the context of the overall response rates produced across all media. Providing the management perspective required for effective decision making within an IDM framework is a prime goal of this book as a whole, and particularly of Chapter 4.

Creative Excellence. To make the most of an IDM media mix, we use distinctive techniques to increase awareness and retention across media and over time. The opportunity represented by interlinking media messages has a potential downside as well—the "house-of-cards" effect that occurs when a poorly executed message reflects badly on the rest of your program.

We strive to create a unified impression through a variety of techniques. For instance, a promotion may have a distinctive name that rings a bell each time it is mentioned, whether in print, or over the airwaves, or on the telephone, or in the mail. We may have an appropriate spokesperson delivering our message. A distinctive graphic element may be carried through, or a sound, or a texture. Anything that makes a positive, memorable impression which can be incorporated consistently across a variety of media will add to awareness and retention of our message, and build positive response.

We will review several examples of well-executed IDM creative efforts in broadcast, print, and telemarketing, and analyze the factors that made them effective.

Development of Database Resources. Integrated direct marketing represents a potential gold mine for database development, through its coordinated use of interactive media. By combining purchase history and other information available through mail with the depth and breadth of data that becomes available in the course of telemarketing contact, we build a marketing resource that grows steadily more valuable.

To make use of all the information gleaned in an IDM program, we must create database resources which are capable of combining data from diverse sources and processing it in a timely, meaningful way. Equally important, we must develop systems which allow us to share information between marketing resources quickly and efficiently. The customer information revealed through a telemarketing contact, for example, must be conveyed to a field sales-force representative quickly and accurately to create a program that deals intelligently and effectively with the prospect. Similar channels of data communication must be established between all media areas as well as within customer-service and fulfillment departments.

At the same time, IDM is only effective when it is precisely targeted in the first place. If we are to focus our media on a select group of prospects, we had better be sure that we have the right group in our sights. We will review the market-research and database-analysis techniques that allow IDM to be undertaken with maximum profitability.

Finally, we will summarize the steps required to achieve integrated direct-marketing success in a detailed checklist that will serve as a schematic for designing a program that meets the distinctive needs of individual companies.

Everything Old Is New Again

In using the word *new* to describe the integrated direct-marketing approach, we may well have waved a red flag to some of you. Admittedly, there is no word so overused in marketing as *new*, and while the specific media we are recommending should be used in their most modern incarnations, they have all been around in some form for years now.

That is precisely the point. We are not suggesting untried and radically different marketing media. The tools are at hand for every skilled marketer, and the chances are good you are using them already. It is the *management* of these resources in a synchronized, coordinated program to produce a unified impact within the marketplace that is indeed a new concept, and one which shakes up the traditional order of direct marketing in very positive ways.

In this book we will not attempt to explain the nitty-gritty of conducting a focus group, or writing a direct-response letter, or staffing a telemarketing center. These core capabilities have been explained well enough in dozens of other books (some of which are cited in the Bibliography at the end of the book), and there are a host of experts available to conduct these operations for companies who wish to avail themselves of outside services. However, the commitment to integrating resources, to managing the total operation in pursuit of a well-defined, tightly focused objective must come from within the company with goods or services to sell. When viewed from this management perspective, all the lessons we have learned about direct marketing to date serve as basic building blocks for an innovative and exciting multimedia discipline. Thanks to the synergy we can create using IDM techniques, everything old truly is new again.

2
Creating Synergy through Media Selection and Deployment

Interrelationships between media exist whether you want them or not. In fact, the world in which your products or services are marketed—the gestalt of the target market—is incredibly complex, and your marketing message is one small voice within this maelstrom of converging and opposing forces. No one can hope to gain control of very much of this flux.

However, as a smart marketer working in an IDM framework, you will manage those resources at your disposal—the precision tools of modern direct-marketing media—to create a cohesive series of *complementary* impressions. There is a predictable sequence of events which must take place in order to reach a purchase decision. Each marketing medium has its own unique strengths to contribute at points along this continuum. By recognizing the required steps and using each medium according to its strengths in achieving these stages, we create the synergistic effect of integrated direct marketing.

In this chapter we will explore three aspects of integrated direct marketing:

- The intermediate goals that must be attained as we move the prospect toward the word *yes*

- The strengths and weaknesses of the media at our disposal for use in achieving these intermediate goals

- The optimal ways to combine these media to achieve our objectives in a timely, cost-effective manner

A good way to start is to review a relevant case history in some depth. The company involved is AT&T, and the subject is computers.

A Case in Point
AT&T Mortgage Line Software

J. E. Gray, *Marketing Communications Manager, Computer Systems Division, AT&T*

The marketing of computers is a multifaceted and complex undertaking. Onthe one hand, computer companies need to encourage the computerization of specific tasks within the business environment. On the other, they need to promote the unique benefits offered by their own brand of computer equipment in a highly competitive marketplace. One key marketing strategy which addresses both concerns is the development of computer applications which are unique, self-contained solutions to business problems—so-called turnkey systems.

A turnkey system consists of a ready-to-run combination of hardware (the actual computer equipment) and software (the programs that make it possible to perform specific tasks). The advantage of purchasing a turnkey system is clear: the complexities of assembling myriad system components from an assortment of vendors are eliminated. The technical side of computer equipment becomes less important in the purchase decision, and bottom-line system performance within the business environment takes center stage. For the company which can assemble a truly worthwhile turnkey system, the financial rewards are equally obvious, since the purchase of a complete system is a big-ticket sale, and an efficient one from a marketing-cost standpoint

AT&T offers an impressive turnkey system for mortgage-processing applications, called *AT&T Mortgage Line*. This system purchase includes computers chosen for the appropriate level of capacity required, the software (originally developed by Flick Mortgage) needed to accomplish a specific function, on-site installation, and training. When the time was ripe to market this product, AT&T deployed its marketing resources based on integrated direct-marketing principles. By doing so, it conveyed information, generated excitement, and produced sales.

Seizing a Marketing Opportunity

In 1986, with mortgage rates lower than they had been in years and refinancing activity at overwhelming levels, AT&T had a significant market opportunity with the AT&T Mortgage Line Software System, developed as one of dozens of turnkey solutions. The time was suddenly ripe for this innovative

package, designed to streamline mortgage financing and refinancing processing. As J. E. Gray, marketing communications manager for the Computer
Systems Division of AT&T, described it at the time, AT&T Mortgage Line
was

> ...a superior automated package that would benefit mortgage bankers, savings
> and loans, insurance companies—all the nontraditional as well as traditional in-
> stitutions providing mortgage financing. The timing was right, the software so-
> lution was right, and it worked with our hardware components. All we had to do
> was figure out a way to maximize the sales opportunity.

There were two distinctive considerations in deciding on a sales approach for
AT&T Mortgage Line:

- *Time sensitivity.* While the AT&T Mortgage Line product has ongoing value
  over time, it was particularly attractive in the then-current banking environment. Given the volatility of mortgage rates and their effect on the volume of
  refinancing business, it was important to strike while the iron was hot.
- *Sales-force availability.* The product was relatively new, so the number of
  salespeople adequately trained in its features and selling points was small.

In order to penetrate the marketplace quickly and to maximize the effectiveness of the salesforce, AT&T decided on an integrated direct-marketing
approach. This was decidedly not business as usual for the company.
  According to Gray,

> In business today, direct marketing frequently falls under the advertising
> umbrella, which means that if you want to do direct marketing in conjunction
> with ads for something like AT&T Mortgage Line, the agency would basi-
> cally put together some version of the ad and mail it out, and that would be
> considered a direct marketing program. AT&T wanted to create a more
> complete, integrated marketing effort for this product. Instead of just mail-
> ing something out and then waiting to see if anybody responded, we wanted
> to actually manipulate the process itself—to mail out a package designed for
> response, with comprehensive follow-up systems to manage the response
> produced, and a sales force adequately prepared in advance. We didn't want
> to just send the sales representatives a copy of the ad or direct mail piece and
> say, "I hope somebody calls you."

This marketing concept was presented to senior management and accepted.
The next step was to bring in outside support services, including an outside
direct-marketing consultant. The proposal outlined several potential ways to
market AT&T Mortgage Line, and urged market research to determine the
strategy with the most promise. This was the course followed by AT&T.

Market Research

Gray recalls

Instead of guessing at who the target market was, we decided to do market research specifically for this product and this project....At first glance, that might not seem necessary. If you're going to sell mortgage software, you go to mortgage bankers. Well that's true, but *who* do you go to? You go to whoever buys computer software. Or do you go to the Treasury Department, or the chairman of the board? Who do you *really* go to? So we did research to answer those questions.

The results of the research helped us develop the marketing package not only [for] the right target companies, but [for] the right person within those target companies. It also gave us the information we needed to set the tone and content of the creative for the program by identifying the potential customers' buying triggers. This is more a traditional consumer marketing technique, and we applied it in a business-to-business marketing situation.

The research offered specific prioritized copy points to be included in all media employed in the program, and the research firm worked closely with the creative team to ensure that their efforts met the demonstrated needs of the prospects. (Additional information about the market-research effort on behalf of AT&T is provided in Chapter 5.)

Program Design and Redesign

Research also conclusively showed that prospects needed to actually see the software in action in order to make an informed purchase decision. This immediately eliminated some of the media options which had first seemed especially promising, including audio teleconferencing and the distribution of a videotaped demonstration of the product.

Instead, a series of face-to-face seminar and workshop presentations was planned, where trained presenters could demonstrate the AT&T Mortgage Line software to groups of qualified prospects. AT&T offices in four key states would be employed.

An additional opportunity was the annual meeting of the Mortgage Bankers Association (MBA). This represented a special marketing opportunity: a large number of key executives would gather in a single location and could be screened and sold by a small number of AT&T sales representatives.

Implementation began quickly on this strategy. Because of the timeliness of the MBA Convention, this became the test site for the program. If this effort was successful, then the IDM campaign on behalf of AT&T Mortgage Line could be rolled out regionally (to the four targeted states) or nationally.

According to Gray,

We went with one list of MBA members and targeted the trade show to do the same thing we proposed to do at the seminars. We set up timed appointments and offered personalized demonstrations at the show. We could have done a traditional mailing nationwide and gotten a lot of leads, but it would have taken years to follow up on those leads—they would have piled up on our salespeople's desks. Instead, we focused our efforts on the trade show.

The media mix to generate timed appointments at the convention was designed to take advantage of the natural synergy of the media. This involved:

- *Print advertising.* Print advertising was used in vertical publications to generate awareness and credibility. The originally anticipated expenditure for print was increased as a result of market-research findings, which indicated that prospective customers needed the additional reassurance and awareness provided by trade-journal advertising before moving on to the next stage in the buying cycle: agreeing to an appointment for a demonstration.

- *Direct mail.* To generate awareness and leads, direct mail was used in the form of an attractive 81/2- by 11-inch folder with extensive copy describing the product features (Figure 2.1). A key copy point was that the AT&T Mortgage Line Software System can help you improve productivity 30 to 100%—a finding that came directly from market research done with current users. A postpaid business-reply card was included in the direct-mail package.

- *800-number.* A tollfree 800-number response option was included in the print advertising and the direct mail.

- *Outbound telemarketing.* Positioned as a follow-up to direct mail, outbound telemarketing was used to generate incremental registrations or sales leads. These calls were scheduled in an unconventional way. Instead of waiting until a week or two after mail was received, which is the traditional approach to mail follow-up by telephone, calls were attempted within a few days of anticipated mail receipt. The goal was to generate a *response-compression* effect—to heighten overall response by coordinating mail and telephone in closely timed sequence. We will explore this concept in more depth later in this chapter.

- *Direct-mail follow-up.* To confirm the timed reservation for the executive at the convention, direct-mail follow-up came in the form of an oversized, bright-yellow postcard, with the specific appointment information entered on it.

- *Outbound telemarketing follow-up.* Participation was confirmed by outbound telemarketing follow-up, timed for 3 days before the convention. This contact provided an extraordinary initial gauge of the program's effectiveness, with over 96 percent of those who had made appointments indicating that they would indeed appear as scheduled. The final confirmation call, hours before people left for the trade show, was undoubtedly also a contributing factor to the result that virtually all those who had confirmed did in fact keep their appointments at the trade-show booth.

Results

The integrated direct-marketing program exceeded all expectations, with an impressive 11 percent positive response from the total universe mailed. This 11 percent response breaks out as follows:

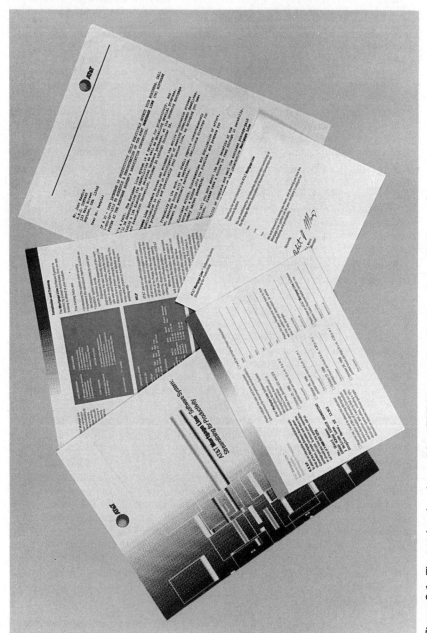

Figure 2.1. The initial mail package of the AT&T Mortgage Line Software System IDM campaign.

A CASE IN POINT

Demonstrations	25.1 percent
No timed appointment, but agreed to stop at booth for demonstration	24.4 percent
Requests for sales-representative follow-up	39.1 percent
Brochure requests	11.4 percent

The synergy created between the media is dramatic, especially when seen in percentage relationships, as in Table 2.1.

In reviewing these figures, it is important to note the effects of carefully integrating the media. The mail-response figures are substantially lower than we might ordinarily expect. This is a direct result of the response-compression techniques employed by positioning outbound telemarketing within a few days of mail receipt. This strategy clearly cannibalized mail response to a certain extent. However, given the 502 percent incremental response provided by outbound telemarketing (based on a comparison of mail-response rate with outbound-response rate), this was more than cost-justified. Outbound telemarketing generated 62.9 percent of demonstration commitments, 72.2 percent of sales-representative requests, 100 percent of demonstrations without timed appointments, and 50 percent of brochure requests.

In summary, the tight integration of the media mix plus the compression of response curves achieved by adding outbound telemarketing earlier than the traditional 7- to 14-day waiting period fueled the effect of media synergy and increased overall response far beyond anticipation.

Of course, the ultimate judgment of the success or failure of any marketing program is the number of leads converted to actual sales. While this figure is confidential, there is no question that AT&T is extremely pleased with the results.

Table 2.1. Media Response Matrix

	Percent of Demonstrations	Percent of Representative Follow-Up	Percent of Demonstrations without Appointments	Percent of Brochure Requests	Percent of Total
Advertising					
Subtotal	5.2	11.3	0	47.7	11.1
800 number	100	70.6	0	33.3	55.8
Coupon	0	29.4	0	66.7	44.2
Mail			0		
Subtotal	32	16.6		2.3	14.8
800 number	48.4	60	0	100	54.4
BRC	51.6	40	0	0	45.6
Outbound telemarketing					
Subtotal	62.9	72.2	100	50	74.1
Total:	25.1	39.1	24.4	11.4	100

A CASE IN POINT

Future Implications

The integrated direct-marketing concept has proved itself dramatically for
AT&T, and there are plans to implement the same kind of approach with
other products in the future. As Gray so accurately notes, though,

> You can't just pick up another product and overlay this kind of program with it
> and be up and running. You have to recognize that the concept does fit, but
> . . . you have to . . . tailor that concept to the needs of the particular product,
> marketing situation, and salesforce capabilities in order to maintain the kind of
> success with different products that we have had with this one.

Gray also offers a fine perspective on integrated direct marketing in a larger
sense—as an endeavor which integrates the resources of a company in a more
effective, coordinated effort than is ordinarily achieved:

> . . . The entire process we used in marketing AT&T Mortgage Line was non-
> traditional for a lot of companies. Too often you get into a mold. The
> salesforce is there, and the multiple sales channels are there, and the roles
> are defined. If your functional responsibility is advertising or direct mail,
> then you do an ad or direct mail piece, hand off a lead, and your job at that
> point is presumed done. You measure your success by how many telephone
> calls you got, or how many leads you handed off, but in the larger scheme of
> things you have to ask what good did you do for the company. Did you really
> sell anything or did you just create paper? Are these leads qualified in any
> way, or are they going to do anything other than sit on a salesperson's desk?
> In many companies that is not a direct marketer's responsibility to care
> about. However, when you do take responsibility for ensuring that the
> follow-up is there, then you have a front-to-back program that's more effec-
> tive because you know with some certainty what's going to happen.

> This particular program has been successful for us because we didn't let the re-
> sponsibility or accountability of the job description limit the program capabili-
> ties. The program went farther than the end of my desk, or the desks of the
> other people associated with this program. And that's why it succeeded.

Goal-Oriented Media Deployment

This AT&T case history offers a fine example of analytical skill in the
choice of media and timing of their deployment. The sales cycle was
broken out into its component parts, and the relative roles of direct mail
and field sales force were determined. Next a set of intermediate goals
was established (generate awareness and enthusiasm for product, secure
timed appointment at trade show, produce actual participation at show
site, etc.), and an integrated media plan was created to employ the most
potent medium available to achieve each intermediate goal. The level of

success attained in the AT&T Mortgage Line program attests to the effectiveness of selecting the right medium to handle the right job.

While there are no hard-and-fast rules to follow across industry and product-line differences, all media choices are based on a common set of goals which must be attained to achieve success.

- *Awareness.* We must make prospects conscious of our offer by attracting their attention. Not only must we overcome the impressions made by our competitors; we must also cut through the general noise and distraction of all marketing messages received, even those in entirely unrelated product or service categories.

- *Information.* The task which takes up most of our time and attention is delivering the information necessary to make an informed purchase decision. This requirement will vary as a function of the product—from the standard product category with well-known features whose only distinguishing buying characteristic is price to new, unfamiliar, or highly technical offers which require in-depth explanation and buyer education before an order can be placed.

- *Action.* The final action we seek is an order, of course, but in programs dealing with more complex purchases, there may be several action steps along the way. For example, the AT&T campaign described above did not ask for a purchase decision at first—the initial goal was to achieve a scheduled appointment at a trade show. The media employed and the manner in which they are used to generate this workshop attendance are very different from the approach we would take if we were closing an order by mail or telephone.

- *Ongoing action.* For most companies it is not enough to make a single sale to an individual. Instead, we seek a regular, ongoing relationship with a customer who will reorder or expand the range of purchases within our product line. Therefore, in assessing direct-response media, we must look at the degree to which each medium encourages the development of a continuing business relationship.

- *Targeting.* Integrated direct marketing is predicated on the existence of a discrete prospect universe, and our ability to identify these individuals or companies. Therefore, another major factor to be considered in our media analysis is *targeting*. To what degree will a given medium help to identify prospects, and how precisely can it deliver our marketing message to a selected group of prospects once they have been identified?

Media Capabilities within an
IDM Mix

Within this framework, let's examine the various marketing media at our disposal, assessing their potential functional importance within an integrated direct-marketing campaign.

Broadcast Media: Television

For breadth of coverage, nothing equals television. For better or worse, television has become the informational backbone of American life, with the average American spending over 4 hours a day in front of the set.

This is not to say, though, that television advertising produces high awareness of your product or service. We are all familiar with the high points of television advertising, the artistic efforts of the few Joe Sedelmaier's of the world who can make Federal Express or Wendy's hamburgers the talk of the nation through brilliant commercials. However, few commercials are brilliant. And even fewer brilliant commercials are oriented toward producing direct response. The medium is there, in the form of the tollfree 800 number, but the message must be finely targeted to produce a useful response.

Direct-response television is increasingly being used within tightly defined market segments to produce direct-response sales and sales leads. The growth of cable television and independent television stations have enhanced our capability to tightly define our target market based on station and program demographics, and to restrict response to manageable levels by buying time selectively. Chapter 5 will explore in some depth a noteworthy IDM campaign conducted by Faultless Starch/Bon Ami Corporation to sell garden tools and rust inhibitors via television, direct mail, and telemarketing.

One interesting aspect of the unique position of television in American life is the degree of credibility we ascribe to a company which advertises there. We see the effect directly in the "As Seen on Television" blurb affixed to consumer items in discount stores. We see it indirectly in the expenditures for image advertising by major corporations, particularly during sports and news programming. In one sense, it seems odd that a medium that brings us professional wrestling, soap operas, and silly situation comedies could enhance an advertiser's credibility. Looking at the matter more closely, though, we see that the context of the programming environment is secondary to the nature of the medium. Television is a sign of power. Everyone knows that it is expensive to advertise on television, and therefore people ascribe a high level of importance to those companies with the wherewithal to undertake a TV campaign. Of course, *what* you say and *how* you say it have undeniable importance in a television ad. However, just the fact that you are using the medium sends powerful signals in its own right.

Broadcast Media: Radio

While radio advertising does not carry the same prestige value as television, it does have advantages within a direct-marketing context. The diversity of radio programming formats and the more localized coverage of each station, as compared with television coverage, combine to allow more precise targeting of a desired group. With the exception of local cable programming, television generally attempts to be all things to all people, and to reach as massive an audience as possible. Radio, on the other hand, has evolved into a medium that reaches niche markets and stresses the local nature of its content. Thus, if we are trying to drive traffic into a particular store or event, radio provides a highly targeted means of reaching the audience within a well-defined geographical market area.

Radio is also far less expensive than television, thanks to lower per-minute charges and production costs. For smaller advertisers, radio is the only broadcast medium that fits the budget. Even companies that are less constrained in their spending may gravitate to radio because of the greater number of individual spots their dollars will purchase, using this frequency to reach different individuals who tune in at different times of day, and to make their message memorable through repetition.

Also worth consideration is the environment in which each medium is received. Unlike the early days when families clustered about the radio to listen to their favorite shows as a group, radio is generally consumed by individuals today. There are various audiences: the drive-time audience on the way to or from work, the audience listening while doing housework or at the workplace, the teenage market listening while engaged in other activities. This solitary listening and high degree of segmentation can lead to highly targeted messages—military recruiting ads on rock stations, financial publications and services during drive-time news programs, home-oriented product offers during afternoon talk shows, etc. And always, for a direct-marketing campaign, the telephone number for response is essential. Rarely will a listener race for a pad and pencil to scrawl an entire address, and then follow up by actually sending a written request. A telephone number, on the other hand, is quick, easy and, if presented in the form of an alphabetic mnemonic (Leading Edge Computer Products' 800 number is USA-LEAD, for example), can be memorized until needed.

IDM Media Scorecard: Broadcast Media

Awareness. High potential, if budget will support adequate frequency. Of course, direct marketing can gain some of the awareness benefit of broadcast advertising by referring through copy and graphics to the company's general-image advertising in order to bolster recognition and credibility for the IDM effort.

Information. Limited. Because of time restrictions, the linear nature of the presentation (i.e., the viewer or listener cannot go back and review information after it is presented), and the lack of concentrated attention on the part of the audience, broadcast media are best used to deliver one or two brief, compelling ideas, without detail or supporting information.

Action. The potential for action is high when combined with an inbound telephone-response option, but is burdened by the fact that responding to a broadcast solicitation is a multistage process. Not only must potential buyers capture the number for response; they must then go to the telephone and initiate the contact. If the TV program is relatively interesting, or the radio is being played during the course of other activities, there will be a delay between receipt of marketing message and response, and even moderately high levels of enthusiasm will be stifled by this delay.

Ongoing Action. Direct-response broadcast ads serve best as a means for focused promotion of an individual product, rather than a choice of offers. The prospect decides whether to buy or not, and that sales contact is ended. Customers who are satisfied with a purchase may respond to a future offer from the same source. However, in traditional broadcast media, subsequent offers will be received on a hit-or-miss basis, according to the customer's viewing habits and the advertising frequency of the promotion. The recent innovation in broadcast direct marketing—home shopping channels and programs—has changed this relationship. These are catalogs of the air, available either 24 hours a day, or at the very least at predictable intervals. We will discuss home shopping channels further in Chapter 7.

A special case in broadcast promotion is the continuity series; witness the success of Time-Life Books, the Franklin Mint, and others. A continuity series purchase is a hybrid—really a single purchase decision that will be fulfilled and paid for over time. These continuity series represent a sale with a high enough profit margin to justify the cost of television advertising, but are perceived by the consumer as a series of individual, relatively inexpensive purchases.

An effective strategy for establishing an ongoing buying relationship for separate, unrelated products is to follow up on broadcast sales and inquiries with written materials.

Targeting. While nowhere near as finely targeted as a direct-response mailing or a telephone call based on demographic and psychographic list selection, broadcast media have become more finely targetable with the growth of cable and local independent stations. This improved selectivity results in more attractive economics for the direct marketer.

Print Media

Once, newspaper and magazine advertising was limited to creating awareness and producing action only from a relatively small cadre of coupon clippers. Used in combination with 800-number response, though, print is a highly effective tool both for delivering information and for producing immediate response.

Choosing the right specialized medium and the right section within more general-interest media is crucial to cost-effective print advertising. Daily newspapers offer a degree of targeting through the division of editorial material into sections, but this is only useful when these sections are meaningful for the product or service being promoted. Thus, financial services, entertainment-related products, and other categories can be effectively targeted to a selected audience within the newspaper environment through placement in the appropriate editorial section. Coupon and 800-number response opportunities turn these ads into active lead- or order-generating devices.

Of course, a lead produced through an ad in a general-interest newspaper is considered a raw lead and should be qualified by other means before extensive time or money is devoted to the follow-up. A few key questions can be asked by the incoming telemarketing operator or included on the coupon to indicate immediacy and intensity of interest, or purchasing authority within a corporation. Strong responses in these areas could justify outbound telemarketing contact; less pressing interest might warrant only mail follow-up.

A more promising and more powerful avenue for marketing communication in print is through specialized publications and trade magazines. The first and foremost advantage is clearly the higher degree of self-selectivity exercised by the subscribers to these publications. It is not uncommon for a single publication to become the bible of an industry, and two or three publications will nearly always cover the entire range of specialists in a given field. If you want to reach librarians, for instance, you can be certain that ads in *Publisher's Weekly* and *Library Journal* will be seen by virtually all the decision makers in that universe. Note too that *Library Journal* is published by the American Library Association, and is just one example of a publication produced by the dominant trade group in a field which achieves preeminence as a news source for its members.

There is another advantage to using highly targeted publications as advertising vehicles within an IDM campaign—the availability for rental of the publications' subscriber lists. Advertising within an editorially appropriate section of a magazine or newspaper is valuable, but it is difficult to follow up actively, since the subscriber list will include readers with diverse interests. Renting the subscription list for a specialized publication, though, allows you to reach out to those individuals who see your print ads through direct mail, outbound telemarketing contact, or both. Further, you can carry the graphic and copy themes used in the ads through to the mailing piece and telephone script. In this way, your print advertising serves to spark awareness, provide an initial amount of information to prospects, and generate a certain quantity of leads or sales from individuals who are particularly excited about your product or service, or especially responsive to print ads. At the same time, IDM takes into account that the majority of people interested in your print ad will not be motivated enough to take action. If your ad were operating in an isolated medium, these positively inclined but inadequately motivated individuals would be lost. With the aggressive follow-up undertaken by an integrated direct marketer, that positive inclination is translated into action through other channels. Thus, the dollars invested in print become far more productive.

IDM Media Scorecard: Print Media

Awareness.   For a dramatic announcement of a product or promotion, print can be a highly effective means of delivering your message. If you are promoting a mutual fund that delivers 18 percent taxfree returns, or a microchip that electronically recreates all the functions of an IBM PC and costs 25 cents, or a tell-all autobiography by Jane Wyman about life with Ronald Reagan, then a print ad in the appropriate publication will produce enormous response.

More often, advertising is tied not to momentous occurrences but to ongoing product benefits. In these cases, even good print advertising will not leap off the page and incite immediate action among a large number of readers. However, given the relatively modest investment required, it is valuable as a means of producing incremental awareness, when used in conjunction with other direct-marketing media. This is especially true when the subscriber list is used as a target list for ongoing contact.

Information.   Unlike broadcast media, information provided in print can be read, reread, and saved for future reference. While too much copy in too small a space is intimidating, we more often see a lack of adequate information. The use of charts, boxes, and subsections to convey technical specifications or statistical details can convey a lot of information without blunting the immediacy of the ad.

Of course, the promise of additional information is a driving force in motivating readers to take action, respond to your ad, and by doing so identify themselves as prospects. Therefore, a coupon or telephone channel for response, clearly and prominently displayed, is a key element of any print ad in an IDM undertaking.

Action.   Thanks to the dual-response devices of coupons and 800 numbers, print advertising can generate large response figures. The audience for print ads is substantial, and the means for replying can be clipped and used at the reader's convenience.

In fact, it is important to consider the level and quality of response you are seeking when you design a print advertising campaign, particularly in a lead-generation program. A lead which is not followed up promptly and professionally is worse than no contact with the prospect at all. Therefore, print advertising decisions must be made based on a careful assessment of back-end capabilities.

In this light, it may not be to your advantage to make responding to your advertisement too easy. Is an 800 number appropriate, or will this channel bring in too many unqualified leads? Can your incoming telemarketing operation complete the transaction with unqualified callers over the telephone, or will you be obligated to follow up by other means, and incur the expense this entails? Should you include screening questions on a print coupon? This will provide further information and screen out less motivated respondents. The balance between quantity and quality of leads produced should be determined on a case-by-case basis, and is often the subject of comparative testing.

This caution holds especially true for bingo-card response devices which allow readers to circle products or services for which they want further information; the responses are then forwarded by the publication to the advertiser. Consider the quality of the lead produced, and your goals in this regard. A bingo-card lead is often worth no more than the modest level of curiosity required to circle your number on the form, yet you are obligated to respond to this inquiry at the risk of alienating a future customer. Clearly it is in the best interest of the publication seeking your advertising dollar to inundate your desk with leads produced by your ad. However, your best interests are served by producing only qualified, cost-efficient leads. In many cases this entails refusing the generous offer of bingo-card service.

Ongoing Action.   Print advertising is a relatively inexpensive means of maintaining visibility. To use this tactic effectively, a regular print schedule must be maintained, with a distinctive graphic format, consistent media placement, and a convenient means of response.

Targeting.   By careful media selection and attention to physical placement within the media used, we can attain a high level of penetration of a targeted audience. This is one of many areas in which market-research results are extremely valuable. By asking qualified prospects or current customers which publications they read regularly, we learn how to target future print-media buyers.

Direct Mail

Direct mail is the traditional backbone of a direct-response effort, and this preeminence continues within the integrated direct marketing framework. However, even seasoned direct-mail experts will have to adjust their thinking when practicing their art according to the principles of IDM.

Direct Mail Plus 800 Number

The area where coordinated media has already become commonplace is inbound telephone response. The ubiquitous 800 number is now business as usual in creating a modern direct-mail piece, although a surprising number of old-school marketers still either resist it entirely or undermine its effectiveness by burying the number in copy or mentioning it only once.

If you are serious about driving up 800-number incremental response, the number should appear within the first two paragraphs of the letter, again in the body copy, in the postscript, several times in the brochure, and prominently on the order form or business-reply card.

This goes to the heart of a crucial question in assessing direct mail: What are you selling? Of course, you are selling a product or service, but there is much more involved.

Individualization

Ideally, you are selling something which has been especially selected to be of interest to the recipient. This is more than a pat phrase to be used in the copy; it is of paramount strategic importance in the implementation of direct mail. This criterion controls your product selection, your choice of target list, and the creative presentation of your offer. In fact, the same product may be presented in radically different ways to appeal to different audiences and, in the process, boost response enormously. The mail package that goes out to a prospect who responded to an ad promoting a new gardening tool in *Modern Maturity* magazine may stress ease-of-use features, perhaps with specific reference to the problems of arthritis. A response to an ad promoting the same tool in *Organic Gardening* magazine might be followed up with a mail package highlighting the speed the tool provides in working the soil. The tool hasn't changed, but the promotional package individualizes the offer to the recipient.

Convenience

Above and beyond the specific nature of the offer, direct mail gives consumers the convenience of shopping at home. Once again, we need to go beyond the tired evocation of that phrase in copy to highlight the benefit this entails. Financial-services marketing is a clear case in point, as in the Citicorp case history presented in Chapter 1. Convenience is a central concern in this instance, functioning as a key product feature for the busy target market. The appeal of this aspect of direct mail is multiplied many times over by the use of integrated direct marketing. The mailing can both reinforce the information provided by other media and direct potential customers to their own medium of choice. Citicorp's mail package offered the convenience of inbound and outbound telephone contact as a benefit of the campaign, as well as the traditional mail response for those more comfortable with this means of reply.

Direct Mail: Catalogs plus
Telemarketing

Catalogs are another prime example of traditional mail vehicles which have had their effectiveness heightened through integrated direct marketing. Print is used to generate catalog requests, often with a toll-free telephone number to encourage response. Toll-free ordering is also used within the catalog to increase response rates. Another aspect of inbound telephone which is very much an IDM marketing tool is prominent promotion of a customer-service number within the catalog, adding a sense of reliability to the mail-order purchase process.

Outbound telemarketing can also dovetail effectively with catalog promotions. One well-known instance of this was undertaken by A. B. Dick in its office-supply sales efforts. To reach low-volume accounts without incurring the growing costs of sales-force visits, a comprehensive catalog was created. A. B. Dick went beyond simply mailing the catalog, though; it created an outbound telemarketing unit which would call catalog customers on a scheduled basis and offer to take their orders over the telephone. This active step turned an ordinary printed catalog into one component in an interactive, and highly successful, multimedia sales effort.

Another lesson from the catalog business which has special significance for the integrated direct marketer is the concept of multiple mailings. Catalog marketers expend great effort on determining the appropriate number of catalogs to issue each year, and on devising different, less costly formats which may be mailed to supplement their major full-color efforts. Even without a catalog mailing, many IDM campaigns include a series of direct mailings, each designed to complement the prospect contacts made through other media, and to fulfill a particular function at a given point in the selling curve. We will explore this multiple-mailing strategy at length in the IBM case history which concludes this chapter. In this instance, separate mailings were used to generate initial interest in the product. For a teleconference promoting the product, they were used to confirm and encourage participation in the teleconference, and to deliver the information required to make the teleconference an effective marketing experience for the participants.

In short, direct mail must be viewed from a new perspective to be most effective within an integrated media mix. This entails the highest standards of quality in design and delivery of each piece, since each element in the campaign will reflect on all the others. It also requires strategic consideration of the role which each direct-mail piece will play within the marketing continuum. Does every mailing have to do it all? Not any more. Instead, we must design the flow we want to achieve, and make sure that each mailing effectively moves the customer along to the next level of decision making, whether that is sending in a response, or picking up the telephone, or meeting with a sales representative, or simply having the background information needed to make the marketer's next active contact proceed efficiently.

IDM Media Scorecard: Direct Mail

Awareness. A powerful direct-mail package is an excellent tool for creating awareness, with or without additional media used to set the stage for receipt of the mailing. Of course, the challenge today is to gain the attention of the recipient, whose desk may well be inundated with mailings. This can be accomplished through the quality of the mail package itself, the precise selection of a target market with special interest in the subject of the mailing, and the skillful use of additional media to create an environment which draws attention to the promotion. When promoting a high-ticket item, for example, you might test a brief outbound call to announce the upcoming mail package. For this strategy to succeed, you will need a distinctive design for the outer envelope that clearly identifies it as the mailing referred to during the telephone contact.

Information. For delivering information in quantity, there is no substitute for direct mail. All the other media we employ are time-dependent. A broadcast ad lasts 30, 60, or 120 seconds, and a telephone contact lasts as long as the connection is maintained. Even print advertising will only hold the attention of the reader for a brief period. Direct mail, on the other hand, is consumed entirely at the convenience of the recipient. A mailing can be perused when the recipient has the time to deal with it. Sections can be read and reread. It can be saved for future reference, or passed along to other interested parties. The general gist can be gleaned quickly, and details consulted when needed. In a multiple-part mailing, the recipients can pick and choose the sections which draw their interest; thus the mailing fulfills the needs of letter readers, lift-note fans, order-form enthusiasts, and even token pokers and stamp lickers in the same mailing.

Action. Direct mail provides a simple and powerful call to action through the combination of mail and telephone response channels. Where it falls short, particularly in the modern avalanche of direct mail, is in creating the sense of excitement needed to produce a reaction. By employing additional channels for communication between mail recipient and marketer, including inbound and outbound telemarketing and face-to-face meetings where appropriate, IDM not only produces maximum response to the mail itself, but translates positive inclination created by the mail into positive response gained through a diverse set of channels.

Ongoing Action.   Direct mail succeeds in fostering an ongoing relationship with customers or potential customers through the personal appeal of the creative package. A good direct-mail copywriter will speak directly to the recipient, creating an atmosphere and appeal which encourages the reader's sense of involvement. Here again, targeting is an important tool. When a mailing has a clear-cut and distinctive audience, the copy can employ a tone and specific references which indicate an understanding of the target group's concerns, and this in turn will encourage repeat business.

Another key aspect of mail in developing ongoing relationships is frequency. Since direct mail is relatively inexpensive, regular contact can be maintained, even with noncustomers from promising market segments. As in our catalog examples, a campaign which uses high-cost mailings may also include less expensive interim pieces to encourage response to the other mailings, highlight special promotions, and generally keep the stream of information flowing.

Finally, direct mail should be designed with retention in mind when used in an integrated direct marketing environment. We do not want a mailing to end up in the trash can under any circumstances, but especially not when we plan to follow up with a telephone call a few days later. As we will discuss in Chapter 5 on creative execution, inventive methods to add continuing value to a mailing are worth incremental expense if that investment increases the effective life of the mailing and by doing so has a positive effect on response to other media.

Targeting.   It is axiomatic to the modern direct-response business that a direct mailing be as finely targeted as possible. While broad-based direct-mail programs (such as magazine subscription solicitations or programs to raise funds for well-known diseases) are a major factor in the overall world of direct response, integrated direct marketing campaigns focus on smaller, more select markets, where the dollar value of a purchase is higher and the long-term value of a customer to the marketer is greater. Integrated direct marketing may be too expensive to use for customer-acquisition purposes if the allowable cost per order is less than $20. However, once you have acquired a customer (or a donor, in a fund-raising program), relationship building and upgrading can be achieved in a cost-effective manner through IDM.

Inbound Telemarketing

The 800 number has fueled much of the growth in the direct-marketing business in the past few years. The shopping trip has lost much of its allure in the age of two-career couples and expanding leisure opportunities. Ordering by telephone eliminates much of the hassle of acquiring the material rewards of all your hard work. The call is free, and if you are ordering from an out-of-state vendor, there is no sales tax to pay. The incremental boost produced by adding the option of an 800-number response to traditional mail-order forms is significant.

As we move into the new age of integrated direct marketing, we look for ways to maximize our investment in inbound telemarketing. To date, this channel has been viewed almost exclusively as a service to the customer. While this is certainly valid, it can be more—a marketing channel in its own right, producing incremental sales and, equally important, additional information to be added to our all-important databases.

Cross-Selling

Any marketing operation which does not attempt some form of cross-selling on an incoming call is, in effect, throwing away money. There is an art to cross-selling (offering additional goods and services to the person calling in to place an order). The cross-sale must be pursued graciously and nonaggressively. The offer must be directly related to the order being placed. And it should be included strictly as a one- or two-sentence suggestion. The last thing we want to do is irritate the individual who has called us in the first place for the sake of convenience. On the other hand, the individual on the telephone is that most precious of direct-marketing commodities, a paying customer with absolute recency, and failing to at least attempt an incremental order is equivalent to a financial sacrifice.

Cross-selling is appropriate within the context of customer-service calls as well. The person calling has a need. The solution may be a related product or service. Even when this is not the case, you know precisely which product or service the customer-service caller is using, and can often suggest relevant additional purchases based on this knowledge.

The other valuable commodity available to the marketer in the course of the incoming call is information. Don't treat the 800-number call as a one-way connection. The telephone is an interactive device: use it that way. Once again, there are limits to the degree you can prolong the call without becoming burdensome. However, it is essential to ask for the source of an order or inquiry, to provide a means for tracking the effectiveness of each medium in the marketing mix. It is also perfectly proper to ask who else might be interested in receiving your marketing materials.

And without turning the call into a market-research questionnaire, you may be able to elicit information with a single question that can impact your future marketing efforts. For instance, you might want to know whether the caller has ever ordered from your company in the past, to gauge the degree of repeat business you are generating. If you are considering a product-line expansion, you might want to know whether the caller would consider the offer of a related item from your company. Or you might ask what it was about the offer that prompted the person to respond; this is a great way to get free, live research information. Data gathered in this way is especially valuable because you are speaking with a proven buyer, rather than an off-the-street prospect.

This active use of incoming telemarketing presupposes a level of skill on the part of the people handling your telephone orders which, frankly, is often lacking today. There are service bureaus which can handle this type of call, though, as long as they devote the necessary time to training their staff to meet your needs. Of course, an in-house telemarketing unit can be expressly developed to fulfill a more demanding role, though here too you will need, first, to be sure that the telephone staff is adequately prepared and, second, to monitor the calls regularly.

Fulfillment

The other distinctive IDM concern in the incoming telemarketing area is fulfillment. This consists of two parts: the speedy delivery of goods and services ordered, and the prompt follow-up of literature requests and other customer-service functions. In product delivery, as in every other aspect of IDM, excellence is the minimum acceptable standard, since every phase of the program reflects on every other phase. There should always be a marketing message delivered along with your package, whether that message consists of a bounce-back order form, a simple thank you for the current order, an explanation of customer-service procedures in case of problems, or all the above. In addition, offering options for special handling via express services is a positive move in many ways. Clearly, it offers an attractive benefit to the customer who requires the promptest possible service. It also makes the company offering this special service memorable as a source for future purchases. And on a more abstract level, it is a service which sets a style and tone for your operation, attesting that your company will go the extra distance in order to satisfy the customer.

Speaking of satisfying the customer, all too often the order-taking service mentality associated with 800-number response has consigned customer service to a second-tier priority. This has extremely negative consequences over the long haul, and it is the long haul that we are most concerned about here. If your company cannot deliver the answer to a simple question, or a piece of paper with product specifications, in a timely manner, why should the inquirer trust you to make good on promises connected with an actual order?

IDM Media Scorecard: Inbound Telemarketing

Awareness. While incoming telemarketing is generally an attractive convenience helping to ease the path to a purchase, there are instances in which it is central to securing the attention of the purchaser. This is particularly true when 800-number service is a distinctive feature within a product category. For example, hotel chains which offer nationwide tollfree reservation service gain a distinct edge over local establishments which may offer similar or superior accommodations, but are less accessible for out-of-town travelers. The same type of competitive advantage is gained by financial-service companies which offer attractive rates while emphasizing the convenience of transactions via mail and telephone.

Information. Inbound telemarketing offers a unique capability in delivering up-to-the-minute information in a time-sensitive environment. In a situation in which availability of products or services is limited, customers can order via toll-free number, learn what their choices are, and place orders based on this knowledge (assuming, of course, that appropriate computer systems to give the toll-free operators current information have been installed). This type of thinking applies for everything from theatre tickets and airline seats to financial transactions in fluctuating markets, to close-out, clearance, and one-of-a-kind retail sales.

Action. Inbound telemarketing is action; it is the simplest, fastest step the customer can take to make contact with a supplier. There is an unspoken contract involved in this relationship—that the company taking the order will deliver with exemplary promptness. There is less of the fuzziness in expected delivery times involved with mail order, in which customers may add a few days to their perceived schedules to allow you to receive the order through the mails. Expectations are higher with telephone ordering, and the smart marketer will devote concerted effort to fulfill those heightened expectations.

Ongoing Action.   The convenience of 800-number ordering tends to reinforce a continuing relationship, if the initial ordering experience was a good one. The expectation of a continuing relationship reinforces the demand for superior fulfillment operations, as well as the necessity for top-notch, fully trained, and monitored individuals answering the telephones.

Targeting.   A moot point essentially, since the person initiating the call is doing the targeting. An issue that should be raised, however, is the question of inappropriate incoming calls, which rack up charges to the marketer even though they do not result in an order. Unclear descriptions of an offer can lead to a host of expensive calls from questioners seeking clarification.

Even more prevalent are calls to an 800 number from customers with service problems. When you publish an 800 number, you provide a pathway to your company with no expense to the consumer and, unless there is clear guidance to the contrary, this number will be the first recourse whenever a customer wants to reach you. When the toll-free number is for ordering only, and other channels are available for obtaining further information, or getting customer service, or making other inquiries, the customer must be told precisely where to turn for help at every opportunity—particularly in your promotional material and your shipping documents. Nothing you can do will totally eliminate unproductive 800-number calls, but prominently providing information about the proper communication channels for nonordering purposes will at least minimize this unproductive expense.

Also pertinent to the subject of targeting is the opportunity to gain information from the inbound telephone call and, by using this information, to hone the focused utilization of media in future efforts. This requires training for telephone communicators to ask the questions, and a commitment to management review and analysis of the results.

Outbound Telemarketing

Once the poor stepchild of marketing media, outbound telemarketing has taken on a critical role in integrated direct marketing. The reason can be expressed in a word—*results.*

No other mass-marketing medium can put a trained sales representative in direct contact with a prospect, and do it at a tiny fraction of the cost of a live sales call. The telemarketing representative has information at hand, can reach a large proportion of the prospect market for most offers, and can economically service accounts from coast to coast.

The range of goods and services promoted through telemarketing has mushroomed. Certificates of deposit, farm products, political candidates, magazines, collectibles, pharmaceuticals, computer software, and maintenance agreements—the list could go on for pages. In fact, it is becoming increasingly difficult to find a marketing area which has not seen a success story through outbound telemarketing.

Why the poor stepchild then? Simply because during the early stages of its development, outbound telemarketing was used by some disreputable companies to bilk the public with offers of swampland, phony jewels, and other expensive hoaxes, many of which received prominent attention in the national media. The potential of the medium was too substantial to be denied, though, as more and more reputable companies employed the power of one-to-one conversation to reach target markets.

In an integrated direct marketing program, outbound telemarketing can be used to close a sale or to move a prospect one step closer to a purchase decision. In either case, the telephone call is rarely the first contact in the chain of marketing events. Instead, it is usually positioned after a mailing has been received, or in response to a request for information from a prospect.

Engaging in a telephone conversation implies some prior relationship, and this is as true for a telemarketing contact as it is for a personal call. This relationship may be as new as the direct mail which arrived a few days earlier, or as well established as a call from the bank where you've always done business.

Sometimes the reputation and visibility of a company or organization is enough to provide the basis for profitable telemarketing contact. Major corporations, well-known charitable organizations, and professional societies have reputations which win the immediate attention of the individuals they call. On the other end of the spectrum, local businesses draw on their neighborhood affiliation to gain credibility with their telemarketing prospects. In either case, the person-to-person contact provided by outbound telemarketing provides a flexible, two-way exchange that can be extremely effective in building new customer relationships, as long as the telemarketing effort is cost-justified by the ongoing value of the customer.

As in our discussion of incoming telemarketing representatives, the quality of the people doing the calling is of decisive importance. There will always be people who absolutely do not want to do business over the telephone, and the only appropriate response to that closely held preference is pleasantly saying goodbye and calling the next prospect. However, a well-conducted telemarketing contact, offering a product or service of importance to the recipient, will be welcomed by a large proportion of the prospect universe, whether this consists of individuals at home or corporate executives at work.

The range of applications for outbound telemarketing is enormous. Here are a few to consider:

- New customer acquisition
- Reactivation of past customers
- Consolidating and cross-selling existing customers
- Upgrading current customers
- Screening and qualifying leads produced through print, mail, or trade shows to determine appropriate levels of sales-force or literature follow-up
- Servicing marginal accounts whose profitability does not justify a personal sales call
- Penetrating geographically remote target markets, testing the possibilities for future expansion, or doing both at the same time
- Building traffic at retail or dealer locations

IDM Media Scorecard: Outbound Telemarketing

Awareness. Outbound telemarketing is a powerful means for focusing attention on your marketing message, thanks to the immediacy of the personal contact. It is simply easier to ignore a broadcast advertisement, or a print ad, or a mailing piece, than it is to ignore a ringing telephone. And once the telephone is answered, your marketing message is brought to life by the trained telemarketing representative who is delivering it.

Of course, with this power comes responsibility. A ringing telephone can potentially be construed as an invasion of privacy. This consideration makes the targeting of your telemarketing contact absolutely crucial. The message being conveyed must clearly be pertinent to the individual answering the telephone and must be conveyed in a concise, low-keyed manner. Outbound telemarketing must be perceived by both caller and prospect as a service to the recipient, bringing a truly important and valuable offer to his or her attention. Otherwise the personal nature of the contact, which is the very power of outbound telemarketing, will serve as an irritant rather than a means of establishing a mutually satisfactory relationship between company and customer.

Information. What is important in using outbound telemarketing as a means of communicating information is to concentrate on the strengths of the medium—the ability to deliver facts which are absolutely up to date and pertinent to the specific needs of the individual receiving the call—and to remember to use other media for your other purposes.

Specifically, lengthy descriptions with lots of detail may be important to your marketing effort, but they will fall flat if delivered over the telephone. There are times when a picture really is worth a thousand words, and it is far better to deliver that picture through print or mail than to try to paint it over the telephone. Even when words are the appropriate vehicle, printed materials which can be looked at, read, and referred to by the prospect are the appropriate means of conveying quantities of complex information.

On the other hand, the interactivity of telemarketing makes it ideal for *answering questions*—a capability unavailable elsewhere. This can be especially crucial when selling complex or unfamiliar products. To take advantage of the ability to deliver immediate answers to individual questions, you must have a well-trained telemarketing staff with fully prepared backup materials at their disposal for ready reference. Telemarketing professionals will quickly identify the questions which will come up most frequently, prepare scripted answers to them, and design a fallback position (i.e., a procedure for handling unexpected questions) that will satisfy prospects quickly and reliably.

This question-and-answer interchange offers a unique opportunity to truly understand prospects' concerns and turn them into sales opportunities. A well-structured telemarketing script will provide answers to a prospect's questions or objections, and will follow up immediately with a sales benefit related to the point which has been raised. This enables the person being called to tailor the sales presentation to his or her own personal needs through the flexibility of a two-way interchange of information.

Of course, the prospect is not the only one who can ask questions. By employing a series of screening questions, the telemarketer can categorize the prospect according to need and purchasing authority, providing highly qualified leads for further follow-up activity through direct-response or field sales force channels. Cross selling and upgrading sales are also supported by the ability to determine the prospect's needs through exploratory questioning.

While the information provided by the marketer is of utmost importance to the prospect, the response coming in from the other end of the telephone has special importance for the company engaged in telemarketing, if the marketer has the savvy to listen. The interactive telephone connection does more than provide a yes or no answer; it enables the marketer to ask "Why not?" if the offer is refused. By analyzing the responses to this question both quantitatively (How many people in each category?) and qualitatively (What specific comments were made by individuals?), we can learn a great deal about reactions to pricing, product features, and positioning relative to competitors.

Action.   Every outbound telemarketing call which reaches the individual being sought produces an action. The immediacy of the contact demands response; in this sense it is the most active marketing medium we have. This is advantageous in motivating those who were positively inclined, but might have forgotten or delayed their response, into saying yes. These fence sitters represent the majority of the positive response generated by outbound telemarketing. The prospects most anxious to respond will already have done so via mail or 800 number. The firm nos will not be convinced by telemarketing, and marketers are wise to train their staff to quickly recognize these people, gently probe their reasons for lack of interest, and graciously terminate the call.

The instant response provided by telemarketing is also valuable within the overall marketing mix as a rapid bellwether of things to come. When something is wrong, it quickly becomes apparent, and thanks to the information provided by the prospect, the steps that may be taken to fix it are also apparent. On the other hand, if the response is positive, we can move quickly to expand our efforts and take advantage of the opportunity we have uncovered. The quick readings on list segments, product features, and marketing strategy which are forthcoming from an outbound telemarketing program make it an invaluable market-testing device, in addition to its obvious function as an order generator.

Ongoing Action.   Use of continued, regular outbound telemarketing contact was mentioned above, in conjunction with the A. B. Dick catalog program. Even in a less structured framework, telemarketing contact leads a prospect to focus on the offer being made. The effect of that sense of immediacy and importance spills over into response to all other forms of media employed. Getting prospects on the telephone, explaining your offer, and responding to questions brings an important, personal customer-service dimension to the marketing program. The next time those individuals see your logo on a mailing, or flip to an advertisement from the marketing campaign that was discussed over the telephone, they are inevitably going to pay increased attention to your message. This has been measured by leading marketers such as American Express and Citicorp in tests of the mail-response rates of individuals who had been contacted via telemarketing and had refused the offer made over the telephone. This group produced 10 to 20 percent higher mail response rates than those who had received direct mail alone.

Targeting. To be cost-effective, outbound telemarketing requires more stringent targeting than other media, because of the cost of making calls and the desire not to irritate people who are not qualified prospects for the offer. Positioning this contact as a part of an established business relationship makes this level of targeting relatively clear-cut, though. If you are calling to follow up an ad response, the respondents have effectively qualified themselves through their initial interest. If you are calling an established customer with a new offer, the prior information about that customer in your files provides a clear basis for judging case by case whether or not a call is justified.

Response Compression

Deciding which media will be most effective in meeting the marketing communication requirements *at each distinctive step in the sales process* is a primary step in implementing an integrated direct-marketing campaign. In addition to knowing *how* to deliver the message and *what* the creative content of the message will be, we must determine *when* that delivery will take place.

We have found that the traditional sequencing of media does not create the maximum synergy from the media being employed. Specifically, the impressions are conveyed over too long a time period, diluting the impact to a significant degree. In the AT&T case history reviewed earlier in this chapter, and in most full-scale IDM campaigns, we create a sequence of ongoing contacts, using a variety of media. These are deployed with short, carefully orchestrated intervals between contacts so that we gain a disproportionate share of the prospect's attention. For a 2-week period in the lives of the financial managers who were prospects for AT&T Mortgage Line, the AT&T product and the upcoming trade show were brought to the forefront of their minds. A sense of event was generated—a feeling that something important was going on. It would be far more difficult, if not impossible, to achieve this effect through isolated media.

We call this tighter time-frame approach *response compression*. By deploying media in an abbreviated time frame, we create an intensified synergy between media that generates much higher response rates. The principle of response compression offers dual benefits—greater total response and faster results.

Response-compression techniques increase results by maximizing the cumulative effect of the combined media. The following figures represent typical results produced through closely sequenced integrated direct-marketing contacts:

Direct mail	1.0 percent response
800 number (30 to 100 percent lift)	0.3 to 1 percent
Outbound telemarketing (100 to 1000 percent lift).	1.0 to 10.0 percent.
Cumulative response rate	2.3 to 12 percent

One prime example of the effect of response compression involves the traditional sequencing of direct mail with outbound telephone follow-up. The industry rule of thumb says to wait 2 to 3 weeks after direct-mail receipt before placing the outbound call. Why? So that the mail response has a chance to come in, and so that those individuals who have responded can be removed from the calling list.

What is the logic involved in this approach? The goal is to avoid duplicating effort, and there is no argument that a call placed to someone who has already responded positively is unproductive. Further, when we see that the cost of a telemarketing call is 5 to 10 times higher than the cost of an average direct-mail piece, we correctly say that a mail response is less expensive than a telemarketing response.

Think about the matter a little further, though, and you realize that the traditional thinking doesn't make sense in today's competitive environment. In an IDM operation we routinely call within 3 days of receipt of mail. What is the downside to this strategy?

▪ *Some people who have already responded by mail will be called for no reason.*   Granted. But since a rule-of-thumb response rate for mail is only 1 to 2 percent, we would be holding off on making a powerful, complementary impact, via telephone, upon 98 percent of our target market if we waited until mail peaked and then began calls to prospects who had by now largely forgotten the mail message. The extra telephone call to those who have already said yes is not burdensome to them; it is a simple matter for them to just say so and hang up the telephone. In fact, since a well-conducted outbound telemarketing call is a positive experience, the additional contact will enhance the buyer's sense of importance to the marketing company, especially if some important product benefit is reinforced in the call to reassure the customer that the purchase decision was a good one. The calls to the few previous positive respondents are brief, serve some useful purpose, and are certainly cost-justified compared with the lost opportunity entailed in waiting for the mail response to peak.

- *Some people who would have responded to the mailing, given a chance, will instead respond by telephone, and a telephone response is more expensive.* In the real world, the majority of responses to a direct mailing occur soon after receipt. The mailing which is set aside for further attention at some later date rarely receives that attention. Therefore, the individuals who might have answered the mailing had they not been telephoned is a minuscule market segment—yet it can stand in the way of reaching the real market in a timely, powerful manner.

On the other hand, what do we gain by timing our telephone follow-up in tight sequence after mail receipt? We have learned over time that adding outbound telemarketing follow-up to a direct mailing will multiply our response rate. The question is, what level of response do we want to multiply—the fresh, hot response rate produced when the offer is new, or the lower level of enthusiasm which results after time has passed? Consider Figures 2.2 and 2.3.

In both cases mail response remains the same, and telemarketing produces the same percentage lift to the overall response. But in Figure 2.3, with outbound telemarketing calls placed soon after mail receipt, this lift occurs while interest and response are still high, creating a far greater total response than in Figure 2.2.

Experience tells us that telemarketing will produce, on average, a 5-time lift over *current* direct-mail response rates. In Figure 2.2, that mail response rate has already dropped to about 0.25 percent before telemarketing is begun, so our 5-time multiplier for telephone only produces 1.25 percent. In Figure 2.3, though, outbound calls begin when mail response is still near its peak—about 1 percent in this example.

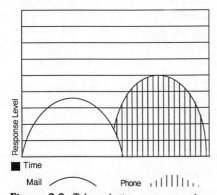

Figure 2.2. Telemarketing response when begun toward the end of the mail-response curve.

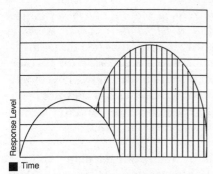

Figure 2.3. Outbound telemarketing follow-up closer to the direct-mail response peak produces higher total response for a longer time.

Therefore, telephone produces a full 5 percent response, and the total response for both media is dramatically greater than in the first scenario.

In fact, there is evidence to suggest that the response multiple produced by outbound telemarketing actually *increases* when calls begin soon after mail receipt, because of the stronger base mail-response rate in effect. At this writing we do not have enough statistical evidence to prove this assertion, but it is certainly a logical premise.

In summary, we recommend direct mail with an 800-number response option to be delivered *within a week* of the appearance of print advertising; outbound telemarketing contact should occur *3 to 4 days* after mail receipt. Mailings should be staggered to allow time for multiple telemarketing attempts and callbacks to those not available on the first attempt. To complete the cycle for maximum customer satisfaction, orders should be fulfilled as quickly as possible. Optimally this should be within 48 hours of receipt—or, at the least, a note confirming the order should be sent within 48 hours.

It takes more effort to make the elements of a marketing campaign click into place within a tight time frame. The required level of precision involved at every phase of media advertising, mail, and telephone contact in this scenario is greater than internal resources or outside vendors are probably used to achieving. However, the reward for excellence in this case is the dramatically higher response rates produced through response compression, and that is a goal worth striving for.

Planning and Executing the Media Mix

To sum up the thinking involved in planning and executing the media mix in a successful IDM campaign, we turn to Robert J. Blair. As manager of direct marketing communications for IBM, Mr. Blair was responsible for an IDM program that employed diverse, highly targeted media to manage an extremely challenging marketing situation. In this example, a new and vastly improved version of a computer software package was released—software which, in its initial release, had not achieved its market forecast.

A Case in Point

IBM System Software

Robert J. Blair, *Former Manager of Direct Marketing Communication, IBM*

The IBM Corporation has a long history of product and marketing innovation and excellence. Direct marketing has been used in various forms for many years, changing as products and customer's expectations have changed, reacting to the increased costs of more traditional forms of selling, and adapting to take advantage of new direct marketing ideas and tools.

One of the newest ideas, which encompasses and utilizes the maximum potential of all the marketing tools employed, is integrated direct marketing. The principles of IDM have been used for typewriter sales, typewriter accessory and supply sales, PC accessory and supply sales, software sales, and minicomputer sales lead generation. IDM has also been used in connection with mainframe sales. It has been used for target audiences as small as 100 and as large as several million, for customers and for prospects, for a wide variety of organizational levels and functional titles.

One interesting example of IBM's use of IDM techniques involved a software security system for mainframe computers. Its basic functions are to establish security, to limit access to layers of information, and to police those layers to prevent unauthorized access or manipulation of data.

IBM marketing, sales, and customer service identified many areas for product enhancement after the initial introduction of the program. This resulted in several releases of enhanced versions of the package. The latest release of the program contained a host of improvements over the earlier version, and was supported by an IDM campaign. The objectives of the campaign were to:

- Make IBM mainframe customers aware of the latest version of the program.
- Highlight substantial price and performance enhancements.
- Involve customers with the product and its benefits.
- Generate high-quality leads for the IBM sales force.

Resource Allocation

Concurrently with setting goals and determining the target market, we had to assess our own internal capabilities (and time constraints) and decide whether this project would be executed totally by IBM personnel or performed outside the company—and if outside, whether by the agency of record or by a specialized IDM agency. Our function's stated charter was to manage resources so as to attain company marketing objectives in a successful, cost-effective manner. It was decided that this project could best be achieved by retaining an outside agency.

We elected, after a search, to assign the campaign to an IDM specialized agency which had prior experience with IBM direct marketing operations.

Management had limited resources for the campaign, but high expectations. They wanted results—high-quality leads for the sales force that would convert, with a minimum of additional expenditure, to sales.

The agency chosen offered us the following advantages:

- Years of experience with IBM
- Thorough knowledge of the IBM customer set
- Understanding of IBM corporate structure
- Ability to plan an integrated campaign
- Ability to enlist the finest talent within each functional area (e.g., creative, design, printing, other related skills)

Once this team was organized, we began to evaluate and assess all aspects of the campaign. Agreement was then reached on the campaign objectives.

The initial target market was expanded. It was determined that within each corporation there were two individuals, each with separate concerns, who ultimately interacted on the buy decision for this software. Market research confirmed that the vice president of information processing and the vice president of finance were the two functional people we must ultimately convince.

The target market was further expanded beyond the IBM database of customers. A regression analysis of the portion of the database matching our criteria was undertaken. The resulting profile was used as a model for selecting outside lists. Criteria included:

- Name (rather than title only) and title
- SIC
- Size of organization (gross sales)
- Number of employees
- Mainframe equipment installed (IBM or IBM-compatible)

Methodology

Methodology is an easy word to pronounce, but it is a difficult concept to agree upon.

At this point in the campaign planning cycle we had all agreed upon the program objectives and ordered the lists encompassing the target market. However, the method of achieving our objectives of awareness, involvement, and action was the subject of much study and review.

A traditional approach would have been to use direct mail to the target market (a very traditional approach would have been to mail to only one executive per company). The offer would have been to attend a demonstration or a seminar on the product. After the demonstration or seminar, each attendee would be contacted by an IBM salesperson.

Ultimately this approach was rejected. Why?

- We felt the target market already knew about the product from previous releases and promotions.
- We knew that there was a certain lack of understanding about the product based upon the performance of earlier releases.

Therefore the use of a traditional product brochure mailing was rejected. Moreover,

- Product demonstrations could only be conducted at IBM customer-service centers having the appropriate mainframe capabilities, potentially creating a situation in which executives might have to travel to attend.
- The customer executive's busy schedules might preclude attendance, especially if considerable time was involved.
- The expense to IBM could be significant, thus driving the cost per sale up and adversely affecting profitability.

Market research was undertaken. Specifically, we asked a representative sampling of our target market what they wanted from a mainframe security system and what they thought about the IBM product. Their answers became the backbone of our promotion. They told us, in their own words, what they wanted to hear about the product. Based on their responses, it was apparent that the new release of the product was right on target. The challenge was how to convince an entire target universe.

We found that, first and foremost, the IBM reputation was our greatest asset.

Therefore, our first objective was to reopen the door to communication about this product. The research made it clear that the improvements must be presented in a straightforward, authoritative manner.

To enhance the effectiveness of this campaign, to underscore the importance of our audience, and to utilize the power of IDM, we arrived at a multiple-stage promotion.

Mailing 1

A 6- × 9-inch format was chosen. The large size offered impact as well as sufficient display space for exciting, eye-catching graphics. The piece was to serve as an invitation, to get members of our target market to reserve space at our event.

Graphics for the invitation were created utilizing an IBM PC-XT (a fact we promoted) in conjunction with an advanced computerized design system (Figure 2.4). The visual was obviously technological: a confusion of bits and bytes which were put through a black box and came out ordered in straight lines. Parts of the graphics were carried through on the outer envelope and on the reply card.

Graphic development had to serve two masters: (1) the objectives of the promotion and (2) our modest budget. The result was a striking two-color design.

The outer envelope was addressed directly to the person, demonstrating a key philosophical point of IDM. We are writing to these people in the most businesslike manner because they are important. We recognize their stature and treat them accordingly. The extra effort is reflected in our offer and rewarded in our response rates. In addition to the synergy created by the planned integration of media, personalization can effect up to a 15 percent lift in measurable response (Figure 2.5).

Printed in bold type on the outer envelope was the message RSVP, implying an invitation and helping to convince our target market to open the envelope.

The brochure formally announced the enhanced version of the product, invited the recipient to be our guest at an audio teleconference to learn how IBM can address the escalating requirements of data security today and tomorrow, and proceeded to enumerate the many benefits of the revised product.

Executives could respond via the enclosed postage-paid business reply card or, for faster service, use a toll-free 800 number. We requested a specific reservation by date and time (four teleconferences were scheduled), and asked for the names and titles of interested colleagues who would also be participating. The offer was time-sensitive, since we asked for all responses by a certain date and time.

The first mailing went via U.S. Postal Service first-class mail, presorted.

The Audio Teleconference

To quote from the brochure:

> At a predetermined date and time, we will connect you and your counterparts at other companies via telephone lines to an interactive audio teleconference on [the product]. Should you desire, you are welcome to use a speakerphone and invite interested colleagues to participate. It should take about one hour.

An audio teleconference is a relatively new concept. Individuals or groups of individuals are linked via telephone lines to a central location where the presenters are located. At each participating location you might have one person at a telephone, or your entire target market at each company's location might be seated around a speakerphone, looking at the visual materials you have supplied, listening to the dissemination of information, and participating in the interactive phase.

Typically an audio teleconference begins with a discourse or product overview. This is followed by an interactive question-and-answer period. This is accomplished without chaos; calls are centrally coordinated, and questions

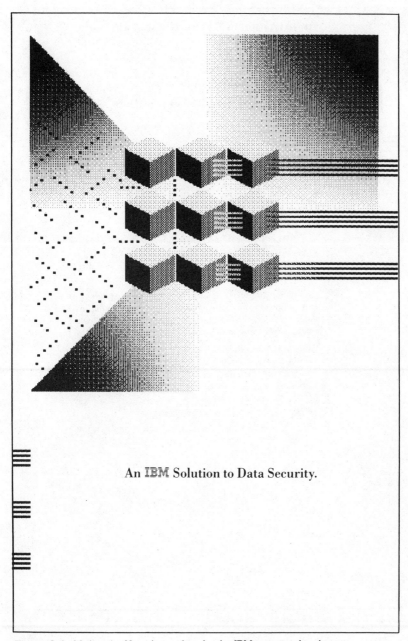

An IBM Solution to Data Security.

Figure 2.4. Mailing 1—Upscale graphics for the IBM invitation brochure.

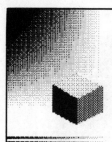

An Invitation to Be Our Guest at an Audio Teleconference.

Learn How IBM Can Address the Escalating Requirements of Data Security...

Today and Tomorrow.

Your corporate data base is a critical resource. Its accidental or intentional destruction, modification or disclosure can have serious, far-reaching implications.

Now, IBM introduces a security solution that can be easy to install and use. It has the ability to delegate control of selected resources to appropriate groups of users, and thus minimize the impact on the DP staff.

Additionally, it interfaces directly with users, displays service options and commands in a menu format, and provides a HELP facility. All to maintain, and possibly enhance, company-wide productivity.

Other benefits include:

▶ *identification and verification of users by password*
▶ *authorization checking for access requests*
▶ *journaling, logging and reporting of security violations and accesses to systems resources*
▶ *the IBM service and support you expect.*

We'd like to tell you more. In fact, we're inviting you to talk to IBM's top data security experts and the program authors from your own office.

Figure 2.4. *(Continued.)* **Mailing 1—A brochure to enumerate benefits.**

At a predetermined date and time, we will connect you and your counterparts at other companies via telephone lines to an interactive audio teleconference. Should you so desire, you are welcome to use a speakerphone and invite interested colleagues to participate. It should take about one hour from beginning to end.

The audio teleconference will be held on Thursday, December 5, 1985, at 10 a.m. and at 3 p.m.; and on Thursday, December 12, 1985, at 10 a.m. and again at 3 p.m.

To facilitate scheduling, *we must have your reply by 5 p.m., e.s.t., Monday, November 18, 1985.*

For a reservation, just call IBM toll free at 1 800 752-5207. Or, if you prefer, complete and mail the enclosed postage-paid card. We'll contact you with all the particulars.

Sincerely,

A. J. Wall
Manager, Product Marketing—DP Professional
National Accounts Division

P.S. Participants will also receive, at no cost, a general information manual and other materials that will help you get the most out of this audio teleconference.

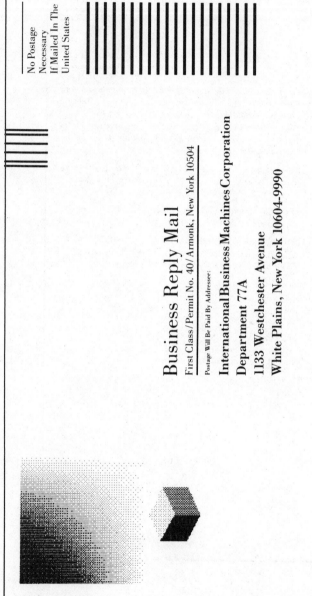

Business Reply Mail

First Class/Permit No. 40/Armonk, New York 10504

Postage Will Be Paid By Addressee:

International Business Machines Corporation

Department 77A

1133 Westchester Avenue

White Plains, New York 10604-9990

Figure 2.4. (*Continued.*) Business-reply card—front.

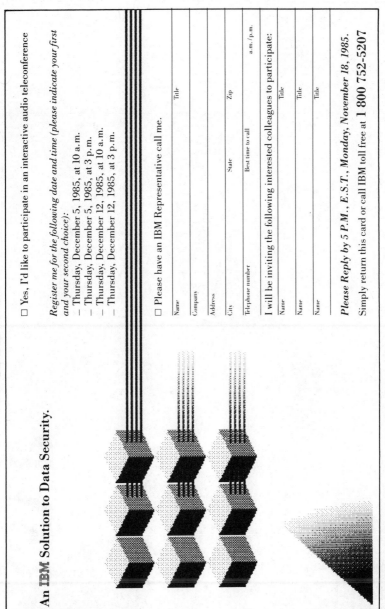

An **IBM** Solution to Data Security.

☐ Yes, I'd like to participate in an interactive audio teleconference

Register me for the following date and time (please indicate your first and your second choice):

— Thursday, December 5, 1985, at 10 a.m.
— Thursday, December 5, 1985, at 3 p.m.
— Thursday, December 12, 1985, at 10 a.m.
— Thursday, December 12, 1985, at 3 p.m.

☐ Please have an IBM Representative call me.

Name	Title
Company	
Address	
City	State Zip
Telephone number	Best time to call a.m./p.m.

I will be inviting the following interested colleagues to participate:

Name	Title
Name	Title
Name	Title

Please Reply by 5 P.M., E.S.T., Monday, November 18, 1985.
Simply return this card or call IBM toll free at **1 800 752-5207**

Figure 2.4. (*Continued.*) Business-reply card—back.

Figure 2.5. Mailing 1—Personalization lifts response.

are entertained on a location-by-location basis. The teleconference host controls the flow of the program without limiting individuals' access to the IBM experts. Records are kept on all callers, including when they hang up. An audiotape of the teleconference is also created.

The audio teleconference was selected because it satisfied key objectives:

- As a new medium it has impact and commands attention.
- It is less costly than a seminar and can simultaneously accommodate many locations.
- *Each location can accommodate many individuals or decision makers.*
- *Each individual or decision maker will be directly, interactively in touch with IBM product experts.*
- *A quality, innovative experience can potentially make a lasting impression.*

To ensure a lasting impression of the product and the media used, we said in the brochure, "We're inviting you to talk to IBM's top data security experts and the program authors...from your own office."

In other words, we were inviting them to talk with the very individuals who had come up with the software design and implementation and who had eventually made it work. These were not sales-oriented people. Further, these experts were instructed to emphasize candor in this learning experience for participants.

Inbound and Outbound Telemarketing

In addition to the option of an 800-number response to the invitational mailing, we began outbound telemarketing to each targeted executive approximately 72 hours after the mail was dropped.

Scripts were carefully developed and tested to arrive at the crucial mix of buying triggers (on the basis of information developed from customer research) to stimulate a decision to participate in the audio teleconference.

It is important to remember just what our objectives were—not just the objectives of the campaign, but the objectives of each individual medium within the campaign. Our overall goal was to generate highly qualified leads that could easily be converted to sales. For this phase, however, our objective was only to secure participation in the audio teleconference—a step on the road to a sale.

Mailing 2

The objective for mailing 2 was the confirmation of an appointment for an audio teleconference. Whether the initial response came by mail, 800 number, or outbound telemarketing, a postcard echoing the program's graphic design was generated and sent within 24 hours of receipt of the registration request. Each respondent's name, title, and address, as well as the date and time of the appointment, were laser-printed onto the postcard (Figure 2.6), which also stated, "Thank you for your interest in learning more about...the IBM

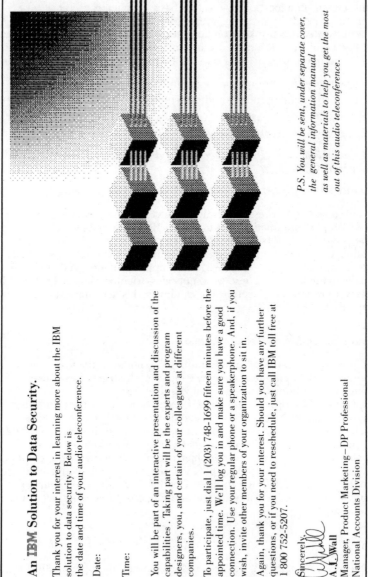

An IBM Solution to Data Security.

Thank you for your interest in learning more about the IBM solution to data security. Below is the date and time of your audio teleconference.

Date:

Time:

You will be part of an interactive presentation and discussion of the capabilities. Taking part will be the experts and program designers, you, and certain of your colleagues at different companies.

To participate, just dial 1 (203) 748-1699 fifteen minutes before the appointed time. We'll log you in and make sure you have a good connection. Use your regular phone or a speakerphone. And, if you wish, invite other members of your organization to sit in.

Again, thank you for your interest. Should you have any further questions, or if you need to reschedule, just call IBM toll free at 1 800 752-5207.

Sincerely,

A. J. Wall
Manager, Product Marketing—DP Professional
National Accounts Division

P.S. You will be sent, under separate cover, the general information manual as well as materials to help you get the most out of this audio teleconference.

Figure 2.6. Mailing 2—Appointment confirmation sent within 24 hours.

solution to data security. Below is the date and time of your...audio teleconference."

Then we told the executives what to expect:

> You will be part of an interactive presentation and discussion of the capabilities of the program. Taking part will be the experts and program designers, you, and certain of your colleagues at different companies.

> To participate, just dial x-xxx-xxxx fifteen minutes before the appointed time. We'll log you in and make sure you have a good connection. Use your regular telephone or a speakerphone. And, if you wish, invite other members of your organization to sit in.

In every case, we attempted to encourage all decision makers to set aside time for the teleconference.

Mailing 3

Of course, our objectives are not achieved by getting a simple reservation for participation. For our efforts to be successful—to achieve a highly qualified lead—the teleconference must be a quality experience.

To ensure this quality experience, mailing 3 was undertaken to all registrants. Timing was critical. This 9- by 12-inch package, with graphics clearly identifying it as part of the promotion, was mailed first-class by U.S. Postal Service to arrive approximately 3 workdays before the scheduled teleconference (Figure 2.7). The outer envelope bore the teaser "Enclosed is the Information You Requested."

Inside, a letter briefly resold the program and the audio teleconference concept and instructions. More importantly, it guided respondents to the enclosures, consisting of:

- A guide to the initial presentation
- Suggested questions for discussion
- The general product-information manual

Not only did we give registrants comprehensive background material on the product and visual material to help them follow along during the audio presentation; we also armed them with the questions research said were critical to the acceptance of the product, covering areas that included reliability, support, availability, performance, logging and reporting, user interface, and resources.

By highlighting these questions—thus prompting the decision makers themselves to ask them—we hoped to firmly establish their level of confidence in our product and thus turn them into highly qualified sales leads for the IBM sales force.

Outbound Confirmation Call

The day before each scheduled teleconference, our outbound telemarketing agency called all the decision makers who had made reservations to remind them of the value of participating. This was done to maintain the sense of

Figure 2.7. Mailing 3—Follow-up background material to ensure program quality.

urgency generated by the communications to date, and thus ensure a high level of participation.

Integrated Direct Marketing at Work—Results

As we have multiple layers of media, we have multiple layers of response. Let's begin, and as we do, please be aware that only the essence of results can be shared—exact numbers would violate confidentiality.

The initial phase of media was aimed at reaching our target market, delivering enough buying triggers to achieve teleconference reservations. We had to penetrate the initial level of marketing noise and educate the market to the benefits of an audio teleconference both as a concept and as it related to the product.

We offered a choice of four teleconferences over 2 days. Although teleconference technology can accommodate up to several hundred sites, we allowed for a maximum of only 75 registrations, considering the market and the level of interaction we anticipated and estimating that 50 sites would actually log on and participate. However, registration for the four teleconferences was filled after only 2 days of response.

Demand was obviously high. We went back to the program presenters, but because of their complicated schedules, we were only able to get agreement for another two conferences on a third day. The registrations for the additional two teleconferences were filled within a week.

The synergy created by combining mail with inbound and outbound telemarketing not only produced high response levels but also compressed the typical bell-shaped response curve. We got more response over a shorter period of time.

The 800 number produced a 200 percent incremental lift over direct-mail response. Outbound telemarketing generated a 2700 percent incremental lift over mail. The total mail and telemarketing response was over 20 percent.

The second phase of media was aimed at getting good participation and ensuring the quality of the teleconferencing experience. We again had to reach the target market, now through two mail vehicles (one to confirm registration, the next to deliver incisive materials) and one outbound call the day before the teleconference (to ensure participation). Each form of communication had to reinforce the messages already delivered as well as imparting its own buying triggers to achieve this next level of response.

Measurement of response for level 2 takes three forms. One is simple participation: How many sites sign on? The second is the number of decision makers and influencers participating at each site. The third is how long each site remained on the telephone. Our teleconferencing agency not only logged each site onto the conference and kept a record of each site's (and decision maker's) participation but also monitored, and kept a record of when each site hung up. Moreover, a tape of the entire hour-long conference was made available to us.

Our goal of 50 participating sites per teleconference was attained, and in certain instances surpassed. We averaged over two decision makers per site, and 85 percent of all sites participated in the entire teleconference.

This quantifiable evidence is proof of the synergy and the momentum created and maintained by the scientific use of integrated direct marketing.

Different portions of our overall message were delivered in a sequence

determined by research, designed to establish a dialogue aimed at our
ultimate goals for this project.

To restate: our target market was the vice presidents of data processing
and the vice presidents of finance at sites that had IBM mainframes installed.
Our objectives were to:

- Make IBM mainframe customers aware of the product.

- Highlight the enhancements, price, and performance of the product,
  creating the most complete and completely useful mainframe security
  system available.

- Involve customers with the product and its benefits.

- Generate high-quality leads for the IBM sales force.

The program was a success. Measured against our objectives, our integrated
direct marketing plan reached a sizable portion of our target market and got
them to respond. Members of our target market became:

- Aware of the product and the many product enhancements IBM introduced.

- Involved in the enhancements and in how the product could benefit their
  companies' computer security operations on the practical level of price and
  performance.

The responders took action and participated in the teleconference. The
question-and-answer period was stimulating and detailed. The quality of the
resulting sales leads proves that our concept of having a dialogue with the
inventors and programmers of the product worked. The IBM technical
wizards were able to address concerns and answer detailed questions with an
honesty that served to dispel much of our target market's hesitation about
talking to a sales representative.

Leads, in fact, were generated and forwarded to the sales force. On our
self-imposed sliding scale of qualification, those decision makers who stayed
on line for the entire teleconference and asked questions were ranked
highest. This ranking held true when logged against sales.

At the same time, the executives who participated in the teleconference
received letters sent in the names of the sales representatives, thanking them for
their participation and telling them to expect follow-up.

Leads were delivered on three-part referral forms. We wanted to present the
leads in a format that connoted to the sales representatives the time, energy, and
cost that had gone into this program, a format that conveyed the importance and
high quality of the leads. The second reason for this format was accountability.
We wanted to know what happened after the leads left our hands.

The lead referral form was in three parts when handed to the local
marketing manager. It detailed the name and title of the lead, the corporate
name and address, the telephone number and best time to call (based on our
experience from the outbound calls), and the audio teleconference attended.
The marketing manager added the name of the assigned sales representative—the account executive (AE)—and delivered the lead.

IBM account executives were asked to list the dates and times of their follow-up efforts as well as the result of each contact. If a sale resulted, we asked for particulars. If no sale resulted, we asked for a reason.

Sales representatives who were interested in further qualifying a lead were welcome to listen to the tape of the teleconference to ascertain who was participating at the site and the exact questions asked by the prospects.

At the end of the first month the AEs were asked to return the forms. They kept one copy, one copy was retained by marketing management, and one copy was returned to us.

Ultimately, sales representatives reported that the leads were highly qualified, that most of their job was now confined to terms, delivery and installation. Conversion to sales was very high, which in my book is true cost efficiency.

3
Strategic Planning for IDM Success

There are two separate and distinct levels of planning required for successful integrated direct marketing.

First we must identify the role direct marketing will play within the overall business plan of the company. This decision making is part of a strategic planning process, a structured combination of research, analysis, and creative thinking that defines *where* the company is going and *why*.

Only after these issues are settled can we tackle the nuts-and-bolts issues of *how* to get there. Once management has specified the goals, we can develop the specific resources to get the job done.

The management issues involved in implementing an IDM plan will be covered in Chapter 4. First, though, it is vitally important that we review the initial strategic planning activity in some depth. This is the stage in which senior management must set the agenda, determine the allocation of company resources, and make a commitment that will enable business-unit management to aggressively pursue direct-marketing success with a clear mandate.

The Special Importance of Strategic Planning to IDM

Strategic planning is a general business tool, rather than a specifically marketing-oriented discipline. However, we will linger on the topic here, and offer some relevant advice from strategic planning experts, because effective integrated direct marketing is nearly impossible if it is not rooted in a strategic plan. The planning phase is even more crucial for success in integrated direct marketing than in traditional direct-marketing programs, because of the unique requirements of IDM.

"Turf" Issues

Integrated direct marketing violates traditional divisions of responsibility, both within the company and between outside vendors. None of the media employed, or the experts who employ them, function entirely independently in an IDM campaign. Instead, each medium must be tightly coordinated with the marketing goals and functional capabilities of all the other media.

For example, a program that includes outbound telemarketing contact to newspaper coupon respondents will be a disaster if too many leads are produced too quickly for prompt follow-up. Controlling the flow dictates distinctive requirements for the print campaign. If the only planned response to inquiries were direct-mail follow-up, then a fast, high-volume response from print ads would be desirable. To make print an effective front end for telemarketing response, though, both the copy and the response devices offered must actively prescreen and qualify responses, cutting down on the response totals but enhancing the quality of leads produced. The media schedule will also have to be tailored to coordinate with the follow-up capabilities of the telemarketing operation.

The same interdependence exists across all affected departments in an IDM environment. And it takes a clear strategic plan, with a decisive mandate from top management, to motivate individual professionals from different disciplines to engage in a fully cooperative undertaking.

Nontraditional Analysis

Compounding the potential problem of cooperation across media and departments is the shake-up in the traditional devices used to measure success or failure in each area.

If a direct-mail piece would draw a 2 percent response on its own, and has that response cut in half by an aggressive telemarketing campaign timed to tightly coincide with the receipt of mail and benefit from response-compression techniques, then the measure of success must be the *combined* response generated by the two media working synergistically.

All levels of management called upon to pass judgment on the direct-marketing effort must accept this standard. Then, and equally important, the direct-mail manager who sees the response rate suffering at the expense of telemarketing response must be fully and entirely reassured that this effect is an accepted part of the overall plan.

The same give and take can be found in many aspects of the overall operation impacted by integrated direct marketing. We may find new stress in the fulfillment end, for example, if we decide to add an overnight delivery option to our traditional methods of shipping. Suddenly the fulfillment manager has a new express-service vendor to deal with, new procedures to develop and train, tighter shipping deadlines to meet—altogether a host of additional problems which can't help but raise the overhead in that department, especially in the short run. There may be a dozen excellent marketing reasons to provide an overnight delivery option, but unless the fulfillment manager knows that the increased costs are an integral part of a strategic plan that makes allowances for the change, self-preservation is the only reasonable response—and the manager will therefore fight the change tooth and nail.

The allocation of resources and the response expectation for each individual medium will frequently be outside traditional rule-of-thumb measures in an IDM campaign. This requires a mutual agreement between senior management and those who will carry out the program, with clear-cut goals and responsibilities delineated. That will only occur in the course of a formal strategic planning process.

Commitment to Testing

Another key aspect of integrated direct marketing that relies on a formal strategic plan is the technique's reliance on extensive and exhaustive testing. Testing different list segments and creative packages is, of course, the hallmark of direct marketing in general, and the ability to accurately track response and make improvements in future efforts based on this information is a major reason for the general boom in direct marketing. When we move into an integrated direct-marketing environment, though, the testing procedure becomes all the more complicated.

Suddenly we are not dealing only with the response generated by a single medium in isolation but with the interactions occurring between media as well. If we are testing several mailing pieces, a number of different strategies for following up on the mailing, and a variety of list segments, the number of potential test cells increases rapidly.

This kind of test management and result tracking increases the initial expense involved, and requires management personnel to devote more time and energy to the back-end analysis process. The reason for undertaking relatively complex testing is the same as the reason for embarking on IDM in the first place—to identify the unique interrelationships between media that create a cost-efficient, synergistic response. A strategic plan that clearly identifies the goals of the program and the philosophy driving the effort will make the apparent vice of complexity into a clear virtue.

Potential for Dramatic Change

Perhaps the most significant reason that formal strategic planning is so essential to successful integrated direct marketing is the potential for major changes in the status quo inherent in the IDM process. IDM has the potential of generating such a volume of business that it can truly serve as an alternate or supplemental channel of distribution. This effect must be carefully coordinated with the current business procedures of the company. Essentially, there are three ways in which IDM methodology can be brought to bear on an ongoing business:

- To maximize existing distribution, i.e., to generate qualified leads for existing sales force and thereby maximize their productivity
- To supplement existing distribution, for example, by still employing traditional methods such as representatives or dealers but also making products or services available directly to end users
- To replace existing distribution, as, for example, in insurance companies that might drop their agent force and become direct writers, or banks that eliminate branch offices and rely on direct marketing to achieve national expansion

These three applications are not mutually exclusive. A manufacturer might use IDM techniques to screen and qualify leads for the house sales force. Simultaneously, the company could move lower-volume customers from sales-representative contact to catalog shopping, and expand into geographical territories not covered by an existing sales force that was using direct marketing vehicles exclusively.

Undertaking this sort of effort, though, or even a more modest shift in distribution, will inevitably cause ripples in the status quo. Sometimes those ripples turn into tidal waves, particularly as the direct-response methods prove their effectiveness.

"But we're only testing direct marketing. Why would anyone feel threatened by testing?" That attitude is all well and good for the individual proposing a test program, but won't do much to quiet the misgivings of employees who see the possibility of major changes if the test program succeeds. If you do not sell the program internally based on benefits to all concerned, then the test will be unfairly burdened from the beginning by a lack of cooperation, or even out-and-out disruption. Consider the difficulties outlined by John Hunter in the Citicorp case history (Chapter 1), when field sales-force personnel disrupted the test program by continuing to call on direct marketing prospects and slowing the processing of applications received through IDM channels. Citicorp was able to overcome this uncooperative start by improved communication with the sales force, explaining the benefits accruing to personnel through a program that streamlined loan closings and allowed them to concentrate on larger accounts.

The Citicorp experience is not an isolated incident by any means. Even at the earliest test stages of an integrated direct marketing program, senior management must have a very clear strategic sense of the program's goals and its implications for all concerned should it succeed. This vision must then be communicated to all relevant employees to ensure cooperation.

Elements of Strategic Planning

The strategic planning process involves finding answers to four key questions:

- Who are we as a company?
- Where are we?
- What future goals do we want for our company?
- How are we going to achieve these goals?

Each of these questions can be answered glibly in a moment or two. The insightful manager, though, will see that these inquiries offer the basis for a probing analysis of a company's entire operation.

One argument frequently put forth *against* devoting substantial time and resources to strategic planning is the difficulty, if not impossibility, of predicting the future. Certainly the anonymous wit who said "Forecasting is hard—particularly forecasting the future" had a relevant point. The volatile nature of both the national and the world economies makes long-range prediction a risky business. That fact, combined with changeable conditions within the individual company itself, will limit our strategic planning to a reasonable time frame, and require us to re-assess the plan elements both on a regular basis and in the event of major fluctuations that impact the business.

However, the answers to the core questions involved in strategic planning do not change so rapidly. While external forces may produce unexpected stresses on the company, the identity and resources of that company are relatively stable. Therefore, the strategic planning questions outlined above are valid as tools for immediate assessment of the status quo, for planning a coherent approach to future economic stability and growth, and for providing the groundwork underlying any ongoing communication with the marketplace.

Who Are We as a Company?   Assessing the company's self-image and, equally important, the image of the company within the marketplace is valuable no matter what economic changes may arise.

Consider the Citicorp home equity loan program. This IDM program, undertaken to move into new geographical markets with new products, was entirely consistent with Citicorp's position as an aggressive, innovative financial institution. For another, more conservative competitor, this level of risk taking would have been inappropriate.

Where Are We?   Bringing objective, factual information to bear in answering this question can clarify both the problems and the opportunities that exist within the company.

The AT&T Mortgage Line experience discussed in Chapter 2 is relevant. By insightfully assessing the opportunity available in the marketplace at a specific time, the company found immediate direction for pursuing its long-term goals: increased sales of computer systems.

What Future Goals Do We Want for Our Company?   The agenda for future growth set by senior management will effectively limit or expand the perspective of everyone in the company.

Tell a middle manager that the company is an aggressive corporation eager to use its marketing capabilities in any profitable channel that presents itself, and that manager will offer wide-ranging suggestions which may prove extremely valuable. Tell the same manager that the company is, was, and always will be a shoe-polish manufacturer, and you won't hear any suggestions that venture higher than the ankle.

This is not to say that there's anything inherently wrong with limiting your company to a single specialty, if that suits management goals.

However, coming to a clear decision about the company's direction and effectively communicating this decision to all concerned will channel the efforts and creative energies of the company toward a common goal.

How Are We Going to Achieve these Goals?   In answering this question from a strategic planning perspective, we are looking at establishing a direction, rather than crossing the t's and dotting the i's on purchase requisitions.

Is the company generally willing to invest capital in developing internal resources, or should work be distributed to outside vendors without increasing overhead?

Is the image to be conveyed in marketing efforts that of a superior-quality supplier, with the ancillary marketing and public-relations expenses this entails, or is cost cutting the operating philosophy?

Without a clear strategic plan in hand, managers are left to their own devices in answering these questions, which in turn encourages timid decision making. And timidity is no asset when it comes to integrated direct marketing.

Developing the Strategic Plan

To provide a step-by-step path for management to follow in developing a strategic plan for integrated direct marketing success, we turn to the Michael Allen Company, a leading strategic consulting firm with extensive experience in counseling major corporations in this area.

A Case in Point
The Michael Allen Company Plan

Steven M. Landberg,   *Vice President, The Michael Allen Company*

Key Factors in Strategy

We have found that there are six key factors involved in developing a "winning" business strategy (Figure 3.1):

- Focus
- Competitive advantage
- Integrated business equation
- Actionable, functional programs (where *actionable* means workable or useful)
- Resource concentration
- Aggressive implementation

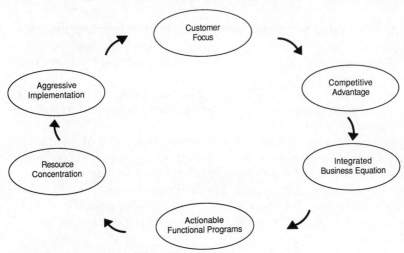

Figure 3.1. A winning business strategy.

Focus

Customer focus is the primary factor in developing an effective strategy since it drives all the other factors. Focus means establishing a clear target market for strategy development.

While most business managers have recognized the need for establishing a target market in their strategic plan, we have found that few have truly integrated that customer focus into all elements of their operations.

The strategic manager understands that winning in today's environment requires clear focus on a set of customers in order to best design products and services to meet their needs as well as understand their price-service trade-offs for selling and distribution determinations.

Customer segmentation has generally stemmed from analyzing demographic characteristics. However, more sophisticated approaches also examine other customer-segmentation frameworks, including attitudes, preferences, buying behavior, lifestyle indicators, and psychological perceptions. These segmentation skills and processes, which are essential for developing a business strategy, are the same ones required for developing a successful direct marketing program. Many of the sophisticated list-segmentation, manipulation, and management techniques used by direct marketers are now being utilized by large corporations to establish customer focus for development of their overall business strategy.

Businesses which have lost touch with their ultimate customers by distributing and selling through third parties are becoming increasingly aware of their vulnerability to the distributor, who controls the customer relationship, and to the competitor who has superior access to customers.

Integrated direct marketing offers a unique opportunity to achieve superior understanding of the needs and desires of the customer. By synthesizing the feedback provided through all marketing channels, we arrive at a coherent, timely, and accurate portrait of the marketplace. This is especially true when telemarketing is employed. This interactive channel offers the opportunity to hear directly from prospective customers, to listen to the objections being raised and the questions being asked, and to act on this information.

Customer focus is not only required for effective marketing: it must also become a guiding factor in all elements of the business. Each function or operation must be customer-oriented to achieve true customer focus.

Competitive Advantage

If customer focus is the primary factor in developing superior business strategy, competitive advantage is the second most important factor. Once a business has a clear customer and market focus, it must understand how it can develop advantages over its competitors in serving that market. A company can develop those advantages when it has a superior understanding of that customer segment or market. Then it can develop the product features, price-value relationship, purchasing convenience, brand image, sales approaches, distribution channels, or marketing promotions and merchandising that will distinguish it from the competition.

The use of integrated direct marketing techniques can represent a competitive advantage for many businesses. IDM can provide a distinctive level of convenience, immediacy, and customer awareness, particularly when used to promote a new product or service. It can also provide a competitive price advantage by lowering distribution or sales costs.

Integrated Business Equation

With a clear market focus and competitive advantage, a business can begin to develop an integrated business equation.

An integrated business equation involves the coordination of all strategic elements into a reinforcing and mutually supportive approach. Each function within the company must be considered. Marketing, sales, product development, operations, customer service, finance, and human relations must all have a consistent focus in order to reinforce each other and develop competitive advantages.

Direct marketing should be integrated with all other channels of distribution in creating the overall business strategy.

Actionable, Functional Programs

Developing an integrated business or direct marketing strategy is not enough; that strategy will succeed only if it can be translated into actionable and functional programs within the resource limitations and corporate culture of the company.

It is difficult enough to execute one strategy effectively, but most businesses have multiple strategies (including direct marketing) that must be executed at the same time. Businesses tend to be organized around functions rather than strategies. Therefore, each strategy must be broken down into specific actions to be taken by each functional organization. Each functional organization must then determine how best to execute the set of functional programs that is required to implement the business strategy. State-of-the-art strategic planning, therefore, requires that all line operations (including direct-marketing functions) be involved in the development of a business strategy. This will not only aid the functional actionability of the strategy but will also aid in gaining management commitment to successfully execute the needed programs.

Well-designed and well-executed direct marketing involves not only the direct marketing specialists, but also other marketing and operational managers, as well as business strategists in all phases to ensure actionability and coordination. However, the direct marketing function is too often a very separate organization that is perceived to be outside the mainstream business operations. In order to maximize effectiveness, direct marketing must be well integrated with a business's strategy and operations.

Resource Concentration

The next key strategic factor is resource concentration, which has its basis in fundamental military strategy. Once an enemy's vulnerability is determined, military strategy would suggest concentrating forces at that point to over-whelm the enemy and develop a competitive advantage through focus. That same principle applies to business strategy.

Once a business strategy has been developed with significant focus, sources of competitive advantage, and integrated and actionable programs, a business must provide sufficient funding or reinvestment to overwhelm competition in that market. Companies tend to spread their resources among markets, strategies, or businesses rather than concentrate them on key aspects. That serves to diffuse their efforts and results in mediocre performance. Competitors that have successfully concentrated their resources behind solid strategies have been able to establish leadership positions in the markets they serve.

The direct marketing industry provides strong evidence of the value of a concentration of resources. Successful participants have concentrated their resources in a particular product category against specific customer targets with a superior offering. If a company wishes to enter or expand in direct marketing, it must concentrate resources in that capability to develop competitive advantage.

Aggressive Implementation

Finally, to achieve superior position, a company must execute its strategies more aggressively than the competition does. A fantastic strategy is worthlesss if it is not aggressively pursued. Many businesses fall into that very condition—having a strategy that is both fantastic and worthless—by not making the needed changes. Aggressive execution of a strategy typically involves changes in a business's organization structure, people, culture, and incentives. The objective in business today is to rekindle an action-oriented and risk-taking environment in which performance and experimentation are encouraged. Those values and the company's strategic direction must be clearly communicated both up and down the organization in order to achieve aggressive implementation. Management systems must also reinforce those changes through planning, budgeting, training, promotion, and compensation programs. To achieve success, a company must

- Develop a dedicated direct marketing operation, distinct from other functions.
- Include the direct marketing function in the initial phases of marketing planning.
- Provide direct marketing training to all parts of the organization impacted by the operation.
- Promote personnel out of or into the direct marketing function.
- Establish the right compensation structure for its direct marketing organization.

Building the Strategic Plan

There are many ways for a company to develop a strategic plan. However, all processes must incorporate the key strategy-development factors discussed above in order to achieve the desired results. Each of those factors requires certain strategic planning skills (Figure 3.2).

Establishing focus requires customer segmentation through market research and analysis.

Developing competitive advantage requires thorough evaluation of the company itself as well as its major competitors.

An integrated business equation can only be developed by determining the key business drivers for achieving competitive advantage for a particular target market and coordinating all business elements around those key drivers.

Translating the integrated business strategy into actionable, functional programs demands the development of a coordinated implementation plan across job responsibilities and departments.

"Winning" Strategy Factors		Required Planning Skills
o Customer Focus	→	o Customer Segmentation
o Competitive Advantage	→	o Competitor Analysis
o Integrated Business Equation	→	o Key Business Driver Determination
o Actionable, Functional Programs	→	o Implementation Planning
o Resource Concentration	→	o Portfolio Evaluation
o Aggressive Implementation	→	o Management Systems Modifications

Figure 3.2. The six planning skills necessary to implement a winning business strategy.

Resource concentration requires decision making based on accurate assessment of the strengths and resources available to the company.

Finally, aggressive implementation usually requires modifications in a company's management systems to achieve the level of expertise and motivation required to make the program work.

Excellence in Strategy Development

The planning skills described above should be melded into an effective strategic planning process that fits the needs of the particular company. The basic skills or efforts needed in a planning process tend to be universal. However, the specific methods for implementing these steps should reflect the particular company's situation, including its planning sophistication, financial performance, industry dynamics, and management culture.

Strategic planning is not effective as a separate process: it must be integrated into a strategic management system, with business managers actively involved and committed. It cannot be achieved just by having a strategic planning staff guide business managers in filling out planning forms. Rather, it needs to be a decision-making tool.

While strategic planning processes generally have a defined time line, strategic thinking must go on continuously. Strategic planning is not a linear process, though it is often so depicted. It is an ongoing undertaking that should encourage management interaction and constructive dialogues. The business climate is fluid and ever-changing. To be useful in this environment, the strategic plan must be regularly revised and reassessed based on current conditions.

The Strategic Planning Process

Strategic planning has come, gone, and come again as business's savior. However, it is not the procedure but rather the disciplined analysis and creative thinking behind the procedure that is most important.

Despite that, businesses still need a framework within which to guide and coordinate the disciplined analysis and creative thinking as well as communicate the decisions and ensure their implementation. Management must ultimately determine the proper balance between "loose" and "tight" control in its systems. With that perspective, the next section will briefly describe the steps in an issues-oriented strategic planning process that is utilized by the Michael Allen Company as a basic approach to be modified for a particular client's needs (Figure 3.3).

Mission

Strategic planning should begin both with a mission statement for the business as a whole and with guidance from senior management for the conduct of the planning process throughout the year.

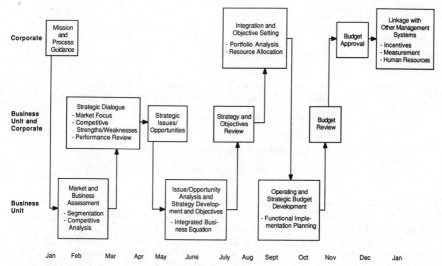

Figure 3.3. An issues-oriented strategic planning process.

A mission statement defines the arena in which a business will operate, including

- The products or services it will provide
- The customer segments it will serve
- The primary means it will use to reach those customers with those products or services

The mission statement forces a company to understand what business it is in, its opportunity or growth areas, and its source of differentiation or competitive advantage. For some businesses, direct marketing will be the primary business arena. For other companies, direct marketing will serve as its primary means of reaching its customer targets or an area of opportunity. Still other companies will not include direct marketing as part of their mission statement but rather as a business function.

Market Assessment

The next stage is the market and business assessment conducted by each business unit. This stage should encompass the analysis and key assumptions of the business environment; evaluation of the industry structure and economics; assessments of competitors and suppliers; and analysis of the products or services, end customers, and distributors (Figure 3.4).

A CASE IN POINT

Industry Size/Growth	Economics	Environmental Factors	Competitors
Revenues Units Concentration	Pricing Margins Returns Resources	Regulatory/legal Technological Societal	Share/growth Financials Strategies Strengths/weaknesses
Products	End Customers	Distributors	Suppliers
Applications Types Brands	Demographic Psychographic Geographic Purchasing behavior and references	Type/class Size Concentration Purchasing behavior and references	Capacity Cost structure Pricing

Figure 3.4. Market and business assessment for better target marketing.

The primary purpose of this stage is to develop a business segmentation framework and analysis for better target marketing or focus. The market focus should reflect not only the attractiveness of a particular segment, but the company's relative competitive position, capabilities, or both (Figure 3.5). A segment's market attractiveness generally reflects that segment's size, growth potential, profitability, competitive intensity, and risks. Competitive position generally reflects

- The company's market share
- Share change
- Relative share versus top competitors
- Current or potential strengths in the key areas of developing competitive advantage, such as
  —Distribution cost
  —Service quality
  —Brand image
  —Pricing
  —Product features

Dialogue Session

After the assessment stage, the business unit and top corporate management should have a strategic dialogue which serves as a vehicle for strengthening strategic understanding, setting direction and market focus, and identifying the key strategic issues and opportunities facing the business. This also provides a session for improving communications, adding creativity, and establishing priorities. At this stage, integrated direct marketing may be viewed as a high-importance issue or as an opportunity for further investigation and strategy development.

Objective Setting

The key strategic issues or opportunities that come out of the dialogue session form the basis for further analysis, strategy development, and objective setting by the business unit. During this stage, focused market research and analysis may be required to better understand the particular opportunity before developing and then evaluating strategy alternatives. The strategies selected must focus on the key success factors for that business opportunity and should establish the integrated business equation discussed earlier.

Once again, the business unit and corporate management should meet to review the selected strategies and business unit objectives. Each business unit's strategies and objectives are then integrated into the corporate perspective and mission. At this point, resources must be allocated and objectives set to meet the overall corporate requirements. The analytical framework used earlier to establish market focus for a business unit (see Figure 3.4) can also be utilized to conduct a portfolio analysis between business units. However, resources should not be allocated to businesses, but rather to specific strategies. The resources a business gets should reflect the sum of its strategies. Likewise, objectives should be established for strategies and synthesized together for a business unit. Conceptually this is appropriate, but in actuality, measurement systems are not usually set up for strategies but for defined business units. Therefore, a business should either modify its tracking systems to measure strategy performance or monitor business-unit performance as the sum of its strategies, and should use specific management objectives that also include factors outside the ongoing tracking system.

Budgeting

With objectives set and resources allocated, business units can establish their budgets through implementation planning. By translating the business strategies into functional programs, a budget can be effectively constructed. However, budgets should include separate funds for operations and for strategic programs. This should avoid the cutting of strategic investments to meet immediate operating-profit shortfalls. This better balances a business's short- and long-term performance, making it possible to avoid mortgaging the future for a temporary problem. This stage is very critical since it necessitates integration of the business strategy, the implementation plan, and the budget.

Figure 3.5. Market focus should reflect market attractiveness as well as a company's relative competitive position.

At this point, the budget process is now underway. Budgets must now be reviewed and approved to set next year's plan into operation. With this process, budgets reflect the business direction and specific strategies developed in the strategic planning phases. However, the budgets and strategic plans must now be linked with the other management systems to ensure their execution.

Applying Strategic Planning Principles to IDM

With thanks for this clear and concise explanation of the strategic planning process, let us examine in more depth some of the concepts specific to integrated direct marketing which should be incorporated into the development stage of your plan.

Corporate Identity

Marketing is above all a communication process, and as in all human communication, the source of information provided is at least as important as the information itself. If we read a headline in the *New York Times* about a dramatic new treatment for cancer, we take the story very seriously indeed. If the same story appears in one of the less reputable supermarket tabloids, we assume the treatment is a fraud. This would be true even if the stories carried identical headlines and verbiage, included the same information, and were written by the same reporter. We have an ingrained reaction to the source of the information, and it would take an incredible effort for the publisher to alter this predisposition.

The same is true in marketing on several levels.

First, we expect certain products and services to come from certain sources. If you are in the market for a computer printer and an IBM telemarketing representative calls to offer you one, you will take the offer seriously. If you received a call from L. L. Bean with the identical offer, it would be nearly impossible for them to make the sale. This doesn't connote a lack of respect for the quality and service of L.L. Bean; we just don't associate the company with computer products.

Product is one means we use to categorize suppliers of goods and services. Price is another. A shopper might be happy to write a check to Carol Wright for inexpensive items, and have no particular predisposition about what type of item it has to be. Anything in a Carol Wright catalog at a significantly higher price, even if it is a name-brand product, would run into a psychological roadblock set up by purchasing habits and the image of the company making the offer.

Assessing your company image with regard to the criteria of image and price, then, is an essential planning step. The hard-nosed part of this exercise is to review the marketing history of the company, along with the market-research data, and to arrive at a solid definition of the company's perceived line of business. The exciting part is to creatively consider the unexploited opportunities presented by the results of this assessment. Can L.L. Bean sell electronics? Absolutely—as long as the products are in some way related to L.L. Bean's central business. Walkie-talkies, shortwave radios, even homing devices to enable campers to locate their campsites if lost in the woods are all worth consideration for a company identified with an outdoor lifestyle.

On a retail level, consider the diverse products offered by Hallmark Cards. While not generally considered a toy or jewelry company, Hallmark has successfully marketed stuffed animals and costume jewelry with seasonal themes, drawing on the Hallmark association with holidays and using established distribution channels.

The ideal opportunities for identifying unexploited product and service categories appropriate to your business are brainstorming sessions. The participants should be drawn from all levels of the company, and outsiders recruited for focus groups should also be included. Begin with a premise—an accepted identification of your company in terms of industry segment, price category, and the consumer's emotional response to the company—and engage in freewheeling "what-if" thinking. Then review the results from a business-strategy perspective. What makes sense given your goals and resources? Based on these decisions, you can move into a testing phase.

Competitive Analysis

Looking inward is the first step. Once you have a clear understanding of your company's strengths and weaknesses, it is time to look outward at the other players in the marketplace. In addition to the standard criteria for this sort of management study, pay special attention to opportunities to use the strengths of integrated direct marketing to gain competitive advantage.

Two key factors to consider:

- What marketing channels are not currently being exploited to greatest advantage within your product segment? If direct mail is standard operating procedure among your competitors, are they using inbound or outbound telemarketing, or both, to increase their response rate?

How about coordinated space advertising, or radio, or television? By creating multiple, synergistic impact through an integrated media program, you produce buyer focus on your offer, gaining signficant competitive advantage.

• Approaching the question from a different perspective, what products or services are not being offered effectively to media respondents? Direct marketers have learned over the course of time that different people respond to different forms of solicitation, and have developed sophisticated lists identifying buyers according to their chosen medium. If we can pinpoint individuals who have made purchases in a specified dollar range through a given medium, we must then ask ourselves, "What is *not* being offered to these people through that channel in that price category?" Proven direct marketing customers are available to us in ever-increasing numbers, with increasingly precise demographic and psychographic data for accurate analysis. Identify a product or service provided by your company which is not being offered to these responsive individuals, and you have found a likely target for an integrated direct marketing campaign.

Internal Communication

It is impossible to overstress the necessity for establishing and maintaining effective communications between all participants in an integrated direct marketing program—and that necessity starts right at the beginning, with the strategic plan.

The plan should exist in written form. It should be distributed as a whole to the key executives at upper management levels of the company who will be responsible for putting it into action.

Of course, there will be items of a confidential nature in the plan and in the supporting documentation. However, a distilled version should be made available to all employees in the divisions affected. The goals you are seeking, the image of the company as a whole, and the distinctive concepts underlying the direct marketing operation will set the tone for the entire undertaking. Everyone involved in customer contact of any sort, from the person who designs the direct-mail materials to the person who handles product returns or answers the telephone to take an order, will have a role to play in conveying a coherent and convincing message to the marketplace. Even those whose roles are strictly internal to the company will benefit from having a sense of where their function fits in achieving the goals of the program.

This communication process can also take the form of formal educational efforts. Direct marketing as a whole, and each separate direct marketing discipline, has its own set of precepts, concepts, and hard facts. Wherever decisions impacting the direct marketing program will be made within your company, it is vital that your people be trained in the task at hand. This is true whether you are trying to build an in-house direct marketing capability or working with outside vendors. At some level, key decisions about your direct marketing program will have to be made by individuals within your company. Without a good grounding in the basics of direct marketing, it is nearly impossible to accurately assess the progress and the possibilities inherent in a program.

There are many sources for this kind of information. As direct marketing has grown, so has the availability of quality literature in the field. We are focusing in this book on the unique aspects of integrating direct-marketing disciplines. The Bibliography at the end of this book contains a selected list of books and magazines which deal with direct marketing as a whole, and with skillful use of the individual direct marketing media. Two of these publications which are notably worthwhile are *Direct Marketing* magazine and *DM News*.

The Direct Marketing Association offers a wealth of worthwhile educational programs in the form of seminars, as well as a rich selection of publications on all aspects of the field. Many universities now offer courses in direct marketing as well, on the undergraduate, graduate, and seminar levels.

Why are we stressing the need for direct marketing education here? Partly because we are acutely aware of the depth and breadth of topics which are not covered in this book. We have chosen instead to focus on the distinctive concepts of direct marketing *integration* which pertain to beginners and experts alike.

Further, we are drawing a very real distinction between education and training. Training implies instruction related to fulfilling a given function, and certainly any direct marketing operation must include consideration of training for the workers involved. However, at the strategic level, it is education in the discipline of direct marketing that allows company decision makers to identify opportunities, select suppliers, recognize trends, and evaluate results for maximum profitability.

As consultants, we work with a wide range of marketing professionals from diverse media backgrounds. No matter how much time and effort we devote to understanding the client's situation and needs, we will never have the depth of knowledge and perspective about an individual company that is available to the executives of the company we are serving. The impetus for action and the final judgments of results must come from internal sources. There is no greater frustration for a marketing professional than dealing with people who are simply not informed enough to understand what is presented to them within the context of modern, sophisticated direct marketing. By contrast, those who grasp the unique nature of direct marketing and are responsive to learning its distinctive principles are valued allies in building integrated programs that work, benefiting the companies they work for (or own) and their own careers as well. Francis Bacon said, "Knowledge is power," and while direct marketing techniques were not very advanced in the sixteenth century when he said it, the lesson most certainly holds holds true for successful marketers today.

Market Research

The first source of information to tap in building your strategic marketing plan is your own corporate history. Just as your past and present customers are your best prospects for the future, analyzing your company's experience in marketing as a whole and direct marketing in particular will provide invaluable information about the external reaction to your marketing strategies, and the success or failure of internal systems to date.

The next most valuable information asset is market research. In many cases, thanks to its dispassionate statistical nature, market-research data may be even more accurate as an indicator of strategic considerations than past performance, which may be cluttered with political ramifications and foregone conclusions.

Market research is a cost-effective means of determining many key components in your strategic plan, including:

- Proper target market
- Product positioning
- Perception of the company
- Perception of the competition
- Price sensitivity
- Media selection
- "Buying triggers" (key phrases and concepts that move prospects to action)

For an insightful analysis of the role market research plays within an IDM program, we turn to Eric Langbaum. His company, Eric Langbaum Associates, is a management consulting firm which employs a variety of market-research techniques on behalf of clients in direct marketing and other fields.

A Case in Point

Eric Langbaum Associates Analysis

Eric Langbaum, *President, Eric Langbaum Associates, Inc.*

Basing current marketing decisions on previous experience is fine if you're in a static environment. For better or worse, though, this is rarely the case. New products are introduced. Your competitive position changes. There are shifts in economic conditions. In the face of a constantly changing marketplace, market research is an effective tool for providing the current management information required for successful decision making.

The primary goal of market research in integrated direct marketing is to identify the *buying triggers*. These are the hot buttons, the phrases that give people a positive feeling about a product. Going out into the marketplace and listening to people describe their view of the product, hearing them defining their own needs—that's how you learn the right words and phrases to use in appealing to them to buy your product. And what you find typically is that the jargon that you use internally to describe product benefits and features is not necessarily the same as the jargon your customer uses.

In addition to tailoring product and message to fit the needs of the marketplace, we must identify which *individuals* need to hear those messages, what *media* we must use to reach those individuals, and what are the *optimum distribution channels* to use in getting those products into the marketplace.

Launching a Catalog for A Major Software Vendor

For example, about 7 years ago our client decided to develop a catalog to list its software products.

A list of pertinent questions from the company's executives had to be answered before the project got off the ground. These questions included:

- Was there a need for a catalog?
- If the answer was "yes," what should the catalog look like?
- How should the products be described? How much information needed to be included?
- How should the catalog be promoted?

We conducted research through customer interviews to learn the answers to those questions. They built a prototype catalog based on these answers, and we went back to the customers for their reactions to the prototype.

We built a successful catalog system from the ground up based on customer interviews. Now we periodically go back to assess the utility of the catalog, and the degree to which it is producing business.

We've used the same technique for directories, brochures, direct-mail pieces, and telemarketing efforts designed to sell software: use customer research for initial direction and then for fine tuning of a prototype.

Skillful Use of Research Techniques

There is a wide range of market-research techniques available, including one-to-one interviews, focus groups, and questionnaires conducted by mail or telephone.

Although focus-group interviews can be very expensive in terms of out-of-pocket costs, they offer a significant benefit in that they afford an opportunity for the client to be present at the sessions and to hear the reactions produced firsthand. I have also taken clients along when conducting research interviews with individual customers. If clients have attended and listened to the interview, the information produced has greater relevance and immediacy for them when they are next faced with a marketing decision.

The specific research approach can be either qualitative or quantitative, depending on the specific situation. Conducting 10 or 12 in-depth face-to-face interviews in client organizations can produce results every bit as solid as doing a study of 1000 people. Whether to go for quality or for quantity is really a decision that must be made on a case-by-case basis.

For example, my company was involved in a major microcomputer marketing campaign that was launched on the basis of a dozen in-depth customer visits. In fact, this is the most successful campaign ever launched to market microcomputers. The reason the research worked so well was that the interviews were consistent. We saw the right people, and the results made intuitive sense. With the results of this research, we could sit down with representatives from the advertising agency and say to them, "Here are the messages, here are the media, and here's the audience that needs to be reached."

The client was more than willing to pay for interviews with more people, but it wasn't necessary. Experienced researchers should be able to evaluate the data produced in light of a wealth of previous experience, guide clients in the efficient use of market-research techniques, and provide a framework for turning the research findings into an actionable strategy.

In shopping for a market-research firm, a sophisticated marketer should understand that you can get a lot more for your dollar than simply a printout of the data. Market research involves a technical skill. But unless the information produced has some practical benefit, it isn't worth doing. The market researcher should spend a good deal of front-end time interacting with senior management and with the people who will have to execute whatever marketing plan is created. For it to have value, market research must lead to a plan which is actionable within the context of the company's goals and capabilities.

Research for AT&T Mortgage Line

The research conducted on behalf of AT&T for the AT&T Mortgage Line program (a complete case history was given in Chapter 2) has all the ingredients of a successful market-research effort that was integrated across the board with all relevant departments.

We started off by learning about the company in depth: what its objectives were, what the product was, who the executives thought the marketplace was, what marketing options were being considered.

Based on this discussion process, we decided that face-to-face interviews with current users was the appropriate research methodology. The product was still very new, and we wanted to understand the dynamics of the decision-making process. This involved learning who was involved in the purchase decision, how these people learned about the product, and what their experience was. We wanted to learn what had worked or hadn't worked in the marketing effort to date, and what would have worked had they tried it.

We selected a cross section of current customers representing different industries, such as banks, mortgage companies, and large real estate firms.

We had multiple interviews at each site: we spoke with the decision makers who had purchased the system, and with the end users of the system.

We took this information and, working with AT&T executives, their outside direct marketing consultant, and the creative specialists for the program, developed the marketing plan and the media to be employed in implementing the plan.

The direct-mail campaign was developed on the basis of research indicating who needed to be reached. The buying triggers were integrated into the creative presentation.

Research also provided the basis for working out the scenario for the trade show: what to say to the prospects, how the product demonstration should be conducted, what kind of support materials the sales force would need.

We also worked out a strategy for doing product-demonstration seminars throughout the country. We laid out the agenda for the day, who the audience had to be, how to extend the invitation, the mechanism for getting the responses back—all based on the results of the research.

The most significant point to remember from the AT&T experience is that market research functioned as part of a team effort. This marketing team started with research, built a marketing plan based on those results, and then executed a creative presentation which incorporated those findings. All the professionals involved, from inside the company and from its various outside resources, worked closely together to create a profitable program. And to a large extent, the close integration of information and talents was the reason it worked.

Measuring Customer Satisfaction

Finally, if you really believe in the principles of integrated direct marketing, then you need some mechanism for evaluating the results of your efforts on an ongoing basis.

Every company should have a continuing market-research program aimed at objectively assessing customer satisfaction, because that is what ultimately determines whether or not your marketing plan works. The importance of establishing an ongoing customer relationship is crucial to integrated direct marketing, and market research plays a key role in measuring your success in this area.

When you systematically measure customer satisfaction, you have the ability to identify weaknesses before the bottom line is affected. Direct marketing response to future efforts will reveal weaknesses in your strategy and execution, but that is an expensive way to learn. Market research provides an earlier reading on problems that may arise, and also provides the detailed information required to fix them.

While this book will not attempt to provide an in-depth education in the art and science of market-research techniques, an understanding of the process from the management side of the table is an absolute requirement for successful strategic development of an integrated direct-marketing program. Marketing research provides an essential window on your market. Therefore, we offer a synopsis of this process prepared by Walbridge Research Associates, a firm specializing in psychological market research. Thanks are also expressed to Richard B. Vanderveer, Ph.D., of the Vanderveer Group, Inc., for his contribution to this discussion. In addition to extensive credentials, this firm offers an appealing outlook on the research process. To quote:

> The bottom line in marketing research is that information is gathered which is maximally useful, by being directly and meaningfully "actionable." While seeming perhaps like a trivial point, all too often marketing research is ill conceived and results in either information which is not useful or blatant misinformation. The costs of the "wrong answer" can be staggering. The job of the manager who is either conducting marketing research or acquiring marketing research services is to insure that the collection of data is conducted in a manner which is cost-effective and usable. Finally, the information obtained must be understood by the intended end users. Arcane, scientific, or academic information, while often interesting, is generally not what is necessary to get a marketing job done.
>
> With the increased emphasis on technology, a tendency for managers to become "technique bound" has developed. Those individuals have allowed the *apparent* complexity of marketing research problems in combination with the wide range of available marketing research techniques and suppliers to confuse them to the point where they lose sight of the actual *simplicity* of the issues under study.

With this reassuring perspective, let us review the decision flow involved in the market-research process, as outlined by Dr. R. Hoyt Walbridge:

Words from the Wise

Dr. R. Hoyt Walbridge on Decision Flow in the Research Process

Dr. R. Hoyt Walbridge, *Walbridge Research Associates*

While the specific needs of different market-research endeavors vary, virtually every project involves a logical flow of events. These events start with problem formulation and carry through to the all-important presentation and distribution of results. In addition, when events or stages in the process are not considered fully, the results may not be visible until the often-disastrous ending of the research project. Perhaps one of the most killing remarks that a reviewer of a market-research operation can make, when the findings are presented, is, "But those weren't the objectives I had for this study."

Delineated below is a scheme for a logical flow of stages in the research process. While this scheme is neither novel nor unique and can be subdivided or collapsed, it does contain the basic and essential elements of each and every research process. These stages constitute the manager's checklist of essential steps.[1]

1. Problem Formulation

- The process by which researcher and decision maker specify the information and action objectives of the market research.

  Defining why research is being done

  Specifying business decisions which will be made based on market-research results

  Refining research questions to eliminate interesting but irrelevant information

2. Determination of Information Sources and Research Design

- Often information has already been compiled which can be useful in answering the key questions at hand.

  Existing information should be checked against current information needs.

  If market researched is required, it should be designed with validity and efficiency in mind.

---

[1] The sequence of stages in the research process is similar to statements referenced by Gilbert A. Churchill, Jr., *Marketing Research*, 2d ed., Dryden Press, Hinsdale, Ill., 1979, p. 17.

3. Selection of Data-Collection Methodology and Technique

- Research can be described as *exploratory* or *confirmatory*. The choice dictates the parameters around how information will be gathered.
- Exploratory research offers the widest flexibility; used to assess feasibility of a larger research effort including logistics as well as substance, often it provides essential baseline information.
- Confirmatory research tests the validity of exploratory work, testing whether findings are sufficiently reliable (consistent and generalizable) and valid (on target) to hold up under cross examination (the real world).
- Confirmatory research generally takes the form of either a *descriptive* or a *causal* research design.
- Descriptive studies are just that: they provide a picture of the market. Terminology encountered in descriptive studies often includes:

  Usage and attitudes (U&A)

  Awareness, trial, and usage (ATU)

  Knowledge, attitudes, and practices (KAP)

- Causal studies involve measurement of the impact of a stimulus or an independent event: they "prove" the impact of things. Impacts are measured as changes in thinking or behavior. Test-market research is the par excellence example of casual research.

Data-collection techniques have specific attributes which may be useful or not, depending upon the study objectives established during problem formulation. The appropriateness of different techniques varies depending on the type of research questions being asked. Specific techniques can be arrayed on a continuum, as shown in Table 3.1, which ranges from greatest to least flexibility and, at the same time, offers greatest confidence in generalization to large consumer populations.

The most flexibile and exploratory type of research available to the marke researcher is the focus group. This is contrasted with analysis of test markets, which provides the most precise mode of data collection but which is completely inflexible. Analysis of test markets is based solely on return data; it allows no chance for either questioning the meaning of the data by asking consumers about the "whys" of their behaviors or for manipulating the way in which information is obtained.

Table 3.1. Technique Selection—The Marketing Research Trade-Off

Flexibility				Precision or generalizability
Focus groups	In-depth interviews (personal or telephone)	Structured interviews (personal or telephone)	Mail self-administered questionnaires	Test markets

4. Sample Design

A sample is a subset of a larger population. The central issue in this discussion is determination of what type of research sample is required, based on study objectives and problem formulation. There are two types of samples: *nonprobability* samples and *probability* samples.

Nonprobability samples are not based on statistical techniques and cannot ultimately be compared statistically with the statistical picture of "true" reality. Nevertheless, the majority of marketing research is based on nonprobability samples, which, as could be expected, come in several flavors.

- *Convenience samples.* People who are available and willing to participate in the study.
- *Quota samples.* People who meet specific screening criteria and are available, e.g., 30 people over age 40 who use automatic teller machines for day-to-day banking.
- *Purposive samples.* Quota samples of specific groups for comparison purposes, e.g., people who do and do not use automatic teller machines.
- *Expert samples, also called key informant samples.* Samples of people known to be opinion leaders in the topic of study.
- *Snowball or referral samples.* Respondents whom the researcher was referred to by other respondents. This procedure is often used in studying decision making within organizations.

Probability samples are scientifically selected, meaning that every eligible individual has a known probability of selection. Individuals are "randomly" selected. Probability samples are the most accurate way to measure true population characteristics and are vastly more costly to implement than nonprobability procedures. Probability samples should be used only when necessary.

Regarding sampling error, the degree to which a sample does or does not reflect the population reality is much more closely tied (mathematically) to the absolute size of the sample than to the proportion of the population being measured. Large nonprobability samples, therefore, are frequently treated like probability samples, because it is assumed that biases are balanced and therefore wash out with larger sample sizes.

Bias. All samples can suffer from bias, error, noise, or being off the mark.

Noncoverage bias refers to the situation in which individuals who should have been eligible for inclusion in the study are not included. The U.S. Census is frequently accused of noncoverage bias by minority groups who feel that they have been underrepresented in the census.

Nonresponse bias is another potential pitfall for the sampler. This refers to bias caused by the exclusion of individuals from a study because of their own unwillingness to participate. For example, in assembling physicians for a focus group, one wonders if those physicians who decline to attend would have expressed attitudes and reactions different from those who attend.

WORDS FROM THE WISE

Bias is an issue which has to be addressed in virtually every study, regardless of where that study falls on the continuum of flexibility versus generalizability. For the most flexible qualitative research, bias is checked in a qualitative way against what is known about the topic. The researcher must ask the question, "Is there any reason to think that this group of individuals differs in any systematic way from the larger group to which the study is being addressed?" At the other end of the continuum, dealing with the most generalizable and inflexible data-collection schemes, the researcher must again answer that same question. The researcher may also be asked to quantify the impact of bias on the validity of the projections of results.

5. Data Collection and Analysis

- The problem that the research is designed to address will dictate how the data are analyzed and interpreted.

  Data collection must be consistent. Questions must be asked of every respondent

  Data analysis must be objective. The results must speak for themselves.

- Results that are not actionable are probably not worth whatever they cost.

6. Dissemination of Findings

- This is the obvious last step that is frequently overlooked, ill conceived, and a frustrating waste. These results are especially likely to occur if the study objectives specified during problem formulation have not been adequately addressed.
- Dissemination of findings includes format and audience considerations. In this communication process, the "selling" of the information is a form of internal direct marketing.

4
Steps for Implementing IDM at Your Company

Chapter 3 outlined an approach to strategic planning which will provide a solid foundation for IDM success. Now we must look at the steps required to take that plan and put it into action.

We will begin by discussing the crucial program-management role within the company. The integrated direct marketing framework places major responsibility for the success or failure of the program on the manager who coordinates the effort. There are unique requirements for this position, and unique rewards as well. We will examine the duties of this critical individual in depth, and consider some of the criteria for selecting the right person for the job.

As we investigate the role of the IDM manager, we will discuss the contributions of key departments inside and outside the company needed for IDM success. At each step along the marketing path, from the senior management level through the operational departments, we will explore the type of cooperative action the IDM manager must secure to keep the program moving forward.

Integrated direct marketing is an information-intensive strategy. The basic springboard for all direct marketing activities is the list. If an appropriately selected and segmented list cannot be purchased or assembled, there is simply no program. Once a list universe has been selected, though, the management of that list can spell the difference between success and failure. This is especially important in implementing outbound telemarketing. Employing a list for a direct mailing is a fairly static procedure: The mailing is generated, with the required level of personalization, and dropped at the strategically determined time. The list used in telemarketing is more fluid, though. When placing outbound calls, we know whether the contact has been completed or not, and we can continue to try until we do make contact. This is a key strength of the medium, but superior list-management techniques and management judgment are required to employ this technique effectively. We will examine these unique procedures and criteria in this chapter.

Finally, we will consider one of the most difficult questions in direct marketing: should you rely on outside vendors or build up your own in-house capability? As IDM proves itself a powerful, cost-effective, and high-revenue distribution channel, many Fortune 500 and midsized companies are discovering there is a business imperative to bring directmarketing services in-house. In this chapter we will consider the pros and cons of in-house and vendor services, and offer guidelines for selecting outside vendors where appropriate.

Managing the IDM Effort

If you will be managing the IDM effort in your company, welcome to the hot seat. Integrated direct marketing is a more demanding management undertaking than traditional single-medium efforts. There is increased pressure for on-time performance of agreed-upon tasks across all media, since the interrelationship of these tasks is key to creating the synergistic effect of IDM.

Management must take a broader, and simultaneously more in-depth, view of the marketing situation when mounting an IDM campaign, since the number of interdependent factors increases in this environment, and fully maximizing the opportunities presented may call for nontraditional thinking and decision making.

The greatest shift in responsibility and pressure, though, occurs for the manager with direct responsibility for coordinating the program. We will call this position the *IDM manager*, though the actual title will clearly vary from company to company. If your company is small enough, this individual could be the *executive vice president of marketing*. If it's large enough, the person who handles these responsibilities could be a *marketing manager* or *product manager*, with several subordinates who are charged with handling the details of the operation. In either case, the person we are discussing will be responsible for making sure the integration of resources takes place.

IDM manager is a position which can be incredibly stimulating and extremely visible, even in a large organization. At the same time, the

IDM manager who is not capable of organizing and utilizing the resources of integrated direct marketing will at best achieve ordinary results, and at worst be responsible for an expensive disaster.

Responsibilities

Corporate size, culture, and operational procedures will dictate many of the specifics of the IDM manager's job functions. However, it is important that a single individual have ultimate responsibility for the areas listed below. If these key concerns are divided up between several executives, no matter how capable and cooperative, it will be nearly impossible to manage an IDM campaign effectively.

The responsibilities of the IDM manager include:

- Explore integrated direct marketing techniques.
- Develop or obtain an assessment of company marketing goals and strategies.
- Prepare a strategic IDM proposal.
- Develop a marketing action plan (MAP).
- Manage program implementation.
- Summarize and evaluate results.
- Develop new applications for IDM resources.

In the following pages we will examine each of these functions in detail.

Explore Integrated
Direct-Marketing Techniques

The IDM manager must be the house expert on direct marketing strategies, resources, opportunities, and procedures.

Clearly, the greater the level of expertise, the better. However, we do not mean to imply that the IDM manager must master all the subtleties of each individual direct marketing discipline. As direct marketing has evolved over time, so have the depth and breadth of knowledge available in each field, and astute marketers today are wise to rely on specialists. The key quality to look for in managers is the ability to recognize good work when they see it.

IDM managers do not have to be able to write good copy but must be able to recognize good copy. They are not expected to know how to conduct a database analysis but must be able to engage the right professional to make the most of this resource. In short, the IDM manager is a consumer of services and must understand enough about direct-marketing specifics to be a "smart shopper." The IDM manager will have to evaluate the opportunities and liabilities represented by three resource-acquisition strategies:

- Rely entirely on in-house staff.
- Rely entirely on outside agencies, consultants, or service bureaus.
- Create an integrated combination of in-house and outside resources.

While the actual acquisition of direct marketing services will not occur until later on in the development process, the relative merits of in-house and outside services must be considered from the beginning of implementation planning. Building in-house capabilities is the more capital-intensive and demanding path; it also offers the greatest long-term profitability *if the company is making a substantial commitment to IDM*. Senior management is responsible for determining this level of commitment, but it is the IDM manager who must prepare an assessment of the relative strengths and weaknesses of the available alternatives.

Develop or Obtain Assessment of Company Marketing Goals and Strategies

The IDM manager may or may not be the individual who sets company goals and strategies, though most likely that responsibility will lie elsewhere. Before the manager's job can be done properly, though, these decisions must be crystalized in a document that encompasses the necessary specifics (see Chapter 3) and carries with it the approval of the chief executive officer (CEO). If such a document does not already exist, the IDM manager should request it.

Prepare Strategic IDM Proposal

With company goals firmly established, the IDM manager prepares a plan to meet the company goals, using the resources and techniques of integrated direct marketing. This proposal should include:

- A statement of purpose
- A summary of strategic considerations in achieving this purpose
- A general outline of the steps to be taken in implementing a program
- Anticipated revenues
- A budget estimate

The manager must be prepared to support this proposal with specifics, while recognizing the leeway required at the early stages of the IDM planning process. This is not the point at which procedures should be set in stone, or budgets analyzed to two decimal places. Rather, the opportunities for using IDM techniques to achieve goals in the business plan should be explained, with general figures indicating the magnitude of investment required to accomplish these goals.

While specific vendors of direct marketing services will not have been contracted at this point, they are good sources of information even at this early stage. For those services which you anticipate bringing in-house, consultants skilled in these disciplines can make an important contribution to the planning process. In addition, it is often worthwhile to bring in a consultant experienced in developing integrated direct-marketing campaigns during the initial planning stages to suggest options and alternatives and to provide an industry overview.

The goal at this stage is to secure a mandate to proceed with the development of a specific marketing action plan. That level of planning involves substantial time, and can entail investment for initial research, consultation, and other services. Therefore, it should be undertaken only when an initial management commitment to explore IDM has been secured.

The Role of the Consultant

Assembling your integrated direct marketing effort entails some difficult decisions. For example:

What are the potential applications for IDM techniques in your company, and how can you pursue them in a cost-effective and timely way?

What is the extent of the decisions involved in planning the program? Have you forgotten anything?

Will existing company capabilities be adequate to meet the demands of an IDM campaign, and how do you expand them if necessary? Will current agencies and service bureaus fit into this new marketing framework, or do you need "new blood"?

With thousands of agencies, service bureaus, and consultants to choose from, how do you whittle down the options to a manageable level?

And how do you structure the interrelationship between in-house capabilities and outside providers to create an efficient, cohesive team?

Many companies faced with these decisions have found that the first outside resource requirement is a direct marketing consultant skilled in building integrated campaigns. This individual or company can play a crucial role from the initial planning stages of the IDM program through its ongoing implementation.

An integrated direct marketing consultant brings to the effort the capabilities discussed below.

Experience.   An IDM consultant offers knowledge of a wide range of media, and understands the potential for applying the varying strengths and weaknesses of these media to the distinctive marketing challenges facing your company. The consultant is aware of positive steps taken in campaigns undertaken by other companies, as well as the pitfalls to be avoided.

You should neither expect nor accept cookie-cutter solutions to your marketing situation. However, the prior experience of the consultant should point out potential avenues to explore, and identify mistakes before they happen.

Perspective.   As an outsider coming into your company, the consultant offers a fresh viewpoint on the marketing process as it pertains to the goods and services you produce. It is difficult for in-house personnel to offer nontraditional approaches to a marketing problem. Even if they are aware of new directions which might be explored, it is often politically safer to propose only modest variations on the accepted recipe. An outside consultant can take a fresh view of the situation, bring a wide frame of reference to bear, and suggest solutions which may deviate widely from the "business-as-usual" norm within a company. And from a purely political standpoint, the suggestions offered by a consultant are likely to be given more weight than internal recommendations, simply because of the consultant's position as "hired gun."

Resource Recommendation.   One of the primary assets the consultant brings to the effort is a knowledge of the resources available to get the job done. This is particularly important in an IDM program. As we have already discussed, even agencies and service bureaus with highly respected records of achievement in their individual specialties may be ill suited to integrating their abilities across media lines. This inability will not be apparent from promotional material, or client lists, or even recommendations from other satisfied customers who have operated within a more traditional framework. The IDM consultant will be familiar with the subset of top agencies, service bureaus, and consultants which also have the distinctive experience of working cooperatively with other experts. That knowledge can save hundreds of hours of screening and interviewing.

Ongoing Management Assistance.   We have emphasized the heavy requirements placed on company management in coordinating diverse resources in an IDM campaign. An outside consultant will have the knowledge and ability to function as a focal point for these vendors, providing coordination, passing along information, troubleshooting the process, analyzing the program as it develops, and generally supervising the implementation process. A busy executive may be hard-pressed to keep up with the extent of activity required to run an IDM program. The consultant can screen and qualify problems for internal attention, and offer a single source for the ongoing reporting structure.

Develop Marketing Action Plan

Developing the MAP entails contacting and evaluating suppliers of all services, as well as evaluating and developing internal resources. We will fully discuss the ramifications of decisions about in-house services versus outside vendors later in this chapter. However, it is important to understand that the implications of establishing an IDM framework go beyond resource acquisition to the heart of management relationships. Integrated direct marketing requires a level of communication and cooperation which crosses traditional "turf" boundaries. This is especially true in the division between the sales and marketing functions. As we have seen in each case history presented in this book, it is vital for a company employing sales personnel to build on the strengths of this operation when instituting an IDM program.

In fact, the impact of IDM on all existing channels of distribution must be carefully assessed. The growth of IDM is an evolutionary process; we cannot cut off established income sources while building the resources required to make a substantial shift to direct marketing. The individuals employed in these existing resource areas must be involved in the planning of the IDM effort, with the impact of the new program openly discussed in a free-flowing dialogue. The marketing action plan must allow for a phased shifting of profit responsibilities, with the successful elements of the current marketing structure maintained, the borderline elements bolstered by direct marketing support, and new profit opportunities developed.

The IDM manager is the standard bearer for the program within the company, and should anticipate resistance to change. The use of direct marketing can cause a significant shift in the overall marketing direction of a company, and those who are firmly entrenched in the status quo will often feel threatened.

Remember also that IDM has far-reaching effects within a company, and each affected area must be considered and planned for. The list of company resources impacted by initiation of an IDM program is extensive, including but not limited to the following:

1. Senior Management.   Upper-level management must sign off on direct marketing activities at several stages of development. At the very least, the initial go-ahead, approval of a plan for testing, assessment of expanding a test program into an extensive rollout operation, and ongoing review of results generated must be undertaken at the top.

2. Sales and Marketing Departments.   Those who currently bear the responsibility for sales and marketing of your product or service must be sold on the idea of integrated direct marketing, and this internal sales job may be the most difficult persuasive task in an IDM campaign. There may in fact be times when direct marketing truly is a threat to entrenched interests—when it is used to replace salespeople, or to cut advertising budgets in favor of direct marketing activity. In all candor, the only solution in such a situation is a strong, clear mandate from senior management and acceptance of the fact that cooperation will probably be very limited. In this case, flawless execution of early programs and successful tests are essential.

More often, however, IDM is used to supplement and complement existing channels of distribution. Problems frequently arise, though, because of a misperception of the role of direct marketing on the part of the existing sales and marketing force. If salespeople hear "direct marketing," they instinctively feel that their turf is threatened and that accounts will be taken away from them by direct writing of orders. Even if the program is as benign as lead generation and qualification to produce better leads, and hence higher sales, for the field sales force, there is likely to be resentment based on a perceived loss of control of the selling process.

The appropriate responses to this understandable unease are education and communication. It is up to the IDM manager to present the program in a positive light to all concerned, including management, sales representatives, and other affected individuals. Written materials outlining the program, its goals, and its limitations will be helpful. So will face-to-face meetings with groups and with individuals, to answer questions and clarify any points of confusion.

3. Finance. The finance department is a key resource. First, at the planning level, finance can help analyze the expenses involved in start-up operations and ongoing programs, as well as the key figures identifying the lifetime value of a customer. You may also be able to develop improved offers for the customer through discussion with the finance department, evaluating the possibilities of improved credit terms, preapproved credit, extended billing periods, and so forth.

Finance will also be the department that senior management ultimately looks to for the bottom-line results of IDM efforts. It is important that finance managers understand the scope of your program, the financial goals, and the appropriate basis for comparison with other marketing strategies.

4. Legal Counsel. The rules and regulations governing direct marketing activity are complicated by legal differences from state to state. This is particularly true for sweepstakes and contest promotions, which are generally conducted by specialists who are not only experienced in the production and distribution of contest materials but also knowledgeable about the legal restrictions that apply.

Additional legal concerns for direct marketers include regulations governing the collection of sales taxes, the time requirements for delivery of mail-ordered merchandise, warranty and return policy restrictions, and so forth. Some industries, notably real estate and financial services, carry their own more stringent set of licensing regulations for sales personnel.

Your corporate counsel should be consulted early on in the development of your direct marketing program, and should see all materials before they go into production. In addition, lawyers familiar with specific regulations regarding direct marketing activity should be consulted for their special input.

5. Data Processing. Accessing information from your customer files and creating a system which allows frequent updating and fast reporting will require the cooperation of your data processing (DP) people. They will be involved not only in dealing with in-house requests for information but also in interfacing with any outside list brokers or database analysts. This consideration can turn into a significant area of aggravation and expense if files maintained by your company are incompatible with the vendor's computer formats. Solicit the expertise of your DP department before committing to any project requiring sharing information between computer systems.

At the same time, don't go to DP people and ask what they *can* do. Instead, tell them *what you want done,* and ask how long it will take and what it will cost. The odds are good that you will be asking for something that hasn't been done before, whether it is a new way of segmenting data for analysis, or increased access to the database, or a more interactive system of entering and retrieving information. It is common to run into technical obstructions, which are sometimes real but sometimes simply reflect an unwillingness on the part of technical personnel to change their standard operating procedures. Firmness just this side of obstinacy may be required to get what you need.

6. Personnel. The personnel department plays a key role in the decision to develop in-house capabilities or use outside vendors. Direct-marketing functions such as telemarketing, fulfillment, and customer service are labor-intensive operations. For any area in which in-house capability is being considered, the IDM manager will need to prepare a comprehensive plan describing personnel requirements. This should include multiple levels of staffing based on the expected level of activity as well as best-case and worst-case scenarios. The personnel department will then be responsible for assessing the labor costs involved in the decision whether to develop in-house facilities or to use an outside supplier.

If the decision is to develop in-house capabilities, this will inevitably mean that personnel will need increased staff and budget in order to undertake recruitment, hiring, and training.

7. Customer service. With a focus on building ongoing customer relationships, the service component of a company takes on increased importance. In an IDM environment, where a prospect may be contacted frequently and intensively, speed and professionalism in the customer-service department are vital to overall success. This department must be thoroughly briefed, familiar with all communications between the company and the customer, and able to respond promptly to questions or complaints.

The customer-service department is also a prime source of feedback. Customer contacts made by members of this department should be incorporated into your developing database, and the department should have access to an up-to-date record of account activity.

8. Fulfillment. The fulfillment function is absolutely critical to long-term IDM success. When orders are fulfilled in a timely and accurate manner, the receipt of goods ordered serves as an invitation to order again. An integrated direct marketer aggressively seeks out new ways to make the ordering process more pleasant and convenient. All the good will you gain during the preordering stages will be wiped out if the customer must wait for receipt of goods or must suffer through returns and complaints caused by inaccuracy in filling the order.

We view the fulfillment operation as so crucial, and so frequently overlooked, that we have asked one of the industry's leading experts, often referred to as the *dean of fulfillment,* to provide a capsule education on the subject.

Words from the Wise

Stanley J. Fenvessy on Fulfillment

Stanley J. Fenvessy, *Chairman, Fenvessy and Silbert, Inc.*

Consumers today are well educated and demanding. They are attuned to consumerism, and they are seeking *convenient* ways to do their shopping. Once they have been enticed to do business with a direct marketer by integrated direct marketing or by any other means, they believe they are entitled to *service.*

The money you spend on merchandise selection, art, copy, photography, advertising, printing, paper, list rental, mailing, and telemarketing will be wasted if you can't efficiently fulfill orders from those who do, or want to do, business with your company.

How do you provide the support needed to make the art and science of IDM become a reality on the bottom line? Like IDM itself, a fulfillment support program requires the coordination of many disciplines, working synergistically, to convert a skeptical consumer into a satisfied and happy customer.

What are the elements of successful fulfillment? There are seven, and to help you remember them, we have captioned each with a word beginning with P: people, policies, procedures, programs, paperwork, productivity, and physical facilities. Snow White had her seven dwarfs. A fulfillment director needs seven giants. Here they are:

1. *People.* Fulfillment techniques, controls, and systems are markedly different from manufacturing or traditional retail operations. You would not employ a factory production manager to be a store manager. Similarly, the people who manage your fulfillment operation must have mail-order distribution know-how. Further, your regular work force must be composed of both basic *full-time* personnel and a regular cadre of *part-timers* who are available to supplement your basic staff during peak operating and selling periods.

2. *Policies.*   These should range from the guarantee offered to your customers to the rules you expect your people to follow in processing problem orders and making adjustments for disappointed customers. Included in the policies should be the *service* goals for the fulfillment cycle and for responding to customer inquiries and complaints. To assure that management's intent is being carried out, all policies and standards should be formally documented and promulgated to all concerned.

3. *Procedures.*   There must be established routines for processing orders; receiving and shipping merchandise; handling returns; and receiving, reading, researching, and responding to customer inquiries and complaints. There should be no duplication, backtracking, or unnecessary tasks. Work flow from order receipt to delivery to a carrier should be scheduled so that a majority of the orders are shipped the day after receipt. A procedures manual containing flowcharts, system write-ups, and sample forms is mandatory for establishing a clear understanding of accepted practices and for training new personnel.

4. *Programs.*   Almost all aspects of fulfillment, from order receipt to order picking, require computer support in the form of efficient and comprehensive programs and reliable and economical hardware. Meaningful and accurate management information for marketing, inventory management, and cost control is also dependent on computer programs. A wide variety of computer packages is now available. This enables a company to employ the capability of its computer in a shorter time and with a smaller investment.

5. *Paperwork.*   Direct marketing can be said to be a *paperwork* business. It starts with the paper of catalogs and other promotions and continues with purchase orders, customer orders, invoices, computer printouts, packing lists, form letters, refund checks, receiving and shipping documents, and a myriad of reports. The efficiency level of your business depends on well-designed forms and streamlined paperwork. To keep reports and forms under control, many companies periodically review all paperwork to determine which is no longer needed and which can be simplified. The amount of paperwork in a company can be dramatized by posting one copy of every report or form on the walls of a large room.

6. *Productivity.*   A byword in the national economy, productivity is also essential in an individual business. High personnel productivity is necessary to provide the convenience for customers and the cost containment that are essential to the success of a direct marketing business. The most efficient fulfillment operations have installed work standards and incentive pay. In many instances, this has increased productivity as much as 40 percent. The fulfillment facet of a direct marketing business employs more people than all the rest of the business combined. Hence, achieving a high level of productivity in fulfillment can have a major impact on the bottom line.

7. *Physical Facilities.*   Adequate office and warehouse space is essential to achieving effective fulfillment. You can't attract good workers with a substandard working environment. Availability of sufficient space also has

an impact on the following elements: supervision, security, introduction of new equipment, worker productivity, records and merchandise storage, and housekeeping. Companies which have moved into larger and better fulfillment space report lower personnel turnover, higher morale, and reduced fulfillment expense.

Those are the basic elements of successful fulfillment. You must have each of them if your integrated direct marketing program is going to entice customers to order more than once.

Manage Program Implementation

Program implementation runs from the initial management decision to consider the potential of integrated direct marketing more fully through the creation of an ongoing, profitable program and exploration of additional uses for the direct marketing resources and expertise developed in the process. At each step along this continuum of program implementation, the IDM manager is responsible for several key functions:

- Maintaining an ongoing dialogue with vendors, supervising their progress, and ensuring that they will meet agreed-upon quality standards and deadlines
- Providing to vendors required information regarding company policies, procedures, history, and internal organization
- Developing the level of expertise and capacity required of in-house marketing services
- Preparing draft recommendations, upon achievement of each developmental step, and reporting to management the results to date and recommendations for further action.

As the program moves beyond planning stages and into actual marketing operations, the IDM manager becomes the hub of communications. A structure must be designed which allows up-to-date information to be passed in several directions:

- The IDM manager must develop the required communication channels between in-house departments and between in-house functions and outside vendors, and must monitor the smooth functioning of this interface.

• A reporting structure must be developed that will work in two ways. Information coming into the manager's office must be analyzed and acted upon, and an ongoing, regular system for reporting to others within the company must be established and maintained. While prompt and complete reports to senior management are obviously important, the first concern, at least chronologically, is sharing information within the functional departments impacted by the IDM effort.

Summarize and Evaluate Results

It is up to the IDM manager to synthesize the results of the diverse elements from an integrated direct marketing program into a report that clearly defines the successes and failures of the effort and recommends a course for further action. Because of the relative complexity of IDM, and the manager's unique position as company expert on the techniques and their implementation, this is a critical aspect of the managerial responsibilities.

Integrated direct marketing capability is an asset with ongoing value to the corporation. The easiest way to gauge results of any marketing effort is to simply compare the profit achieved with the expenses incurred. Even if this measurement indicates that an IDM effort has succeeded, though, it is selling the technique short. If an initial effort does not show profits from goods or services sold equal to or exceeding the cost of direct marketing in the short term, it is entirely possible that the long-term effects of the campaign will lead to substantial profits. To prove this point, we need a systematic way of assessing the value of a customer over time.

The methodology has been summarized neatly by Richard J. Courtheoux, president of Precision Marketing Corporation in Chicago. "The lifetime value of a new customer," he writes in the *Direct Marketing Association Manual*, "is the net present value of all future contributions to profit and overhead expected from the customer." In the following excerpt from the *DMA Manual*, Courtheoux explains how to derive this figure.

Words from the Wise

Richard J. Courtheoux on the Lifetime Value of a Customer

Richard J. Courtheoux,   *President, Precison Marketing Corporation*

Accurate calculation of lifetime value requires considerable thought, effort, and serves as a base of information on customer performance. The methodology described below attempts to project future customer performance using historical patterns as a base. In changing businesses, these patterns should be adapted to reflect current expectations.

Lifetime value can be computed by executing the following steps:

1. Segment customers into a manageable number of cells. These cells can be based on recency of last purchase, frequency (number of purchases), dollar amount of purchases, merchandise purchase categories, or other criteria appropriate to a business. Alternate cells may represent customers with similar formula scores from a statistical technique such as multiple regression. The number of cells should be:

   • Enough so that genuine differences in customer responsiveness can be represented.

   • Not so many that the amount of work explodes and the accuracy of the statistics for each cell deteriorates.

   Accurate lifetime value calculations typically use 25–100 cells.

2. Choose a time period for tracking results. Six-month seasons are a good balance between too much and too little detail.

3. Estimate the contributions to overhead and profit which are derived from the starting period of the customers in a cell. For example,

   • Track all the revenues and costs which can be associated with those customers during the period.

   • Tracking cell performance by medium (or offer) for each cell is not advisable by itself, since some customers move from one cell to another within any given time period.

4. Describe the movements of customers among cells from the beginning of one time period to the next. For example, a cell may have 1000 customers at the start of one season, and have those identical 1000 customers at the outset of the next season. This is often the most sensitive and complicated part of the analysis.

5. Project the movement of 1000 new customers over a number of periods into the future, using the customer-movement patterns described in step 4. The projection should be planned far enough into the future so that only a small amount of discounted contribution is being observed.

6. Use the number of customers in each cell for each period projected in step 5, along with the financial performance information from step 3, to calculate contribution per period.

7. Apply a cost of capital (or discount rate) which represents the rate of interest that your company needs to justify an investment. The cost of capital is a means of equalizing current and future cash flows. It reflects both the time value of money and the uncertainty of future cash flows. For example:

   • A company with a 12 percent annual cost of capital will require a $112 return next year for a $100 investment this year.

- If no projected number is used in your company, an annual real rate of 12 percent (which covers inflation) is a reasonable number to apply.

Projected cash flows in all seasons after the initial one are adjusted to their equivalent in season one dollars. An example illustrates how these steps can be executed.

1. Segment customers by recency of last purchase. Group in 6-month intervals all customers who have purchased in the last 3 years.

2. Use 6-month seasons as the time period for the analysis.

3. For each cell:
   - Identify the customers in the cell at the start of the season.
   - Add up all revenues obtained during the season from these customers.
   - Compute the costs for these customers during the season, including promotion, merchandise, and fulfillment.
   - The contribution is the difference between total revenues and total costs.

The total contribution should be divided by the number of customers in the cell at the start of the season in order to produce a contribution per customer. A typical table might look like this:

Recency Group	Contribution per Customer
0–6	$4.39
7–12	2.20
13–18	1.02
19–24	.57
25–30	.07
31–36	(.09)
37 +	—

4. At the end of the season, movements of customers among cells can be summarized as follows:

Start Cell	End Cell	Probability
0–6	0–6	0.25
	7–12	0.75
7–12	0–6	0.17
	13–18	0.83
13–18	0–6	0.12
	19–24	0.88
19–24	0–6	0.09
	25–30	0.91
25–30	0–6	0.06
	31–36	0.94
31–36	0–6	0.03
	37 +	0.97
37 +	37 +	1.00

WORDS FROM THE WISE

Table 4.1. New customer lifetime value calculation

Customers	Season									
	1	2	3	4	5	6	7	8	9	10
0–6 months	1000	250	190	154	130	108	86	62	48	37
7–12 months	0	750	187	142	115	98	81	64	46	36
13–18 months	0	0	622	155	118	95	81	67	53	38
19–24 months	0	0	0	547	136	104	84	71	59	47
25–30 months	0	0	0	0	498	124	94	76	65	54
31–36	0	0	0	0	0	468	117	89	72	61
37 + months	0	0	0	0	0	0	454	568	654	724
Contribution	4390	2743	1877	1458	1060	818	685	521	401	310
Discounted contribution	4390	2588	1671	1224	840	611	482	346	251	183
Cumulative discounted contribution	4390	6978	8649	9873	10714	11325	11808	12155	12406	12590

SOURCE: Reprinted from *DMA Mail Order Manual*, Release No 620.4, with permission from Direct Marketing Association, Inc., New York, 1986.

5. The calculations displayed in Table 4.1 show the movements and financial contributions from 1000 customers in a recency group 0–6 at the start of the season. A cost of capital of 6 percent per season (12 percent per year) is used for discounting future season contributions. The key figure is the cumulative discounted contribution of $12,590 from the 1000 new starting customers.

The calculation shows a lifetime value per new customer of $12.59 (= $12,590/1000 customers). This could be expanded to include:

- Acquisition season contribution. The analysis shown ignores all first order revenues and costs, in effect allocating them to the customer acquisition process.

- More time periods. However, the additional discounted contribution by period 10 is quite small. Carrying the analysis to more periods will only add slightly to the estimated lifetime value for this business. In many firms, the projection should extend as much as 10 years.

- Detailed financial calculations. Contribution could be broken down to show revenue, list rental income, cost of goods, fulfillment costs, etc.

- Loss of some customers from the file due to attrition.

This analysis becomes a base case which can be modified to evaluate various business options.

This is, admittedly, a complex calculation (sources for more detailed explanations of the figuring process can be found in the Bibliography at the end of the book). It demands not only the financial sophistication to carry out the calculations but also database records sufficiently complete and organized to provide the fodder for the figuring. Still, whether you follow the procedure outlined above or simplify it to deal with only a few individual market segments (tracking buying behavior over time and factoring in the net present value of the revenues produced), deriving a quantitative figure for the lifetime value of a customer is critical.

Of course, the process doesn't stop with the presentation of a neat figure on paper. Once you can identify the long-term value of a customer, this must become a key element in top management decision making. The purpose of IDM is to create an ongoing relationship between company and customer. For virtually all sellers of goods or services, it is repeat business over time that not only provides the bulk of the profit but also brings in new customers through referrals. By identifying the key segments of the marketplace and pinpointing their continuing value to the company, we can accurately apply the resources of IDM at appropriate levels. For a particularly active segment of the customer base, or a segment that has the potential for becoming very active, more frequent contact employing a greater diversity of media may be warranted. For less frequent but still steady buyers, less intensive but regular contact through a single medium may be cost-justified. It is up to the IDM manager to put together the market-segmentation data with an eye toward establishing acceptable marketing expenditures for each segment, and to make program recommendations to senior management on the basis of this rationale.

Develop New Applications for IDM Resources

Integrated direct marketing capabilities are a business asset, and should be viewed as such. While the learning curve may seem steep during a company's first direct marketing experience, it actually flattens out very quickly. After the initial effort involved in gathering resources, identifying and solving operational problems, and understanding the management techniques required to profit from direct marketing activities, future programs are conducted on a different level. Marketing strategy becomes the major area of change once the operational resources are in place.

This holds true whether you are building up in-house operations or using outside vendors for all services. The management team members are developing their own expertise, and identifying sources of expert knowledge and operations outside the company as well.

The IDM manager should actively seek out new ways to exploit thecompany's IDM resources. As the in-house expert on the techniques involved, the manager should confer with product-marketing executives, discussing potential applications for IDM as they relate to individual promotional activities. There is a definite benefit to increasing the amount of IDM activity undertaken by the company. With increased expertise and volume usage of mail, telephone, and broadcast resources, prices per contact decrease and marketing efficiency increases.

Choosing the Right Person for the Job

While there is no single profile for choosing an individual to serve as IDM manager, there are some key criteria to keep in mind:

Direct Marketing Experience

Direct marketing is its own distinctive discipline, different from general advertising. While advertising is accountable in its own way, it does not approach the level of definitive feedback at the heart of direct marketing. "Reach" is an important concept in both advertising and direct marketing, to be sure, but completed transactions are the stock in trade of the direct marketer. For this reason, a radically different set of criteria applies both in the design of a campaign and in its evaluation.

Any prior experience with direct marketing is better than none at all, since the underlying decision-making factors are common to all direct-response media. Ideally, managers should have had some exposure to at least direct mail and telemarketing. No matter what their previous experience, though, these individuals should be open to all possible media. Preconceived notions about direct-response media, whether they are positive ("A glossy, impressive mailing never fails") or negative("Telemarketing will never fit in with our company image") are deadly when it comes to evaluating options for an IDM effort.

Years with the Company

There is plenty of opportunity for bringing new blood and new ideas into a company in conjunction with an integrated direct marketing program, whether as new employees or as outside vendors and consultants.

However, the person who manages the effort should have some track record and an established position within the corporate hierarchy.

There are two good reasons for this. The first is entirely pragmatic. Experienced company veterans will know the strengths and weaknesses of the organization firsthand. They will be responsible for bringing outside experts up to speed on the marketing history of the company; its previous successes or failures; and its goals, aspirations, and culture. Not only will these individuals be able to draw on personal experience within the organization, but also they will know where to turn for more information as the need arises. Newcomers, in contrast, will be hard pressed to learn enough, and to learn it fast enough, to adequately integrate a new marketing campaign into the ongoing stream of company business.

As we stressed in Chapter 1, adopting integrated direct marketing is a more sweeping change than merely adding media to the marketing mix. It is a philosophical outlook on the way your company does business, and as such, must be developed as an intrinsic component of the corporate culture. A company is more than an institution for making money; it has a personality, a "corporate culture." IDM draws upon and enhances the best elements of a corporate culture. It stresses service, customer satisfaction, and long-term growth through superior performance. It is also a focal point for corporate interaction, bringing individuals with diverse job responsibilities together in pursuit of a common goal. IDM managers who bring an understanding of the existing corporate culture to their new position can both employ the existing strengths of the company in the new undertaking and help to enhance these positive characteristics in the process of building a profitable direct marketing enterprise.

The second concern in this area is political, and we must never underestimate the importance of corporate politics in the successful implementation of integrated direct marketing. We are bringing a powerful new technique to bear, one which will inevitably infringe on the established order. IDM managers must have enough clout and access to sell the program to their superiors.

At the same time, IDM requires unprecedented levels of cooperation throughout the company, from the executive suite down through the shipping dock. A "company person" has a much greater chance of achieving this level of joint effort than a "new hotshot" brought in to shake things up, no matter how impressive the newcomer's credentials may be.

Entrepreneurial Inclination

The concept of an individual applying entrepreneurial thinking within a corporate environment (sometimes referred to as an "intrapreneur") is especially appropriate for integrated direct marketing. This is an aggressive, modern strategy with high levels of potential profit and, consequently, high visibility within the corporation. IDM management is an ideal spot for managers who are willing and eager to stake out a distinctive niche within the company and to take responsibility for the success or failure of their programs.

On the other hand, it is important that company management reward and encourage the IDM function adequately to attract and retain the necessary talent. An appropriate level of compensation and perks and an upward path within the company from the IDM management position are essential to motivating an entrepreneurial individual.

Profitable Telemarketing List-Management Techniques

Integrated direct marketers expend tremendous time and effort developing carefully targeted lists of prime prospects. Through coordinated media efforts, we can reach these selected individuals with greater impact and produce a higher market penetration within these high-potential segments than through traditional single-media efforts. To maximize the effect of our multimedia strategy, though, it is essential that the prospect list be handled with proper respect for the importance of each name.

This is especially true when outbound telemarketing is part of your media mix. Outbound telemarketing can deliver messages not only on a specific day but at a predetermined time of day. It is even flexible enough for your message to be delivered at the day and time specifically requested by the recipient.

At the same time, a telemarketing contact is more expensive than a direct-mail contact. To be employed profitably, the medium requires a tightly targeted list and maximum list penetration. We demand the highest possible income per thousand names in a telemarketing program. This requirement places a significant burden on your ability to control and manage your target list.

As Liz Kislik, president of Liz Kislik Associates in New York, observes:

For a direct mail campaign, the list management process is often fairly static. The names are segmented, merged and purged against other lists, and the mailing is generated.

In the telemarketing process, though, list management is dynamic. Names must be batched according to time zones and list segmentation criteria, then constantly reshuffled depending on the results of calling attempts as the program progresses. Completed calls must be grouped separately from incomplete attempts, and detailed reports regarding the results of these calls must be generated. Depending on the design of your telemarketing program, you should allow for callbacks at a specific time—this is important from the prospect's point of view, but represents greater complexities in list handling.

The efficiency of your telemarketing effort, in the actual telephone operation and in all the clerical support functions, has a major impact on the overall economics of the program. To illustrate, let's build a test case comparing mail and telephone response rates in a consumer environment (Table 4.2).

These figures may or may not represent a profitable application of telemarketing, depending on the costs of the operation and the profit margin per sale. Still, they are impressive for several reasons:

- The telemarketing response represents incremental response over mail.

- Telemarketing generated 21 orders out of 420 completed contacts, versus 900 messages "delivered" by mail. This points up a significant difference between mail and telephone: for each completed contact in telemarketing, we know that the message was delivered to the prospect. We have no way of knowing how many of our mail packages were actually read and the offer considered, and how many were summarily discarded.

- At the same time, when *projecting* telemarketing response based on a percentage figure, that projection should be based on reaching not

Table 4.2. Test-Case Comparison: Direct Mail versus Telemarketing

	Direct mail	Telemarketing
Total universe	1000	1000
Undeliverables or nixies (10%)	(100)	(100)
No telephone number (30%)	—	(300)
Unable to reach by telephone after multiple attempts (30%)	—	(180)
Total messages delivered	900	420
Projected response rate	1%	5%
Total orders produced	9	21

100 percent of the list but a much smaller segment of the total (in our rule-of-thumb case above, 42 percent).

Now that we have a projected baseline response, let's analyze the change in telemarketing effectiveness based on fairly modest adjustments to some of our parameters. Specifically:

- Improve the productivity of telephone number look-up by 20 percent, so that instead of losing 30 percent of the list, we lose only 24 percent.
- Improve the reach rate by 30 percent, so that instead of reaching 70 percent of the callable names, we contact 90 percent.

What effects do these changes have on our telemarketing program? See Table 4.3.

By improving telephone number look-up and reach rate, we have increased our total telephone orders by *43 percent.*

Are these improvements possible? Absolutely. Do they represent additional operational expense? Marginally yes, although the costs are variable and are cost-justified given the 43 percent increase in orders.

Take the telephone number look-up operation, made necessary by the lack of telephone-number listings in many commercially available lists, as an example. One easy road to improvement here is simply to seek out those lists which do include telephone numbers wherever possible.

More to the point, remember that we are functioning here in an integrated direct marketing environment. If outbound calls are being made as follow-up to a direct-response mailing, it is a simple matter to request a telephone number in the mailing. This is also a good example of the residual value of each direct marketing program: a telephone number, once gathered and entered into the customer or prospect database, becomes a valuable asset for future programs, eliminating the operational expense of looking up the number and increasing the ultimate response rate produced by the telemarketing phase of the campaign.

Table 4.3. Revised Test-Case Results

	Direct mail	Telemarketing
Total universe	1000	1000
Undeliverables or nixies (10%)	(100)	(100)
No telephone number (24%)	—	(240)
Unable to reach by telephone after multiple attempts (10%)	—	(66)
Total messages delivered	900	594
Projected response rate	1%	5%
Total orders produced	9	30

Even improvements which do add to your calling costs, such as additional clerical effort needed to improve the percentage of telephone numbers found, or more dialing attempts to increase the percentage of completed calls, may well be justified. You will have to plug in your own cost and profit-margin figures to determine whether the increased expenses are justified by the increased performance, but given the magnitude of improvement based on relatively modest production gains, the possibility is certainly worth exploring. Testing in an IDM environment is not simply a matter of acquiring and segmenting lists of names; operational testing is another prime consideration in the search for optimal response rates.

Developing Resources and Suppliers

There are two levels of decisions involved in choosing and using direct-marketing resources:

- Develop in-house capabilities or use outside vendors?
- If outside vendors, which ones?

The integrated direct marketing perspective does not radically alter the criteria which would be employed in making these decisions for single-media campaigns. There is one overriding concern in making IDM work, though, that is more stringent than in traditional direct marketing operations—the necessity for unimpeachable quality and reliability throughout the operation. The reason we adopt IDM techniques in the first place is to make a positive impression based on intense and persuasive contact. Timing is a key element in creating this impression. So are the tone, style, and content of each phase of marketing communication. Drawing attention to oneself is clearly self-defeating if the message is not being conveyed in a convincing fashion. Therefore, we demand top-of-the-line quality in all we do in IDM, whether it is a printed piece or a teleconference or a broadcast spot for radio or television.

In-House or Outside Vendor?

In a sizable company, or even in a relatively small company which has decided to make direct marketing a significant channel of distribution, the question whether to develop in-house capabilities, to use outside marketing services, or to combine the two options is an increasingly significant issue. Integrated direct marketing provides a powerful, coherent marketing message which can produce significant revenue streams. As reliance on this technique increases and as the profits also grow, two key considerations emerge: cost and quality control.

The cost issue is largely a question of volume, particularly as it relates to telemarketing. Direct-mail costs are largely front-loaded: the creative and production expenses are incurred in a fairly brief time frame, and the use of these services is periodic. If there will be a regular stream of discrete direct-mail packages to be written, designed, and produced, then developing these capabilities in-house may be desirable. Few companies actually need this dedicated capability, however.

Telemarketing is a different story. While there are certain front-end costs involved, the major expense items are the regular, ongoing costs of maintaining a facility and paying salaries. Under these circumstances, it will often prove efficient to develop in-house telemarketing operations, since the costs will drop below service-bureau charges when the calling volume is large enough to ensure efficient use of staff and physical plant.

Of course, volume is only part of the equation. There will be times when only a dedicated telemarketing facility will provide the level of product knowledge and interaction with the prospect to satisfy the needs of the program.

A case in point was the experience of Cessna Aircraft Company when it attempted to create an 800-number hot-line lead-generation program using a service bureau. The number was included in the advertisements, and the service bureau started receiving calls—and promptly ran into problems. To quote Philip M. Michel, manager of marketing communications for Cessna, from an article he wrote for *Direct Marketing* magazine:

> The problem simply had to do with the qualifying process. Regardless of the level of qualification of a telemarketing sales consultant, it is practically impossible to impart a sufficient amount of knowledge about a very highly technical industry and involved product like aviation to enable them to engage in give and take. There have been some very successful experiments conducted with outbound telemarketing with well-trained sales representatives in some highly technical areas, such as calling on physicians and laboratory technicians when the objective is primarily to impart information.
>
> Our problem was that the callers were all pilots and aircraft owners. They envisioned in their mind they were going to be talking to somebody that could talk to them about airplanes. We immediately got into an horrendous problem, because the people answering the telephone, for the most part, didn't know very much about airplanes.
>
> Inside of about a two-week to three-week period, the whole thing collapsed of its own weight. Although telemarketing as a lead generating and information cap-

turing device can be highly effective, using a service bureau when you are going to be involved in a complicated dialogue between the prospect and the telephone sales representative is asking for trouble....

As a result of that episode and also our launching of a new flight training program, we decided to move our telemarketing efforts in-house. From the beginning, we staffed our center with pilots who were familiar with our flight training system and knowledgeable about our product line.

This is a case of a telemarketing operation which, in order to be successful, placed extremely heavy demands on the knowledge of the person answering the telephone. Well-qualified representatives working for a professional telemarketing service bureau can provide a surprising degree of information to callers, when provided with appropriate training, carefully crafted scripts, and reference materials. Sometimes, though, there is simply no substitute for a full-fledged expert.

Evaluating the Economics

The bottom-line criteria for deciding on in-house versus outside-vendor services will be based on the financial resources and risk-taking position of the company. Certainly, employing outside vendors allows greater control of the level of expenditure. At the same time, the risk involved in developing in-house facilities will be rewarded with greater profits for a program that utilizes these resources efficiently. Here again, we see the importance of a clear strategic plan that states the corporate strategy for investment as well as the goals for the development of integrated direct marketing.

There is special value to using outside vendors during the testing and development phase of an integrated direct marketing operation. A proven level of expertise is assured, and you can tightly control the costs incurred without funding the overhead of a start-up operation.

The role of consultants is also worth considering in this regard. While some of the intricacies of launching an in-house direct marketing operation are readily apparent, others are only revealed over time. Consultants bring the advantage of experience to your venture. They have seen operations which run smoothly, and others which do not. The consultant is aware of mistakes made by other companies, and helps to insulate you from these pitfalls. At the same time, a consultant should be able to recommend suppliers for designing and constructing physical facilities, creative services, and other short-term requirements.

Consider the total investment involved in establishing your direct marketing facility, and weigh the expense of making mistakes against the fee of a reputable and experienced consultant.

Checklist for Decision Making about In-House versus Outside-Vendor Services

A brief rundown of the considerations involved in choosing either in-house or outside-vendor direct marketing services is given below.

Advantages of in-house operation

Control. The major advantage of developing an in-house operation is the level of control which can be exercised over its functioning. In some instances this is absolutely critical, as in transactions in which salespeople must be licensed by a government authority. Even if there is no licensing requirement, the individuals involved in writing copy, answering telephones, or even fulfilling orders can be more intensively trained and, hence, more knowledgeable about the company's product or service if they are employees of that company rather than an outside agency or service bureau.

Database access. It is easier to draw from, or add to, an ongoing central database from within a single corporate facility than to spread information gathering and dispersal over several vendor companies. This is not to say that it is impossible to enter data from a service bureau into your central files, or to provide ongoing data updates to field operations. However, a centralized operation is more convenient and up to the minute in its database functions.

Employee commitment. If properly structured, an in-house operation can produce higher levels of employee enthusiasm and involvement than an outside vendor. This assumes that the employees in the direct-response departments are fully integrated with the company as a whole, receive adequate compensation, and see the opportunity for advancement.

Learning-curve effects. In an in-house operation, the individuals involved develop a unique level of experience working with the distinctive concerns of the company. Their efficiency and productivity increase over time, as does their value to their employer. The same is true of the operation as a whole: as it continues over time, whether as one long program or as individual campaigns, efficiency and productivity increase, with resulting improvements in profitability. The company develops a special-purpose tool, shaped to meet its own marketing requirements, which can be applied to a wide range of direct-response opportunities, often on short notice.

Advantages of vendor services

Expert capabilities.   The rapid growth of direct marketing in the past 10 years has created a shortage of professionals with the expertise and experience required to design and manage direct marketing operations. Even companies with the desire to start in-house operations and the willingness to offer substantial salaries to managers may find it difficult to hire the necessary personnel. However, an established agency or service bureau will have a team of experts in place, thoroughly trained and experienced in a variety of programs conducted for many clients.

Minimal capital outlay.   The start-up expense involved in setting up facilities and hiring personnel for a direct marketing operation can be enormous. An in-house telemarketing facility involves real estate, furniture, telephone lines and equipment, hiring, training, and more. Fulfillment operations are also labor- and space-intensive. By using a service organization, the company avoids these up-front expenses, and the overhead expenses involved in running a direct marketing operation are spread by the vendor over a range of concurrent programs.

Faster start-up.   Clearly an existing direct marketing vendor will have systems and people in place, eliminating the substantial lag time involved in initially setting up operations.

Easier shutdown.   If a direct marketing program is not going well, it is relatively simple to call a vendor and have operations suspended. In a facility staffed with your own employees, even a temporary hold on a program can mean layoffs and extra expenses.

Staffing considerations.   While in-house or outside marketing executives are generally well-paid professionals, there are several areas in direct marketing operations which require less skilled labor in fairly large quantity. The expense involved in hiring telemarketing personnel, or additional warehouse help to handle single-item fulfillment, will prove exorbitant unless your facility is running at near-peak load on a regular basis. Unusual hours (such as 24-hour operator service) and peak-period staffing requirements (pre-Christmas shipping, for instance) also make direct marketing labor requirements distinctively demanding.

Union versus nonunsion labor. Finally, there is the question of union versus nonunion labor. If additional personnel hired by your firm would be union members with the associated benefits and expenses, it may well prove less costly to farm out the work.

In general, it is wise to rely on outside resources as much as possible in the initial phases of involvement with direct marketing. Up-front investment is minimized; experienced, talented individuals are available at all levels of the operation; and the program can be started, stopped, and restarted more or less at will. Once direct marketing has proved itself as a valuable tool within your marketing plans, then serious consideration should be given to bringing some or all of the functions involved in-house, perhaps drawing on vendors who have proved their abilities in the role of consultants.

Selecting Outside Vendors

Someday there may be a direct-response agency that truly brings together all the services required for integrated direct marketing under one roof—but it doesn't exist today, and creating a single source of that sort would be a massive undertaking. Consider the breadth of media encompassed under the IDM umbrella, ranging from broadcast media through direct mail, print advertising, inbound and outbound telemarketing, audio and video teleconferencing, to the creation of premiums and incentives. And that only covers the media mix: additional specialty services include market research, database management, fulfillment, and consulting services to help bring order and direction to the program as a whole.

It is clear that in a program of any size, you will have to work with several vendors. A primary criterion for selecting these vendors for an integrated direct marketing program is an understanding of, appreciation of, and enthusiasm for the synergistic nature of the program being undertaken.

Some companies—even many with unquestioned expertise and a superb track record in their chosen field—find it extremely difficult to integrate their operations effectively with other media practitioners. The problem may be attitudinal. *There is no "star" medium in an IDM media mix; everyone is a supporting player.* The marketer gains from this ensemble approach, but the agency demanding an individual spotlight loses out.

Rigid internal systems may also spell trouble for a vendor working in an IDM environment. We demand a free flow of information between vendors, so that the strengths of each medium and service function can be appropriately employed, and the response generated through each medium can be used to fine-tune the use of the other media in the mix. This does not imply a loss of confidentiality, since the client supervises this interchange, and no information goes beyond those with a "need to know." However, the number of individuals who do need to know is greater in IDM than in traditional marketing, and a vendor unable or unwilling to engage in an open interchange of information and ideas will only impede the process.

Above all, look for a sense of enthusiasm about the project at hand. There are two very good reasons that a vendor who understands the IDM concept should demonstrate an intense level of interest in your program: it's a matter of dollars and sense. The demonstrated potential of IDM as a major distribution channel for goods and services makes an IDM program a good bet for rapid growth, and with growth comes program expansion, increased use of the vendor services, and greater profits.

Second, integrating resources into complementary, synergistic programs is clearly the direction our industry will be following for the foreseeable future. Every opportunity to undertake a program on behalf of a client interested in pursuing this approach represents the chance to build up the knowledge base in this area. Experience and expertise in meeting the unique requirements of an IDM program is an increasingly important aspect of any agency's offer to a potential client. Now is the time to build up credentials in this regard, and it makes sense to devote extra time and energy to clients who wish to pursue this methodology today.

Checklist for Selecting an Agency or Service Bureau

Figure 4.1 is an adaptation of a questionnaire developed to nelp clients choose outside marketing vendors. It can help you to organize the wealth of choices available so that you will be able to select the agency or service bureau that best meets your needs. We have included both general areas to be considered in assessing the capabilities of any direct marketing service supplier, and specific criteria involved in choosing a direct marketing agency, telemarketing service or fulfillment operation.

This checklist is presented in a format that makes it ready to be photocopied and filled in during the selection process.

Agency name_____ Telephone number_____
Address_____
Name and title of agency contact_____
  (1)Corporate affiliation_____
  (2)Length of time in business_____
  (3)Current clients_____
_____
  (4)Clients competitive with your company_____
  (5)Past clients_____
  (6)Current or previous experience with your company_____
_____
  (7)Previous experience with similar product or service_____
_____
  (8)Previous experience with IDM campaigns_____
_____
  (9)Membership in Direct Marketing Association_____
(10)References:
    Three current clients_____
_____
_____
    Three past clients _____
_____
_____

For Direct Marketing Agencies
Areas of media expertise_____
_____
Level of executives assigned to account_____
_____
Organizational structure_____
Assessment of creative samples_____
Adequacy of resources_____

For Telemarketing Agencies and Service Bureaus
Communicator training and turnover_____
_____
Communicator compensation (hourly or commission)
_____
Number of communicators_____
Ratio of supervisors to communicators_____
Organizational structure_____
Capacity (hours per month)_____
Scripting (structured scripting versus call guides)_____
Automation (What is automated? Scripting?
  MIS? Telecommunication?)_____
MIS (manual or automated? How detailed?)_____
Security of clients' names and other information_____
Creative thinking (creative or strategic versus operations shop)
_____

Figure 4.1. Questionnaire: choosing an outside telemarketing vendor.

Verification procedures_____
Lead time to program start-up_____
On-site monitoring_____
FOR FULFILLMENT BUREAUS
Personnel training and turnover
Number of employees_____
Ratio of supervisors to employees_____
Organizational structure_____
Size of physical plant_____
Equipment_____
Days of operation per week_____
Automation_____
MIS (manual or automated? How detailed?)_____
Inventory-control procedures_____
Security_____
Customer-service capabilities_____
Delivery services available_____
Lead time to program startup_____

Figure 4.1. *(Continued)*

5
The Creative
Challenge of IDM

An integrated marketing effort presents a set of unique creative challenges, both for the writers, producers, and graphic artists responsible for designing the program materials and for the managers responsible for coordinating and overseeing the effort.

The eternal rules of direct marketing, of course, remain valid in an integrated media environment. You still want to offer benefits, benefits, and more benefits. You still need to pack that envelope with a variety of pieces of paper so that order-form readers, letter readers, brochure skimmers, and lift-note aficionados can all find their favorite bits. Telephone communicators still need prepared answers for the most common questions and objections. Some things never change.

Traditionally, though, the creative effort in each medium exists in a vacuum. Each media contact is expected to convey a complete, self-contained marketing transaction. The prospect's attention is gained, the offer is explained, and a response device is presented.

Integrated direct marketing adds another major consideration to the planning and execution of the individual media: the interrelationships between the messages conveyed across the various media employed. By skillfully weaving together these impressions, we create a level of awareness and response far beyond that achieved through a series of unrelated advertising, mail, or telephone efforts.

We will concentrate here not on the basics of good direct marketing creative treatments in general, but on the distinctive aspects of preparing the creative treatment for an integrated direct marketing campaign.

Managing Creative Resources

The first potential stumbling block, before a word or image is put on paper, is assembling a team that can share information and ideas, communicate effectively among themselves, and envision each individual component as part of a marketing whole.

The responsibility for coordinating the creative effort will depend on the resource allocation and corporate culture of the marketer. The one absolute requirement is the company IDM manager for the project. As discussed in Chapter 3, this individual is responsible for making sure that the multitude of elements which go into an IDM campaign come together for maximum synergistic effect.

In addition, many companies which pursue integrated direct marketing with a high level of enthusiasm and intensity employ a consultant to assist in designing and implementing the effort. This consultant's responsibilities include recommending creative resources capable of functioning effectively within an IDM framework, as well as overseeing the relationship between various media specialists and between the specialists and the marketing company.

Finally, there is the creative director. Though the same title exists in the traditional ad agency, the IDM creative director is a very different creature. This individual must be a skillful practitioner of a host of media disciplines, while bringing the larger perspective of integrated direct marketing to bear on all. Frankly, there are not many creative directors in the country today who can fill these shoes in an IDM campaign, and it is sometimes necessary for the IDM manager or consultant to supervise the individual creative efforts of several media specialists directly. However, the integrated creative director is a force to be reckoned with and a major asset to the IDM team. We have asked one of the best, Scott Hornstein of Hornstein Associates in Connecticut, to provide some insight into the job, and into the creative process as it is undertaken in an IDM framework.

Words from the Wise

Scott Hornstein on the Integrated Creative Director

Scott Hornstein, *President, Hornstein Associates, Inc.*

The discipline of integrated direct marketing is a composite, drawing upon the strengths of different disciplines to form a new and more powerful methodology. So the IDM creative director is also a composite, drawing upon many different experiences, contributing to many areas to form a more perfect union.

WORDS FROM THE WISE

The IDM creative director is the resident magician, managing ideas and people, graphics and words to an end which is the physical embodiment of all the planning—an end which the market sees, touches, and listens to, and to which the market responds.

But how? Let's begin by smashing a shibboleth: that (account) management and the creative effort are separate and never the twain shall meet; that the two camps are mutually exclusive and usually engage in open warfare, if things are running "right."

Contrary to this belief, if things are truly running right, what we have is a good, honest exchange of ideas—not always comfortable, not always adversarial, but always productive.

It is important to realize that, while management may be primarily concerned with "business," the business and the creative work are the two good arms of the body politic. The two hands at the ends of those arms, like those of a concert pianist, may be striking different notes on different keys at different times. And in integrated direct marketing, as in the concert hall, the end product should be music.

Indeed, we must take a hard look at the goal we are seeking. More than likely, it is success: attaining what we set out to achieve, by project, by campaign, by career. And that success is achieved through the integration of disciplines. The creative director, therefore, must embrace and have a good working knowledge of, if not be an active participant in, all the processes that come before and after creative execution.

The very model of the modern IDM creative director must necessarily include expertise in the areas discussed below. Indeed, the experience of being a part of these areas results in the cross pollenization of ideas that is critical to the IDM methodology. The sharing of ideas, the internalization of strategy, results in a creative product that is truly on target.

- *Strategic planning.* What are the goals of this program and how do they relate to the goals of the company and the goals of the individuals involved? How can the goals be achieved within the framework of the company and its bureaucratic structure? What is the product or service? What is the offer or series of offers? How will the program be measured by the agency, by the client, by senior management?

- *Market research.* What is the target market? What are the concerns of its members? What do they buy? When do they buy it? And why do they buy it? Moreover, if you pay attention, your target market will tell you what benefits they need to hear, how to spoon-feed them the benefits, what kind of offer they will respond to, and how they wish to respond. You'll also find out who currently has the product or uses the service. What kind of success are these people or companies experiencing? How can that success be quantified?

- *Market planning.* What exactly is the real-life situation? Who are the people in your target market, and what can you offer them? What tests need to be conducted and what can you realistically do? What do you need to learn?

- *Account Management.*   Who are your clients, as people and as a business? What are their internal personalities, their strengths and foibles? How can you work with them? What is the bureaucratic structure? What does the company sell? How is it brought to market? How does the company make a profit? Is there a sales force involved?

- *Media.*   This certainly includes print advertising and direct mail. It also includes both inbound and outbound telemarketing, along with teleconferencing, audiotapes, billboards, premiums, radio, television, videotext, and any other means of getting the message across. The question is, how to deliver the message? To successfully accomplish that, you must be aware of the power, and the weaknesses, of different media and how each can address the target market.

- *Database.*   If direct mail can be called the backbone of IDM, database is the backbone of direct mail. It is the sophisticated computerized construction of a company's client base, the selection, referencing, and qualification of its prospects. The database is worth knowing; the list you mail to accounts for most of the success of the mailing. You can have a wonderful offer with wonderful creative treatment, but if the list is wrong, nobody will care.

- *Production.*   Making it happen is critical. Making it happen well is an art. And as in the practice of any art, there are methods that will enhance a specific idea, fine shadings that will boost response, "tricks" that will help make a difference.

The Creative Product

Of course, the creative product is the creative director's ultimate responsibility.

Here's where all that accumulated experience and involvement comes into play—because understanding the goals, participating in the choices, and incorporating the results of all previous steps builds the bridge to the successful attainment of the project's goals.

Integrated direct marketing is first and foremost a visual medium. If we do not stop our target market from turning the page, if we cannot get them into the envelope, if we do not arrest their attention, we do not get the opportunity to deliver our message.

And once we've stopped them, once we have a moment of their attention, it is up to copy to extend that attention span.

A Word about Graphics

It is worth going the distance to create the graphics that are uniquely relevant to the company, the product, and the market. The up-front costs are somewhat higher than those usually associated with direct response, yet the results generally prove to be dramatic.

Not only do high graphic standards "stop" the target market so that we may deliver our message; they also impart their own message. And that message can be one of innovation, of high quality, of aggressiveness, of the ultimate worth of the product or service.

Graphics can also accomplish the important task of continuity. Remember, IDM utilizes different media to leverage response. The target market may be more aware of the continuity of your message if you use selectively repeated graphic images.

When promoting the latest improvement of an expensive software package to data processing professionals (see the complete case history in Chapter 2), we built a campaign that utilized three visual steps. The first was an invitation to be part of an audio teleconference and talk with the inventors of the software. Graphics were computer-generated, reminiscent of random bits of data being put through a screen and coming out orderly and arranged. The second step was a confirmation—telling registrants,"You are in fact registered, and we're looking forward to your participation." The third step was the delivery of insightful background documentation. Not only were the graphics relevant to the company and the product, but selected images were repeated on each mail piece to let the recipient know, as soon as the package arrived, that this package was an important part of an ongoing dialogue.

In promoting a line of personal computer printers, we selected images that explained technology in more human terms. These images were echoed throughout the print and mail portions of the campaign. When speaking of our efficiency, we showed a frame full of carefully organized, sharpened pencils. When speaking of print quality, we used fountain pens, then flowers (daisy wheels).

A Word about Copy

The closer to the bone you can cut, the more people will pay attention. And I mean people: Even if the campaign is business-to-business, each of us, underneath our business uniform, is a person, with the full range of emotions and motivations. And I mean close to the bone: Make the copy relevant. Give people the reasons they need to respond. If you are making a claim, back it up. For instance, in the AT&T Mortgage Line promotion (see the complete case history in Chapter 2), the manufacturer of a software system for mortgage bankers claimed that it would improve productivity, a major concern for any institution. Research showed that beta test sites had experienced a 30 to 100 percent increase in productivity. That became our headline, and the headline worked.

Back up the benefits whenever you can. Another case in point, this time for the sponsor of seminars concerning the changing legal situation that hospitals face. Our target market was hospital CEOs. Testing proved that the addition of testimonials of hospital CEOs who had attended previous seminars, providing solid substantiation for our product claims, boosted response significantly. To emphasize the importance of testimonials we developed a separate testimonial pamphlet.

A Word about Offer

The offer must bring the product or service and the target market together in a win-win situation. It is one of the great creative challenges, arrived at in consultation with marketing and product management.

A series of offers was successful when promoting the IBM software to data processing professionals. Earlier versions of this software system were generally not well regarded. Market research proved that the new version resolved all previous complaints. To convince the DP market of this, we offered them a teleconference—a chance to talk to the actual inventors of the package without salespeople present. We even supplied them with a set of questions that addressed all previous complaints. Only after attendance at the teleconference was the offer to buy introduced.

A Word about Format and Production

Different formats, obviously, accomplish different ends. The choice bears scrutiny because format, too, implies importance and demands attention. Production, when planned with experience and creativity, can work hard to increase response. Of course, our format and production decisions must always be true to our overall objectives. With one hand firmly grasping these goals, and the other hand wrapped around the principles of IDM, we are in a position to balance formats and production. For instance:

- A junior page, with editorial surrounding the creative treatment can often be more effective (in terms of price and performance) than a full page.

- Certain continuous form mail packages so closely emulate the look of first-class mail that response rates can be significantly improved.

- When promoting a copier to office managers, we were faced with an essentially parity product and an arena of fierce competition. Our piece had to instantly distinguish the product, position it as "unique," and capture attention long enough for us to tell our story. The format became an intricate series of die cuts which illustrated the features of the copier. Our story was one of modularity: that all you really need is the basic box. The first die cut addressed the automatic document feed. If you need it, it's easily attached. But lift it off (and the die cut hinged where the machine hinged) and you still get the same high-quality copies.

- Some advances in copy and graphic production bear further investigation. The first is computerization. It can save you time and money. Hard to beat.

Time .   Producing copy using word processing is equivalent to coming out of the dark ages. Sharing copy through a network (on screen) enhances communication and reduces paperwork. And the tools of design are faster once they are automated.

Money .   First, remember that time is money. Second, compare the costs of computer typesetting with conventional methods. Compare the ultimate cost of doing the separations in-house, on the same computer, with conventional methods.

There are also some techniques that will increase results. For instance, laser printers allow you to personalize (selectively!) with high quality, and personalization increases qualified response.

Putting It All Together

Whether you choose to employ a single, large, integrated direct-response agency to handle most components of your multimedia campaign, or to use several smaller agencies, each with its own area of expertise, you will still be dealing with an assortment of individual media specialists. Different parts of the same parent agency will almost always operate as independent units—in effect, separate agencies within a single corporate structure.

Traditionally the creative team of one media group becomes top dog in a multimedia effort, establishing the theme and copy approach that work for them, and the rest of the media experts become the tail that gets wagged. Within certain limitations, this approach can work. In fact, direct marketing as a whole is often added to an ongoing marketing campaign late in the game, in which case the direct marketing team has no choice but to make use of the established theme and tone of the campaign and translate it to a direct-response idiom.

Politics is very much a factor here. If there is an established relationship with a media specialist, whether an agency or an in-house team, it is difficult to avoid having that group call the shots.

Whether you establish a team which can work together closely from inception through the completed creative product, or must live with a dog-and-tail arrangement, there are certain essential factors in successful integration of your creative efforts to produce maximum response. The underlying concern is opening and maintaining channels of communication among the various creative resources employed. It is unreasonable to assume that these individual professionals will take it upon themselves to build these relationships on their own. Rather, it is up to the marketing coordinator to insist on creative integration, monitor the level of cooperation being achieved, and impose order if need be.

Accept the Philosophy

The first step toward achieving a unified, synergistic creative package for an integrated direct marketing effort is to make clear to all participants that there is a distinctive IDM philosophy guiding the program as a whole. As we have discussed in the introductory chapters, accepting an IDM framework represents a significant shift in viewpoint and evaluation criteria. The writer must ask not only "How well does my copy sell the product?" but also "How well does my copy fulfill my medium's function within the larger multimedia marketing effort?" Consistency and integration across media take precedence over a single highly original concept that offers no coherent linkage to other media.

For example, an entirely visual pun might be perfectly acceptable in a mailing piece, but useless for radio broadcast or telemarketing. An automobile service company offering a special on brake repair might consider a mailing suggesting "You Deserve a Brake Today." However, a radio spot promoting the same special would be unable to make use of the copy line, and hence unable to help build recognition and awareness across the media; nor could a telemarketing representative calling previous customers use a script including the "break-brake" pun.

The creative process is inherently democratic: Each writer, artist, or producer will have a unique approach to a marketing task, and no two individuals will ever arrive at precisely the same result. In contrast, integrated direct marketing is not democratic: The enthusiasms and individual exuberance of one creative media team may have to be tempered to bring their work in line with the overall thrust of the unified program. The marketing coordinator is responsible for setting detailed goals for the creative effort, communicating them effectively, and seeing that they are met.

Setting and Communicating Creative Goals

In a military campaign, the finest strategic planning on the part of the generals is worthless if it is not clearly communicated to the troops in the field. Communication is no less essential in an integrated direct marketing campaign, where diverse components must work in a complementary fashion toward fulfilling the strategic goals.

There are two distinct facets to consider:

The goal of the IDM program as a whole

The goal to be pursued by each individual component.

Assuming you have done your homework when designing the program, the first part of this requirement is relatively simple. You should already have a goal statement on paper, and this document should cover both immediate targets and longer-term goals, since both will have an impact upon the creative strategies employed.

The goal statement must convey the position your company seeks within its competitive category. Is your strong suit pricing? Quality of goods or services? Service? Selection? Reputation? This information may be based on the work of your research department, or outside consultants, or years of tradition, or a Ouija board. A method for achieving this goal statement without resorting to the spirit world is outlined in Chapter 3. It may even come about in the course of brainstorming with the creative team. Whatever the source, though, the company positioning in the marketplace must be arrived at and agreed upon by management up front, and clearly conveyed to the creative team.

Set Goals for Each Medium

It is not enough to determine the overall goals to be achieved—the role of each individual media element should be considered, agreed upon, and put in writing.

Is inbound telemarketing going to complete a transaction, or merely trigger outbound mail? If you do expect to close on an incoming call, will there be mail available for those who request additional literature, and what will that mailing entail? Careful consideration of the stated goals for each component of the campaign will determine copy approach and structure for each message delivered.

Establish Timing of Program Components

Timing is another crucial factor in the success or failure of an IDM program, and this too should be made clear to the creative team. There is an enormous difference between a follow-up mailgram that arrives 24 hours after an initial inquiry is received, and a bulk-rate letter that arrives 2 weeks later. A letter that refers to an outbound call to be made on a specific day will have far more impact than a letter that says "Our telephone representative will be in touch soon." Clockwork timing is not always easy to achieve, but it can be a powerful marketing tool, and the creative effort can enhance the effectiveness of that tool if it is properly prepared.

Gather Ye Data While Ye May

Program goals will vary widely, and therefore the strategic function of each media component will vary from one campaign to the next. However, there is one goal which each and every integrated direct-marketing effort will share—the gathering of data.

As we will discuss in detail in Chapter 6, the care and feeding of your database is of prime importance in IDM. Making a sale or producing a screened and qualified lead is wonderful; it leads to immediately quantifiable results and creates instant marketing heros. However, in an IDM context, information is the coin of the realm, and your creative presentation should consistently be geared toward fulfilling this goal for both short- and long-term benefits.

On the most basic level, this means including a prominent request for telephone numbers when you make up a mail-response form. It seems so obvious that you might wonder why even AT&T forgot to include a space for the respondent's telephone number in a program that specifically incorporated outbound telephone follow-up to mail respondees.

Actually, it isn't that difficult to understand how this kind of error can occur. Traditional direct marketers are taught to live, eat, sleep, and breathe their own particular medium. Any tie-in to another channel of communication is essentially an afterthought. Integrated direct marketers substitute forethought for afterthought. The toll-free 800 number is not tossed into a patch of available white space in your mailing piece after the copy and design have been created to elicit coupon response. It is an integral part of the offering from the start, crucial to the planning of copy and art departments.

The same is true for the coupon lines that ask for telephone number, or for additional information. We are not suggesting that you slow down the mail-response process by turning your response device into a survey questionnaire. However, a few short questions integrated into the coupon can yield substantial dividends down the road.

Consider the company marketing investment vehicles to a list selected on the basis of income level. What additional information can be gleaned from a direct-mail piece, or a telemarketing contact, that might pave the way for future targeted marketing efforts on behalf of other products? Simple check-off boxes on a coupon-response form, or a few quick questions over the telephone, will reveal whether respondents own their own homes (for future home equity loan or second-mortgage solicitation), whether they have children of high school age (to identify college loan prospects), how many cars the family owns (to help you spot automobile-financing prospects), and whether the respondents carry a particular credit card (for use in marketing credit-card protection plans). And of course, these and other factors can be vital to the database constructors in assessing the demographic and psychographic makeup of your marketplace.

The point here is not that the writer or graphic artist should be responsible for determining the information to be gleaned from the direct-response contact, but rather that ambitious goals should be set for gathering data from any direct marketing effort, that these goals should be clearly communicated to the creative departments, and that the writers and designers in turn should skillfully integrate the fulfillment of these database goals with the other considerations inherent in the effort.

Creative Strategy and Execution

Once the creative department has a clear idea of the goals it must achieve, the specific creative strategy for achieving these goals must be considered.

In a world where purchasers are bombarded with hundreds of conflicting and confusing images, establishing a unified creative platform and sticking with it across a variety of media are essential. There are many facets to be considered in achieving this goal, though.

Gaining Perspective

First and foremost, you must assess the current status of the company's relationship to the prospect, since this immediately sets a number of "givens" in deciding on a creative strategy to follow.

Is the current effort the company's first contact in any medium with the target audience? If so, then you have a relatively clean slate to work with, and can omit the history lesson. Most often this is not the case. If there has been prior exposure to the company, then a trip through the archives can be very instructive. Even if you are introducing an entirely new product, or a whole new creative direction, or dealing with a separate and distinct division of a larger corporation, memories are long, and mental associations linger. Before you can begin to work toward reaching your goal, you have to know where you stand.

If it is at all possible, physically check out the creative treatment which has been used in the past. At the same time, find out what response it drew, and how management felt about the piece. One of the most frustrating experiences in any creative assignment is attempting to be a mind reader. There are numerous ways we blunder into taking on this psychic responsibility. Management may truly have no idea what it wants, but that is rare. More likely, the responsible individuals either cannot express their desires verbally or have not taken the trouble. One shortcut around this roadblock is to examine previous projects that have been approved, and to probe for management reactions to these projects.

The value system underlying this management judgment can also be gleaned in the process, and this knowledge is invaluable. In one instance, an agency produced a direct-mail package for Christie's Fine Art Auctioneers that proved cost-effective, yet cost a Christie's manager her job, and the agency a client. The reason? Senior managers did not approve the piece before it was dropped in the mail, and were entirely dissatisfied with both the look and the tone once they did see it. The response rate and financials were fine, but because the package did not take into account the corporate image and the creative standards it imposed, the mailing was unacceptable. This disaster could have been avoided if the creative team had accurately assessed the qualities that made previous mailings successful (according to management standards), and if the lines of communication from top to bottom and bottom to top had been more effective.

Reinventing the wheel by relearning lessons already made clear from older campaigns is simply a waste; reinventing the flat tire by repeating previous failures is even worse. Ask to see not only those pieces which were judged successes, but also the disappointments buried in the files.

Remember also to assess the company's previous marketing efforts not only in the medium you are pursuing, but in all related media as well. There are often valuable lessons or inspirational creative insights to be gathered in one medium that can be carried over successfully into an integrated effort tying together several media.

The Value of Research

The other source to tap for information about the company's present position in the hearts and minds of customers is research. As detailed in Chapter 3, market research can provide a clear reading of the prospect's "hot buttons"—the words and phrases that will generate a positive response. This type of research also teaches us the jargon employed by the end user to describe the product or service being offered, since this language can be far removed from the vocabulary of the producer of a product or service.

Research data must be read with an open mind—a task far more easily said than done. Most of us open up a research document with a preconceived notion in mind, and search for the paragraphs that bolster that idea. This is especially true in a creative endeavor, since there is always at least one idea that leaps to mind immediately upon approaching a new project. Those initial ideas are cherished, and for good reason—as often as not, they prove to be the germ of what is eventually created. However, putting real weight on market research should counterbalance the enthusiasms of initial inspiration with the grim realities of the marketplace.

Scoping the Competition

We must also assess the competitive environment within the company's business segment. Here again, it is valuable both to evaluate research documents and to actually read, view, or listen to the messages being delivered by the competition. In this way, a distinctive positioning may become apparent. Look for messages that are not being delivered—potential benefits going unexploited—media channels not being employed within a marketplace.

Fitting the Message to the Medium

Finally, the IDM professional evaluates the distinctive qualities of each medium, and tailors the presentation to exploit the strength of each to greatest effect. The unique capabilities of each medium are discussed in depth in Chapter 2. It is important that both project managers and the creative team understand these strengths and limitations, and work within them. You simply cannot deliver the quantity of information available in a long-copy brochure in the course of a telemarketing call, nor can you answer every question and objection posed by consumers in your space advertising.

The individual or individuals managing the overall campaign strategy are responsible for combining media wisely. While these decisions are based largely on target-marketing and budgetary considerations, it is also vital to consider what messages must be delivered, and what type of medium and level of exposure will be required to get these messages across.

The creative team must then make the most of the communication strengths of each medium in preparing copy and graphics that convey adequate information with maximum impact. Ideally, the creative team does not receive a media mix that is fait accompli, but is involved in the up-front planning of the effort, and consulted about how each medium can be used to complement the other. In the real world, a host of media decisions are often set in stone before the first copy line or graphic element has been considered, and it is up to the writers and artists to make the most of the established strategic mix.

A Case in Point

Loan Depot—Combining Media to Sell Second Mortgages

Strategically planning the creative presentation as a unified effort allows you to focus on the strong points of each medium and use each to best advantage.

A brief example, and some analysis:

A frequent advertiser on New York news radio stations is a company called the Loan Depot, offering second-mortgage and home equity loans to homeowners. The company very astutely realized that most people hearing the message will either be driving a car, and hence in no position to start taking notes, or using the radio as background to some other task, and therefore disinclined to drop everything to pick up a pencil and paper. They focused on a simple goal for the radio spot: make people remember the 800 number.

The number itself is key to this strategy; it is 800-USA-LOAN. While this number is memorable in and of itself, it becomes virtually unforgettable through the use of a jingle. The lyrics are repeated several times: "Call 800-USA-LOAN, if you're a home owner, and you need a loan."

The president of the company does the announcing honors, with a voice and reading that successfully combine clarity with the sincere appeal of a nonprofessional. The broadcast copy does not dwell on specific loan rates or competitive terms. Instead, the president identifies himself by name and lingers on two distinct benefits: ease of acceptance and ease of application. If you own a home, he tells you, the Loan Depot will almost certainly be able to grant you a loan. And the entire application procedure can be handled conveniently by calling 800-USA-LOAN. Then it's back to the jingle and out.

The company also places newspaper advertisements—moderate-size space ads, two columns wide by 5 inches deep—in the classified section of the newspaper. Here again, the 800 number is loud and clear, but a different aspect of the offer is highlighted.

In this medium, the major selling point is the rate. In fact, the numbers are nearly an inch high. A quick glance at the competing ads on the page reveals the reason for this approach: in a dozen ads from competing companies, only one includes a rate quote, and it is an extremely small ad. Someone clearly scanned the competition and made a smart creative decision. There is a small flaw in the ad: the 800 number should be set in larger type. However, the number is still the only channel for responding to the ad, both the company name and the 800 number are prominent, and there are clear reasons for picking this ad out from the competition.

Some points to consider:

1. A broadcast medium is employed to create awareness and open a channel for personal communication. A common weakness in generating 800-number response through broadcast is overcome through the use of a mnemonic number, its repetition no less than 6 times in a 60-second spot, and a well-written jingle that gives the number an irresistible beat for increased memory retention.

2. The newspaper ads tie in through the 800 number to the radio campaign. They also make use of a bold presentation of the current loan rate, which is lacking in virtually all competitors' ads, making the print campaign stand out within its environment.

3. Both media drive the prospect toward the 800 number to carry the burden of making the sale. Financial transactions require a person-to-person connection, but we have seen in many telemarketing programs that the telephone can substitute effectively for the personal meeting at a branch office (for example, the home equity loan program conducted by Citicorp

discussed in Chapter 1). The media advertising consistently draws prospects into that one-to-one contact by leading them to the 800 number.

The goal is clear: to generate second-mortgage loan commitments. The creative package approaches this goal on a short-term basis, with ads that highlight a specific loan rate, as well as on the longer-term basis, by establishing the company name and telephone number in a memorable way. For many of us who might one day consider borrowing against the equity in our homes, it would be difficult not to think of the chorus jingling "Call 800-USA-LOAN."

Achieving Awareness

An integrated multimedia campaign offers a unique opportunity to build awareness in the marketplace. Taking advantage of this opportunity requires a unifying element in the campaign. The more memorable the thread that weaves together the disparate media impressions, the more your offer will be noticed, the more powerful it will appear, and the greater the response.

The most important creative task is isolating the single, central benefit offered by the product or service and finding a concise, memorable way to explain it. Every marketing medium employs words, whatever its other techniques. Once you arrive at a single compelling verbal explanation for your unique selling proposition, it can be employed across all media, with appropriate variations on the theme, to ensure a consistent and synergistic message.

Let us say, for example, that you are marketing industrial solvents used to cut grease in cleaning factory surfaces. You must look for not just the right benefit to emphasize, but the right way to phrase the description of your benefit. If superior performance over competing products is the key product benefit, for example, there are several ways to express this. You may offer the results of tests against your competition, particularly if the competition is well known in the marketplace ("The one that beat Greas-O brand in independent laboratory tests").You might dwell on a unique ingredient contained in your product ("Googone, our patented fibrilating agent, employs technology developed by NASA to clean residue off returning space shuttles"). If it is significant, you might dwell on the smell ("Unlike other industrial solvents on the market, Acme Degreaser will not leave offensive odors that linger on the factory floor for days or even weeks after cleaning").

Once you have developed this creative positioning and the core phraseology to convey it, be sure it is carried through in each of the marketing media. Of course, each marketing medium requires its own distinctive presentation. A direct-mail package is a controlled creative environment: you can provide the facts as you see them, reinforcing the positive and ignoring the negative. In a two-way telemarketing contact, on the other hand, you must deal with a host of potential questions and objections, scripting appropriate responses.

The type of information incorporated into each media presentation differs, and so does the quantity of information conveyed. A 30-second broadcast spot, for example, must be lean and carefully focused, generating interest and excitement but leaving the details to other media. Even telemarketing has limitations in the amount of information to be conveyed. Some transactions require the consumer to linger over the facts for a while, and printed material offers the opportunity to study data at length which is unavailable through other media.

Still, no matter how the media presentations differ, that central benefit explanation should be used prominently and consistently in each.

The outer envelope of your mailing about the industrial solvent could strongly promote the independent-laboratory-test results enclosed, and the mailing would then lead with the test results in a letter and include a reprint of the laboratory findings, with suitable excerpts, highlighting, or both. A mailing might even provide a small product sample with instructions enabling recipients to conduct their own informal tests. Alternatively, a tollfree 800 number in the mailing could be used to order a sample, opening the way for an interactive question-and-answer opportunity about the product.

Having established a head-to-head test theme and conveyed it strongly, scripts for outbound telemarketing calls following up the mailing can refer to the dramatic test program and gain high recognition with the individual on the telephone, instead of starting cold.

Nor is creative consistency limited to direct marketing media. If there is a simple test procedure that can be duplicated quickly, it could be the theme of a booth at a trade show, with live demonstrations of your product's superiority. A kit could be developed for your salespeople, allowing them to bring to life the benefit their prospect has read and heard about.

This is not to say that your sales presentation should be limited to a single benefit. Particularly in the more copy-intensive media (direct mail, product brochures, long-copy ads), you will want to convey as many significant benefits as possible. However, the core thematic promise, skillfully conveyed, is what will stick in the mind and strike a resonant chord when it is reiterated in each separate marketing media contact.

The specifics of a product-comparison test are not the point here; the consistency is. The central benefit of your industrial solvent can be conveyed in many different ways, each potentially viable and all referring to the same quality. However, to reap the maximum benefit from integrated direct marketing, you must decide on the most effective capsule presentation of the core benefit offered, using creative judgment and consumer opinion testing, and must stick with this presentation as the centerpiece for all your media efforts.

The Look

As we work to maximize awareness and response by developing a creative treatment that achieves a unified, recognizable impression across multiple media, thematic graphics provide a powerful tool. The explanation of benefits must be there; even the most gorgeous piece will not draw a response if it is merely fancy gift wrapping around an empty box. However, graphics produce a more immediate response than words, serving in effect as the gatekeeper to your message. If the presentation doesn't look right, the message won't be read.

Equally important, the graphics you employ can be used across several campaigns, with appropriate variations but with distinct consistency. On a simplistic level, if every envelope your company sends out is purple with pink polka dots, the recipient will quickly learn to pick your envelope out of the pile of mail. Assuming that your envelopes have contained information of value in past experience, that awareness is extremely valuable.

While purple envelopes with pink polka dots could be the seed of an award-winning campaign, let's focus on something a bit more modest—such as a logo.

A great logo is a thing of beauty and a joy forever. We remember great logos. We even wear them; just look at the success of the Coca-Cola line of clothing. In a very real way, familiarity breeds content. Are McDonald's hamburgers necessarily better than the ones served at Fred's Luncheonette? Of course not. But if you are driving through a strange town, you are likely to stop at McDonald's, thanks to the familiarity of the golden arches and your sense of security in dealing with a consistent, known commodity.

The Past as Building Block

As a creative tool, then, we make the most of whatever familiarity we have succeeded in generating over time. If you are blessed with a familiar company name, logo, or both, use them generously in your IDM creative approach. This applies especially for new ventures or unfamiliar subdivisions of larger companies. Identifying yourself as "a division of" a known company and employing that parent company's familiar graphic image goes a long way toward breaking down credibility barriers.

On the other hand, if no familiar company image exists, you can attempt to create one by establishing a distinctive graphic look and carrying it through.

Take ChemLawn as an example. This franchise company markets lawn-care services through extensive use of direct-mail and direct-response broadcast ads, along with selective print during the peak season. Everything ChemLawn touches turns to green. The print ads, the mailing pieces, even the uniforms and truck decorations are graphically tied together. The truck you saw parked outside your neighbor's house refers back to the uniforms on the people pushing the spreaders and the bright-green logo on the television commercial and the bright-green mailing piece on your kitchen table. ChemLawn achieves high visibility, builds cumulatively by remaining consistent in a multimedia effort, and distinguishes itself clearly from competitors, who may well offer a competitive service at a competitive price but who lack the familiarity produced by the integrated-marketing effort.

An attractive and distinctive graphic approach carried through in all customer contact is self-reinforcing. It builds recognition and also conveys a message about the company. We want consistency in our dealings with a company. If you take the trouble to present a consistent look, you make a statement about your ability to deliver a consistent level of service.

The Search for Personality

In a multimedia campaign incorporating both sight and sound, one of the strongest unifying elements available is a spokesperson, preferably a celebrity. The use of an immediately recognizable spokesperson is more common in general advertising than in direct marketing, but it can be an extremely effective tool in the direct marketer's repertoire as well.

The marketer seeking to maximize the integration of multimedia efforts, and thereby build synergy, will find special importance in the role of the spokesperson. The famous face can instantly tie together the disparate elements of a campaign. The face becomes an icon in its own right, instantly recognizable in either print or television messages. The voice associated with the face can be used effectively in broadcast advertising, but creative marketers can integrate it into their direct mail and telemarketing as well.

Consider perhaps the most famous celebrity direct marketing effort—the use of Ed McMahon as corporate spokesperson for American Family Publishers. The American Family campaign combines two proven elements—a big-money sweepstakes with a top television star endorser. Today consumers immediately recognize the "Ed McMahon letter" when it arrives. Television commercials featuring the star prompt consumers to look for their package in the mail. The package itself features repeated images of McMahon—on the outer envelope, on an internal letter, and on an additional flyer featuring photographs of the star awarding checks to previous winners. The media-event nature of the sweepstakes is magnified with a clever payoff: the winner is actually chosen on the air, in a commercial spot run during the *Tonight Show* which McMahon cohosts. American Family even gets bonus exposure thanks to the star's unique role in American culture, for Johnny Carson routinely makes jokes about the "Ed McMahon letter" on the highly rated *Tonight Show*.

Another industry which routinely uses celebrity spokespeople to keynote direct marketing efforts is the insurance business. In certain insurance categories, in fact, celebrity endorsement has become second nature. Insurance and hospital coverage to supplement Medicare (per-day payments for hospitalization periods) are routinely offered in television commercials starring such older celebrities as Art Linkletter and Danny Thomas asking prospects to call an 800 number for further information. Direct-mail packages, either active (to targeted mailing lists) or reactive (in response to the 800-number call) also feature these celebrity spokespeople.

For additional insight into the selection and use of celebrity spokespeople in a multimedia campaign we turn to Kurt Medina, vice president of marketing for National Liberty Marketing. Medina, who is in charge of the marketing of insurance and other services for the 65-and-over market, employs a variety of celebrity spokespeople in a range of direct-response media.

Words from the Wise

Kurt Medina on Celebrity Endorsement

Kurt Medina, *Senior Vice President of Marketing, National Liberty Marketing*

The use of an endorser is never a "given." It must fulfill some definite function within your marketing plan. In addition to the strategic considerations, there are financial ramifications involved. An endorser will want to be paid, either in a lump sum, by a fee per order generated, or with a combination of the two. Understandably, most celebrity endorsers on a national basis wish to be reasonably well recompensed; therefore, you need to have a relatively major campaign before you can use them effectively.

National Liberty Marketing uses celebrity endorsers in promoting several different insurance products in the life and health fields. These endorsers presently include Art Linkletter, Ed Asner, Roger Staubach, Glenn Ford, Patricia Neal, and Tennessee Ernie Ford.

We utilize an endorser to create credibility with the public for an insurance company which is not a household name. The use of a well-known endorser overcomes this barrier. With an endorser, a large percentage of the public says, subconsciously, "This endorser is a wise and trusted individual, one whom I believe in personally, and one who would not put his or her own reputation on the line for something that is not worthwhile. Therefore I can trust the company, because I trust the endorser."

The secondary, more short-term reason we use celebrity endorsers is to create an immediate attention factor. If we have Lorne Greene saying, "Hello there, let me tell you about this product," the prospect is more likely to listen than if an unknown actor or announcer delivered the same message.

Selecting the Right Endorser

If you ask the public, as National Liberty has done, "Are you more likely to buy this product if a celebrity endorser recommends it?" the public will probably tell you "no." Individuals in a focus group will tell you that they "can't be fooled. We know that you are paying the endorser, therefore we're not going to believe what he or she says." They don't want to appear gullible to their peers. However, the truth is that, if the endorser is good, they will pay more attention to the commercial and—assuming you have a good product—be more likely to respond.

I don't think any endorser is going to lead directly to a purchase decision. However, what the endorser accomplishes is to persuade the individuals to read the material and make up their own minds, as opposed to ignoring it right from the start. Use of an endorser breaks down a perceptual barrier and helps deliver the marketing message.

I referred a moment ago to a "good" endorser, and that is an important concept. The endorser must be appropriate to the product or service being marketed. In selecting endorsers for National Liberty, we go through several research panels, selecting people who are representative of our target audience and presenting various celebrity names to them both on a pure, unaided basis and in relation to the product we will be advertising. We want to see if there's trust, credibility, and an association with the product. For example, an instance where the product and the personality didn't mesh for us was Doris Day. In our tests, we found that Doris Day was extremely credible and well liked. However, she was not viewed as an appropriate endorser for insurance by the older market. They preferred a male "authority figure." Thus research led us away from producing a commercial which would have been well liked but not necessarily effective.

Endorsers and Corporate Identity

One final caveat regarding the use of endorsers involves the development of a brand-name identity.

The product my group markets within National Liberty is called Secure Care Medicare Supplement insurance. When we asked the public what they were buying, though, I'd have to say nearly 60 percent were buying celebrity endorsers, 35 percent were buying Secure Care, and 5 percent were buying National Home Life. Once they have been policyholders for a while, they switch over to an identification with the company name. At the initial point of sale, though, it's going to be the endorser first, and the brand name only secondarily.

Ideally, we'd love to have the company name become a stronger presence in the consumer's mind. We're certainly moving in that direction by strengthening the presence of the brand names of our insurance products in our promotional materials. This is an incremental move on our part, though, and not a major upheaval in our marketing strategy: endorsers are still a key element in our creative presentation. So if building a prominent company image is a prime strategic consideration for you, then you should consider whether or not an endorser really is your best route.

The Personal Touch

The element you want to maximize in creating a campaign hinging on a celebrity spokesperson is the personal nature of the appeal. You might want to introduce another member of the celebrity's family in the piece, to add human interest. Trying to sell cars? Want to make a point about safety? Your celebrity spokesperson might hand over the keys for one of your models to a member of his or her own family in a broadcast spot and then offer an 800 number for free information about the unique safety features of your model. You can then fulfill the offer with collateral that includes a personal cover letter from the celebrity endorser.

For mail packages, personal stationery has become an accepted practice, particularly in fund-raising appeals. Even if it does seem a bit contrived, it succeeds in distinguishing your package from everything else in the mailbox.

Lending an Ear

Verbal messages can also be carried through the mails in the form of flexible plastic records (such as Evatone soundsheets) or, more popular now, tape cassettes. They can also be delivered with great success by telephone, in both inbound and outbound telemarketing program. This was proved time and again by Murray Roman, the father of modern telemarketing.

Strategically, the prime consideration is the relevance of the speaker's name or title to the target universe. When raising funds for the Public Broadcasting System (PBS), for example, taped messages featuring Alistair Cooke, Julia Child, and other on-air personalities who exemplify the PBS programming philosophy were employed. When the American Management Association wanted to promote marketing seminars targeted to CEOs and other top-level management figures, the CEO of the American Management Association recorded a taped message.

The functioning of the system was quite simple but effective. The endorser would record a brief message. Over the course of many years, it became clear that brevity was a key to making this technique work. The important factor was not so much what the endorser said as the fact that he or she was saying anything at all on behalf of the product, service, or charitable cause.

On the delivery side we are not talking about high technology. Telemarketing representatives played the taped messages over the telephone using inexpensive cassette recorders attached to their telephones with donut-shaped induction coils available at any Radio Shack for about $5.

This technique bears no relation to the automated telemarketing machines that dial incessantly and automatically play their message to anyone who answers the telephone. The telemarketing communicator is still the key element in the call. When a prospect answers the telephone, the communicator introduces himself or herself and the company or organization sponsoring the call, and asks whether the prospect would be interested in hearing a taped message from the executive or personality. After the message, the communicator returns to the line and attempts to close the transaction. The taped message gives the contact clout and a certain sense of drama, but there is still a one-to-one human interaction between the communicator and the person answering the telephone.

Calls incorporating taped messages have been made on behalf of a wide variety of clients. The foremost users of this technique are fund raisers, both for charitable institutions and for political campaigns. However, there is much more to this technique than asking for donations. When the Louisiana National Bank wanted to introduce its customers to a new bill-paying service, they sent out a letter from Jerry Turk, vice president of marketing for the bank, explaining the features of the service, then followed up with a telephone call including a taped message from Turk that requested a sign-up commitment.

The American Management Association has also used taped-message telemarketing, following up direct-mail packages to senior executives which included a seminar catalog and a cover letter from the association president with a telephone call incorporating a taped message from the president urging participation. Even so august a body as the American Bar Association followed a similar tack, with a letter and telephone call from the president of the association urging membership renewal for lapsed members.

Note that in this sense, the "celebrity" endorser does not have to be Bill Cosby for the program to succeed. Celebrity is relative. The president of an association or a company is a celebrity in his or her own right and can be used very effectively in a direct-mail effort. In fact, a lesser-known figure with the appropriate title may convey more sincerity than a "glossier" celebrity could.

The use of taped telemarketing messages from endorsers has fallen by the wayside today, though there is no reason it should not be revived.

Copy with a "Voice" of its Own

Consider, too, the sense of personality that can be communicated through skillfully crafted words and pictures, creating character without the use of a two-legged character.

The best catalog marketers have proved especially skillful on this score. When you leaf through a catalog from the Banana Republic, or Fredericks of Hollywood, or L. L. Bean, you are immersed in a distinctive environment which says as much about the products being sold as the individual catalog item descriptions. Bean is notable, from the media integration viewpoint, for its use of regionalism. The customer knows that L. L. Bean is in Maine. For many years the company even resisted establishing a tollfree 800 number for ordering, preferring a local Maine number. In addition to the renowned quality of L. L. Bean products, there is a reverse chic appeal that makes a Bean watch appealing to a corporate executive in a $400 suit. The space ads, catalog, and telephone contact with L. L. Bean all integrate to enhance this appeal.

The Downside to Consistency

"It worked in the last campaign. Let's use it again."

Is there a downside to creative consistency? Absolutely.

On one level, of course, you run the risk of generating boredom rather than pleasant recognition. Ideally, the answer is to maintain some element of the creative package constant across campaigns but still achieve a distinct and individual impression each time. Starting entirely from scratch, with no reference to what has gone before, may be tempting to the creative individual seeking to make a personal statement, but it is rarely the way to go. Instead, take a theme, an image, or a look from something familiar (assuming there is a marketing history from which to draw) and incorporate it in something new and exciting.

Sometimes the facts of the case may make consistency inadvisable. Take the experience of a prominent New York bank attempting to expand its geographical base into middle America. Company management insisted on a campaign that incorporated prominent references to the bank's New York base of operations. The bank's own research indicated that the target audience did not particularly like New York or New Yorkers and, in fact, a substantial percentage actively disliked those east coast bankers. Still, management insisted—and the managers got what they asked for, including a television commercial featuring the bank's architecturally striking headquarters building on the New York skyline. What they didn't get were positive results. The campaign displayed admirable consistency with the bank's previous marketing efforts but, given the radical shift in target audience, failed at achieving the new goals entailed in a geographic shift.

Playing for Keeps

The time-honored practice of offering premiums for response, or enclosing premiums with a mailing, takes on added significance in the integrated direct marketing environment. It is often desirable to have your prospect keep some sort of souvenir of your existence. Within the context of an IDM campaign, that premium item can be the memorable creative element that ties your program together.

A premium does not have to be expensive to be effective. In fact, ink on paper often makes the best possible premium, in the form of information. Meaningful reference guides are particularly effective, since good ones are likely to have high perceived value and frequent usage.

Consider going beyond familiar one-dimensional presentations, even in an inexpensive premium program. Any three-dimensional mailing immediately generates additional recall and interest. One company we know offers an intriguing hexagonal pop-up that instantly springs open into a 14-sided spherical object when it's pulled from the envelope. These have been used by a variety of advertisers to create an impression and leave a tactile keepsake on desktops. One tried-and-true route to earning an object like this a continuing place on the desktop of a prospect is to print a calendar on it, but that barely scratches the surface of inexpensive-to-produce yet valuable mailers.

If your target market is select enough and the profitability of a sale great enough, then a relatively expensive enclosure can be appropriate. This tactic makes two major statements to the prospect: You are important to us, and we are financially sound enough to spend a significant amount to gain your attention.

Besides gaining the prospect's attention, the premium also serves as a focal point for future contact. A telemarketer can begin a conversation by asking whether the premium arrived. Future mailings can use the premium as a thematic device. And a series of mailings, each of which incorporates part of a larger whole, is sure to generate continued interest.

CertainTeed Fiberglas employed a dramatic multipart mailing to increase business from established customers. The theme was the many uses of the company's fiberglas reinforcement products, attempting to foster substitution of inexpensive fiberglas for more expensive materials in manufacturing settings.

To bring the point to life, the company commissioned an artist to create a three-part, three-dimensional wall hanging. The triptych was then cast in fiberglas, finished to resemble a metallic surface, and sent in three separate mailings to target customers. Literature describing potential uses for CertainTeed Fiberglas was enclosed with each shipment, along with an invitation to call the CertainTeed sales representative.

The project was an aesthetic success, and has proved to be a valuable business tool as well. Not only did the mailings generate substantial immediate contact with the sales representatives, but the artwork is now found on the walls of several customers, providing an interesting point of departure for conversation about CertainTeed products.

Cross Referencing Media for Greater Effect

The tactic of referring directly to other components of a multimedia campaign has several advantages.

Consider the outbound telemarketing call in which the communicator says, "I'm calling from Acme Enterprises. We sent you a Mailgram the other day about our special September savings offer. Did you receive it?"

Assuming the prospect did in fact receive the mailing, the telemarketing representative has established a context for the telephone call. One problem telemarketers must routinely overcome is the perception that they are strangers calling, possibly with no more to back them up than a telephone in a sweatshop somewhere. Referring to the mailing piece gives them a connection with some physical evidence of solidity.

If there is some preexisting relationship between the caller and the person called, then the mailing piece has refreshed that contact in the mind of the person answering the telephone, making the telemarketer's job easier.

Of course, a precept of integrated direct marketing tells us that there are some people who respond best to mail and others to telephone, and that, therefore, some of the people you call simply will not say "yes" to a telephone solicitation. However, while the call may appear to be wasted because it produces no immediate results, it can spur mail response by referring back to the mailing. Most decision making about a mail offer occurs almost immediately after receiving the piece. The telephone call can give that mailing an additional life, if it has not already been discarded, and provide an alternative channel of response for those who may reconsider after the telephone contact. Of course, the telephone contact also allows recipients to engage in a question-and-answer dialogue, supplementing and clarifying the information conveyed in the print media.

The above example assumes telephone follow-up to mail. We can also integrate two direct marketing media by using one to pave the way for the other. Consider the sequence in the Publishers Clearinghouse subscription campaign, in which massive television advertising is employed to call attention to the forthcoming sweepstakes promotion. In that instance, of course, the audience is extremely wide, and television is an appropriate vehicle.

Channeling Response

As integrated direct marketers, we attempt to open up as many channels of communication as possible between prospects and the company. The assumption is that different people have their own preferred response vehicles, and offering a multiplicity of choices will lead to greater overall response.

At the same time, it is important to remember that the creative presentation will have a strong effect in directing the channel of response, and the writers and designers should understand any preferences and advantages the company may be seeking before they undertake their tasks.

Inbound telemarketing response offers several distinct advantages:

- Ease of response promotes increased response rates.
- Faster receipt of responses provides faster cash flow, particularly when taking credit-card orders.
- Speed of response provides a quick gauge of overall response, permitting adjustments if necessary and providing the basis for quicker, more accurate forecasting (particularly important in the testing stage).
- Interactive contact provides valuable market-research information, pinpointing consumer questions and objections.
- Inbound telemarketing puts prospects into one-to-one contact with a human company representative, promoting relationship building, allowing give-and-take question-and-answer dialogues, and facilitating the acquisition of information by the telemarketing representative for database building.

In some instances, encouraging mail response is preferable. For example:

- Mail response is far less expensive per contact than telemarketing.
- Certain transactions may require a signature on the part of the customer, which would entail a two-step process for a telephone respondent.

Once the relative desirability of the different response channels has been determined, the creative team can help encourage response in the chosen manner.

The prominent placement of a tollfree 800 number in all broadcast and printed material is, of course, the prime method for stimulating telephone response. When Citicorp created an integrated direct marketing program to produce home equity loan commitments in geographically distant markets (see Chapter 1 for details), encouraging telephone response was a significant goal. The loan application required was extremely intimidating on paper—with over 70 separate fill-in items. By getting the respondent on the telephone with a trained telemarketing representative, the application process could be handled painlessly, eliminating confusion and minimizing hassle. However, as John Hunter, vice president of Citicorp, explains, there was more to increasing telephone response than simply emphasizing the 800 number.

A Case in Point

Citicorp—Loan Applications by Telephone

John Hunter, *Vice President, Citicorp*

There were two versions of the newspaper ad we created as part of the integrated direct marketing program. The first uses "Citicorp Hassle-Free Home Equity Loan" as its thematic line; the second emphasizes the "Citicorp Home Equity Loan Hotline."

All the research leaned toward the hasslefree aspect of completing the loan process as being the program's most attractive benefit to the consumer. In the second ad, the number itself is the predominant message, with the actual product benefits relegated to the body copy. In addition, the hot-line ad was very cramped in terms of density of information, and it provided consumers with less of a feel for what they would expect to get once they did reach a telemarketer. So while the tollfree number was printed in very large letters to push telephone response, the hasslefree theme of the first ad proved to be the more successful of the two creative approaches.

The direct-mail package (see Figure 5.1) contained a letter highlighting the hot-line number for the targeted mail audience. Note that right up front in the first paragraph of the letter, the tollfree hot-line number is featured in order to drive response into the telemarketing center.

In addition, Citicorp tested a coupon in some of the mailings, inviting customers to either call the hot-line number or send in the coupon and have a Citicorp account executive contact them. The hot-line approach allowed us to offer expanded hours of operation, from 8:30 a.m. to 7:00 p.m., far beyond normal banking hours, which further conveyed the convenience feature of the product.

In reviewing these pieces you will note that both the mail and the newspaper ads reinforced the use of the telephone. The newspaper used the hasslefree telephone application concept, and the direct mail reinforced the telephone by the use of the hotline tag.

On the other hand, to increase mail response while still offering inbound telephone as an alternative response channel, you can make the printed matter the focus of attention. Tokens, stamps, punch-outs, tearoffs, glue-ons, stickers, buttons, and any other physically manipulable devices you can think of will encourage respondents to handle the paper and send in the response.

Coupons have the same effect. While the same discount or premium may be offered on a coupon and over the telephone, the existence of a physical coupon to be returned with an order will increase mail response. This is particularly true if the coupon appears to be specially numbered, with a red-ink serial number or similar device.

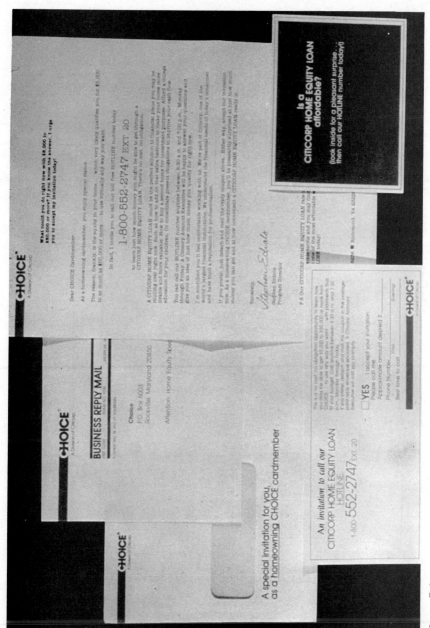

Figure 5.1

A Case in Point

Faultless Starch/Bon Ami

To demonstrate how the elements of a creatively unified IDM campaign combine to achieve a powerful, synergistic result, we will examine the broadcast, print, and telephone experience of Faultless Starch/Bon Ami in promoting its Garden Weasel and Noverox products.

The program sought to introduce new products which offered innovative solutions to tasks for which familiar tools already existed. The Garden Weasel is a unique gardening tool which breaks up and conditions soil. It has distinct advantages over a common garden hoe, but also carries a significantly higher price tag, retailing for about $35.

Noverox is a rust-removal product that uses a one-of-a-kind chemical approach to the problem. Instead of simply taking the rust off the surface of a metal item, Noverox bonds chemically with it, leaving a rustfree, paintable black surface.

The original Faultless Starch/Bon Ami approach to promoting these hardware-oriented products was to send a dedicated field sales force to call on hardware dealers. However, this strategy failed for the Garden Weasel (the first of the two products introduced). The hardware trade was unenthusiastic about an unknown product sold at a relatively high price.

The company reassessed their position and shifted both its promotional strategy and its prime channel of distribution.

- Instead of simply selling the Weasel to hardware stores and leaving it to the retail clerks to sell the product, the company would presell the Weasel through extensive regional television advertising.
- And instead of trying to gain distribution through expensive personal sales calls on individual hardware stores, the company decided to concentrate on sales through chain drugstores.

The chain-store concept was crucial to streamlining the marketing of the Garden Weasel. Instead of relying on a field sales force, a few company sales executives could make presentations at the headquarters of major retail chain stores. If they made the sale there, they had achieved forced distribution in their marketplace.

Of course, there had to be a compelling reason for the chain store to stock a product which had no demonstrated track record in the United States and no public recognition. The answer was television advertising.

The strategy adopted by Faultless Starch/Bon Ami was to go into regional markets with a major television advertising campaign demonstrating the tool to the public. At the end of each spot they would run a tag directing buyers to their local chain store.

This new approach to marketing the Garden Weasel was a tremendous success. To build on their proven ability to sell through chain stores using spot television, the company acquired exclusive distribution rights to Noverox Rust Eliminator.

While chain-store sales for both products were profitable, there was now a logical channel of distribution being ignored: the hardware stores. The company had proved its ability to create customer demand using dealer-tagged television commercials. To expand the market for Garden Weasel and Noverox into the hardware market (which is, after all, the logical place for a consumer to look for both items), Faultless Starch/Bon Ami would continue its consumer TV promotion but send consumers to their hardware store to make a purchase.

The hardware marketplace is structured very differently from the chain-drugstore market, though. Whereas the drugstores are true chain operations, with a central buying office and management-level product-stocking decisions, hardware stores are organized into buying cooperatives, such as True Value, Ace, and Servistar. A central office sales call is still required to win initial acceptance of the product, but then it is up to individual members of the buying cooperative to decide whether or not to put the product on their own store shelves.

Noverox product manager Richard Orr recalls the first efforts to get Noverox onto hardware store shelves. "We started off initially with what we called the 'A-Team Approach,' which was just taking a group of salespeople from our office and sending them into a city to call on every hardware store in that city. That was expensive, believe me."

To bring the expense of promoting the two products to the hardware trade within profitable levels, Faultless Starch/ Bon Ami initiated an integrated direct-response campaign aimed at independent hardware store owners who belonged to one of the major hardware buying coopera-tives.

As with the chainstore distribution strategy, the cornerstone of the consumer marketing effort would be television advertising. These commer-cials would be tagged with the name of the hardware store cooperative. For example, "Available at your local participating True Value hardware dealer."

The initial acceptance of the product and the marketing push came from the central buying offices of each hardware cooperative. In meetings with Faultless Starch/Bon Ami sales executives, the cooperative would agree to have its name used to tag the commerical spots, and to announce the promotion to its dealers. The form of the bulletin varies from one set of stores to another, but all are basically publications or single-sheet listings of upcoming product promotions. As Web Thompson, product manager for the Garden Weasel, puts it, "That's one piece of paper out of thou-sands that go out to dealers every week announcing manufacturers' programs and promotions." An additional push from the manufacturer would be required to ensure large-scale distribution of the Garden Weasel and Noverox.

The task in the direct-response segment of the program was to reach all the hardware-store owners in the target market that had been chosen for TV advertising, alert them to the fact that the TV campaign was either right on the horizon or already under way, and convince them to stock the product. This would be accomplished through a combination of 800-number incoming lines for ordering product, outbound telemarketing calls to each dealer, and in the case of Noverox, a direct-mail package.

Television

The creative core of the Garden Weasel and Noverox campaigns was the television advertising. This focus stems not only from a belief in the drawing power of television, both for the consumer and for the retailer being asked to stock the product, but also from the nature of the products themselves. A commercial for the company's more familiar products, such as a starch or a cleanser, is attempting to find a compelling selling proposition for the individual product within a familiar product category. The consumer's question is not "Should I buy cleanser?" but rather "Which cleanser should I buy?" In contrast, there was and is only one Garden Weasel, and at the time of its introduction, there was only one Noverox rust preventive. Therefore, product management felt strongly that the only way to effectively sell these products was through a demonstration-style presentation. This essentially mandates a 60-second format, since you can't show very much in the way of product performance in a smaller time unit—especially with a 10-second tag required to send consumers to participating retail outlets.

With this in mind, the commercial for the Garden Weasel is straightforward, but effective. Set in an attractive, established garden, the product is shown doing what it does best—loosening soil and doing the weeding "with half the effort, twice as quick." The different applications of the tool are all demonstrated, from working in big areas and wide rows to tilling narrow spaces between plants and even aerating the lawn. Finally the 10-second tag provides the names of participating retailers.

This spot has proved its effectiveness in many markets across the country, and Faultless/Bon Ami has chosen to stay with a winner; the same spot has run for 9 years.

The television approach to advertising Noverox has been more diverse. The original spot was set in a laboratory, proclaiming the amazing scientific breaththrough that had just been discovered. More recently, a campaign created by the Shooting Gallery has been used, featuring a warmer, friendlier atmosphere. The star of these spots is Walt, a local hardware retailer. The subject for each of these 50-second dramas (with its 10-second tag) varies. In one episode, Walt is demonstrating to an antique dealer how to refurbish rusted metal treasures quickly and easily. In another, he actually agrees to stop by a customer's house on the weekend and demonstrate how to use Noverox to fix the rusted patches on the customer's car.

While the subject matter may vary, the visual style is consistent throughout the campaign. In each case, the camera "is" the customer, seeing the action from the customer's perspective, and even having a hand reach out into the frame from behind the camera in some cases to hold the product or shake hands. This immediacy is an effective technique in that it allows Walt to address the viewer directly.

One typical example of the Walt series is entitled "Air Conditioner," and goes like this:

We come in on a friendly gray-haired hardware-store owner wearing a blue smock as he adjusts a Noverox display. The display, incidentally, is boldly emblazoned with the word "NEW" and a television-shaped panel that says "AS SEEN ON TV."

The store owner turns as the camera approaches and smiles in recognition, shaking hands with his customer.

WALT: Well, hello, Don, what can I do for you?

DON: Well, I was checking out our window air conditioner and I noticed some rust starting. You got something that can help me?

WALT: Sure do. It's called Noverox. It's a rust eliminator. I even sell it to the big companies for their cooling systems. C'mon back, I'll show you how it works.

(Cut to a tight shot of a hand holding a bottle of Noverox for a live demonstration. We see a rusty metal rectangle being sanded, washed, and painted with Noverox as the voice-over continues.)

WALT: See this rusty metal panel? Just sand the loose stuff off, flush the area with water, then apply Noverox right over the remaining rust.

DON: It's starting to turn black.

WALT: (enthusiastically) That's Noverox eliminating rust.

(Cut to an animated segment, which is standardized, except for minor differences in the voice-over, for all the Walt spots. The cartoon brush applies Noverox to a metal surface, and we see the tiny rust particles bonding with the Noverox to form a black coating.)

WALT: (voice-over) When you apply Noverox, it combines with rust to transform it into a stable black metal organic compound that makes an excellent primer for most paints. After a second coat of Noverox, you just paint it!

(Cut back to hardware-store scene. The customer is holding a bottle of Noverox in a blister pack.)

DON: Noverox...sounds great. You the only one that carries it?

(Walt takes the Noverox out of the customer's hand and drops it into a brown-paper bag.)

WALT: No, no, it's in other stores, and getting real popular too. (Turning playfully aggressive.) Are you goin' somewhere else to buy Noverox?

DON: Heh, heh, c'mon, Walt.

(Walt smiles warmly for a freeze-frame as the 10-second tag with participating retailers' names appears.)

This ad accomplishes a lot in the course of 60 seconds.

From the consumer's point of view, it provides a surrogate figure with a specific problem and dramatizes the resolution of that problem through the use of Noverox. There are two separate product-demonstration segments: First, a live hands-on application of Noverox, shown in close-up, teaches the consumer a lesson about ease of use. Second, the animated segment provides a scientific basis for the superiority of Noverox to other rust preparations on the market. Viewers may not have the faintest idea what "a stable black metal organic compound" might be, but it sounds sufficiently technical to convincethem that they are getting more than just another paint-over-rust product when they buy Noverox.

There is another major audience for this commercial, though, and that's no coincidence. The hardware-store retailers in the target market also receive a very powerful message when they watch this commercial.

First, of course, there is the personification of hardware-store owner as hero. Walt is an attractive character, friendly and extremely helpful, with a somewhat corny but appealing sense of humor. And "good old" Walt saves the day for the customer, providing the solution to the problem as easily as reaching for a bottle of Noverox. The depiction of a personal relationship between retailer and customer is important too. The handshake of recognition in the opening seconds, the familiar chatty tone of the discussion, even the bit of joking at the end of the spot indicate that these two are regular acquaintances—exemplifying the sought-after ongoing relationship between retailer and neighborhood resident.

Finally, in this spot, there is an implied threat to the retailer. Walt indicates that the product is in fact available in other stores, and questions whether he is about to lose his customer to another outlet. This part of the message has no signficance whatsoever to the consumer, except for whatever slight humorous value it may provide. For the hardware-store owner, though, the message is loud and clear: my customers want Noverox, and if I don't have it, they'll go somewhere else.

The 10-second tag at the end is enough time to allow for two name cards to be displayed, each of which can contain up to three or four participating retailers. If there are more than about eight outlets in a given area, separate versions of the commercials are distributed with different tags, and the spots are run in rotation.

Direct Mail

The mailing package urging retailers to stock Noverox consists of six pieces.

The 6- by 9-inch envelope may not win any beauty contests, but it is striking. Printed in full color, it is covered front and back with a background close-up photograph of badly rusted metal. Emblazoned across the front in ¾-inch letters is the question "DON'T YOU JUST LOVE RUST!?"

Three of the internal components of the mailing repeat this rusted-metal background as a page border: a letter from Richard Orr, the National Accounts Sales manager, a pricing sheet, and a business-reply envelope.

The letter carries the Noverox logo at the top, along with the product slogan, "The one solution to RUST." The return address slug also indicates that Faultless Starch/Bon Ami Company is the sole U.S. distributor of the product.

The letter is worth reading:

March 4, 1985

SELL THE RIGHT PRODUCT!!

NOVEROX is the *original, patented rust eliminator. No other product applied directly to a rusty surface will eliminate* rust, *prevent* further rusting with the *lasting* characteristics of Noverox. That's because Noverox is an *oil-based* emulsion which penetrates, bonds, eliminates and prevents rusting far better than the competition. See the enclosed comparison sheet.

NOVEROX is heavily advertised on *television*. Our preferred retailer-tagged commercials have produced square foot sales four times greater than the average of hardware paint departments. That's product turnover and that's the kind of product that can improve your bottom line and return on investment. This

---

year we have four new commercials that will help you turn rust into cold hard cash.

I am writing to alert you to a major advertising blitz starting *April 1, 1985*. As a member of a major buying group, you may be tagged on television and we want you to be one of the many selected retailers who are ready for the Noverox campaign against rust. I have enclosed comparison results from a natural weathering test, a pricing sheet, our "Cold Hard Cash" brochure, and an *order form*.

We make it so easy to order Noverox. Either contact your buying office or, to expedite your order call our Action Line: 1-800-821-5563. We'll do everything else.

Yours for a rust-free spring,

(signature)

Richard M. Orr

National Account Sales Manager

P.S. *Order now* and turn rust into cold hard cash and receive 60 days dating and prepaid freight on three cases or one floor display.

This letter introduces the product benefits up front, follows with the strong promise of television advertising, offers a simple ordering channel, and in the all-important postscript points out the special offers of payment structure and prepaid freight. The reference to previous experience in producing "square foot sales four times greater than the average of hardware paint departments" is a clear and powerful argument for stocking the product. And, as noted in our discussion of the television spot, there is the implied threat that the competition, "the many selected retailers who are ready for the Noverox campaign against rust," will have a distinct advantage if the recipient does not carry the product.

Another one-sheet, four-color piece in the package has the headline "RESULTS FROM A NATURAL WEATHERING TEST" and displays two metal panels, one nicely clean and black after treatment with Noverox Rust Eliminator, the other rusted and pitted after using a competitive rust treatment. A paragraph of copy offers technical details of the test, and the closing paragraph asserts, "The exclusive NOVEROX formulation, protected by U.S. patent 4086182, is unduplicated in the industry."

With the product benefits fully described, the product pricing sheet, also printed in four colors, pictures the product packaging in three sizes along with the counter and floor displays, with their prominent "AS SEEN ON TV" message. The standard pricing, terms, and freight information are included, along with the generous return policy: the product may be returned in the original unopened carton for a full refund, freight prepaid.

Finally there is the order form, which folds and glues into a prepaid business-reply envelope. At the top of the order form is our old friend Walt from the TV commercials, holding a blister pack of Noverox. The prepaid freight offer is reiterated, with a time-sensitive call to action (the offer expires on May 1, about 2 months after the letter date).

Finally, after the initial telemarketing calls were completed, a simple follow-up mailing went out to all prospects, consisting of a postcard reminding the retailer that Noverox was currently being advertised on television, and providing another opportunity to order by placing a call to the company's toll-free number.

Telemarketing

CCI Telemarketing of New York City created sets of telemarketing scripts for the Garden Weasel and Noverox programs, with different versions for customers and noncustomers. Each script was first tested with a few tape-recorded telephone calls. These calls were then analyzed for refinements and adjustments to the script. If a particular question or objection was raised frequently, an answer was formulated and added to the script. Different sales presentations were tried and evaluated as well, in an effort to produce a scripted telephone presentation that communicated the marketing message effectively and efficiently, taking only as long on the telephone as required. Faultless Starch/Bon Ami was consulted throughout the scripting process.

Each script developed for an individual market segment and product is different in the specific offer it makes, the way it flows, and the language used, but all the scripts follow a similar logical flow in the process of questioning, informing, and attempting to take an order. We'll follow this flow, using as an example a script written for prospects who had never carried the Garden Weasel.

The first goal in the scripted presentation is information gathering. The telephone communicator is instructed to record on the call-record form the way the store is identified when the telephone is answered. Then, after introducing himself or herself, the communicator asks to speak to "the person who is responsible for buying garden equipment" and records that name on the record forms as well. This information has value to the client, who can use it to update the files for future solicitation through direct response or even a personal sales call. On a more immediate level, the telemarketing program includes a provision for calling the store back at a scheduled time if requested, and for making a follow-up call a few weeks later to all the prospects. In these future contacts, the communicator will have an up-to-date record and be able to proceed knowledgeably.

Assuming the proper prospect is reached, the communicator identifies himself or herself as calling for the the Bon Ami Company—a recognizable name for most buyers. While the television spots don't mention the name "Bon Ami," and the direct mail includes it only in the return address and then linked with Faultless Starch in the full company name, mentioning the familiar Bon Ami name up front in a telemarketing call is important to establish credibility and recognition.

The presentation then immediately mentions the television advertising campaign: "We're in the midst of our biggest television advertising campaign ever, and by the way, the program has been approved by [name of individual] at your buying group."

Having employed the twin "hooks" of television advertising and buying-group approval, the communicator goes on to a brief product explanation, wrapping this up with a reiteration of the importance of the television advertising: "With all the added national TV coverage we'll be having, your customers will be hearing a lot about the Garden Weasel so they'll be looking for it."

The communicator goes on to explain that the product is shipped directly from factory to store for fast delivery, with prepaid freight. The TV tagging is mentioned a third time: "To help build store traffic, our TV spots carry local dealer tags." The communicator then suggests an order for a case of 12 Garden Weasels (priced at $314.52).

From here the scripted approach branches out. If the prospect wants to order, the communicator flips to the "Process Order" section of the script. If there is a definite "no" answer, the communicator moves on to ask, "Just for my records, is there any reason why you're not ordering the Garden Weasel at this time?" and records the answer. Even this is not necessarily a dead end. The script includes answers to many anticipated objections, and the communicator is prompted to offer one of these answers if appropriate and try again for the sale.

For those prospects who seem hesitant at the initial offering, there is a step-down offer of a case of 5 Garden Weasels for $131.05. This offer is bolstered with a fast recap of benefits in the offer: "The Weasel comes in an easy-to-carry package and is *fully guaranteed* by the Bon Ami Company. And we can have your shipment to you within just *10 days*. Remember, [name of prospect], we added a lot of network TV coverage. So that means you can make sales through early fall. So, would you like to start with a case of 5?"

If the step-down offer is refused as well, the communicator asks for a reason for the prospect's refusal, offers a tollfree number for asking questions or ordering in the future, and ends with a polite, "Thank you for speaking with me today and have a nice day."

The basic sales-presentation script is supplemented with an extensive series of scripted answers to questions and objections. For the Garden Weasel script we are discussing, the questions and objections that may be raised by the prospect include:

"What are your terms?"

"What's my margin?"

"Bill me direct."

"What comes with a 12-pack?"

"What comes with a 5-pack?"

"Is this available through my warehouse?"

"Is there a minimum?"

"Can you drop-ship?"

"What's the shipping cost? Shipping time?"

"What's the suggested price range?"

"I know all about the Weasel." (Providing a shortcut past the product description)

"How does it work?"

"Is it like a Rototiller?"

"I get a discount through my distributor."

"It's too expensive."

"I saw it advertised for less."

"It sounds like a hoe."

"I need line art (or ad slick)."

"I have it in stock."

"What about returns?"

"What about those defective handles?" (Addressing a previous product problem)

"I never heard of the Weasel before."

"I had a problem with Bon Ami."

"I haven't seen my tag on television."

"Is there co-op advertising?"

"What channel are your ads running on?"

"Who are you?"

If the prospect asks questions the communicator can't answer, an offer is made to have a Bon Ami representative call at a later date.

Faultless Starch/Bon Ami Lessons

The creative campaign on behalf of the Garden Weasel and Noverox demonstrates several points we have raised in this chapter.

Timing.   The retailer solicitation is tied to both a seasonal buying cycle and a heavy television media buy within a set time period. Therefore, both the direct-mail package and the telemarketing program emphasize the timeliness of the communication. This emphasis on timing holds true in the creative package itself, and in the timing of the delivery of the mailing and outbound calling as well.

Cross Referencing.   From the rack display with a prominent "AS SEEN ON TV" message to the retailer's order form with a picture of the fictional product spokesperson, the messages used in the different media are clearly tied together to recall and reinforce previous impressions.

Sending Messages Using Appropriate Media.   The mailing packages emphasize benefits throughout, as does the initial telemarketing presentation. However, in the telemarketing script are the answers to tough questions which may be on the prospect's mind. If the retailer has never had a problem with defective handles on the Garden Weasel, there is no reason to bring up the question. However, if there *was* once a problem, the interactivity of telemarketing provides the only reasonable channel for providing an answer.

On the other hand, Noverox claims were backed up by scientific test results. These findings would not have made much impact through a verbal description over the telephone, but when demonstrated in a full-color mailing insert, they are a powerful marketing tool.

6
New Tactics for Database Marketing

Direct-marketing techniques that were once considered quite extraordinary are now not good enough.

In less demanding times, the ability to personalize a direct mailing with an individual's name was quite a feat. It commanded attention, added impact to the mailing, and made a lot of money.

Today everyone has surpassed this level of sophistication—not only the marketers but, more important, the purchasers we are trying to impress. We can do tricks with laser printing, inexpensive embossing, and other technological wonders that make it clear we have jumped through hoops to prepare a mailing specifically for John Doe. Mr. Doe may be impressed enough to pay extra attention to that heavily personalized envelope, and response rates may increase. But it's not enough.

The real focus of personalization is not the mechanics of production but the selection of individuals to receive the offer. The more accurately a direct-response contact addresses perceived needs of the individual who receives it, the greater the response rate. As database compilation and manipulation become increasingly sophisticated, the resources for precise targeting are at hand, waiting for marketers insightful enough to use them. And with cost per contact increasing across the board, the requirement for accurately delivering the message to select segments of the population grows ever more demanding.

The Database Imperative

There is a type of direct marketing which differs little from general advertising. It is used to sell products with few qualifying buyer characteristics, employing mass-marketing media (broadcast and print) to make a large audience aware of the offer, and 800-number and coupon response to take the order. These general merchandise offers—the bamboo steamers and Ginsu knives of the direct-response world—are one-shot, inexpensive purchases which may rely on some demographic data when it comes to buying marketing media, but generally appeal to the public en masse. This is certainly a good, profitable strategy for a limited range of products. Most direct marketers, though, are looking for something more than the single sale.

John Groman, senior vice president of Epsilon, explains it well in the following excerpt from *MDM Review.**

Words from the Wise

John Groman on Database-Driven Marketing

John Groman, *Senior Vice President, Epsilon*

The principle of database-driven marketing is to spend promotional money on those customers and prospects who offer the greatest return on promotional investment.

For example, when one researches and analyzes buying behavior for a given product mix, one soon discovers that most often the Pareto Principle applies: satisfied, qualified customers with a repeat purchase cycle account for 80 percent of net profits. Usually this select group, often called the *core group* represents less than 20 percent of the customer universe and an even smaller fraction of the target-prospect universe. The corollary here is that often 80 percent of advertising and promotional money is spent on prospects who generate 20 percent of the revenue. This is particularly true in terms of the wasted circulation of mass-advertising programs.

Database marketing can dramatically improve marketing profitability by helping companies better allocate marketing resources for the highest return on investment; segment their markets and personalize marketing communications; and build customer loyalty. Marketers are discovering that combining media, direct mail, and telephone with general image advertising can greatly improve sales efficiency, if the various approaches are integrated and proceed from the same strategy. The marketing database lies at the heart of this integration.

In integrated direct marketing, a key concern is developing *ongoing* customer relationships. This is a two-part process:

*"Database Driven Marketing," *MDM Review*, April 1986, pp. 2–3.

1. Prospecting for buyers who have the potential for continued purchases

2. Developing and expanding the purchase activity of existing and past customers

To be economically effective, both of these activities require a precise profile of those characteristics which distinguish our potential customers. We have already discussed (in Chapter 2) one of the tools used to acquire this crucial information: market research. Using interviews and questionnaires provides one means of differentiating real or potential respondents from nonrespondents. The second, complementary discipline directed toward achieving this goal is the development and employment of database resources.

Database marketing involves two stages:

1. *Gathering and categorizing information.* This is done to provide meaningful, actionable characteristics for marketing decision making.

2. *Analyzing this data.* The purpose of this stage is to determine the patterns which are significant indicators of purchase behavior.

The underlying goal of database marketing—the variable we are trying to maximize—is *relevance*. With the right information at our disposal, and the appropriate methodologies for analyzing the information, we can focus our marketing efforts on those with the *means*, *willingness*, and *readiness* to respond. This is true direct marketing efficiency. Given increasing costs and expectations, this efficiency is desirable even in traditional single-media marketing programs. For integrated direct marketing, it is more than desirable; it is absolutely essential.

The Special Significance of Database to IDM

Integrated direct marketing is the current state of the art in target marketing. Instead of merely identifying a reasonably qualified prospect for contact with an individual medium, we are creating incremental media impressions. However, we are raising the ante per prospect each time we add another medium to the mix. Therefore we need to target each prospect with an increasingly surgical skill. IDM bases its profitability on identifying that target universe which merits intensive contact, and on determining the frequency of contact required to produce a given response.

Marketers using IDM techniques are concerned with cross selling the full range of products and services our companies have to offer. To accomplish this, we need a database structure to provide in-depth information about these customers. A bank's checking-account customer who has a 17-year-old daughter should be contacted via direct response about the possibility of a college loan, for instance. That targeted offer can be made if we have compiled adequate information on the prospect and have organized a database which is responsive to marketing needs.

Meeting the Demands of IDM
Testing

As mentioned in previous chapters, the distinctive nature of testing in an integrated direct marketing environment places new demands on the marketer. Since we are tracking the interrelationships between media across a variety of test cells, the number of permutations and combinations grows geometrically. This leads to increased costs in designing and executing the test program, and to more extensive analytical requirements on the back end.

To keep testing to a reasonable level, we rely on our predictive capabilities. It is economically impractical to conduct actual media tests to explore all the possibilities. The burden therefore shifts to accurately identifying prime prospect groups *before* the initial test contact. This is an area in which sophisticated use of database technology and analysis is crucial. By developing an accurate profile of our target audience through database analysis, we can focus our testing on the other significant issues in designing an effective IDM campaign, such as timing and frequency of contact, optimizing the selection and sequence of media employed, and producing the most compelling offer and creative presentation.

IDM as Database Builder

While IDM makes greater demands on sophisticated database techniques than does traditional marketing, it is at the same time a valuable tool in building more useful and, hence, more profitable databases.

We are establishing multiple channels of communication with prospects through IDM. We may have an 800-number response, plus mail response, plus outbound telemarketing contact, plus a personal sales call, seminar attendance, or teleconference participation for a given individual on the file, all within the course of a single campaign. Each point within this continuum is a rich source of information about that prospect. The goal is to aggressively use this information resource by capturing the data as it is uncovered and analyzing it to uncover the trends and significant patterns it describes.

Tracking the medium through which a response was generated for an individual customer can be a signficant factor in segmenting the database in the future. Individuals who consistently respond through one medium may exhibit a significantly different purchase pattern from those who use another channel. You might, for example, discover that those who consistently respond through inbound telemarketing order more frequently than those who choose mail response. This would justify testing more frequent mailings to the telemarketing-responders segment of the database.

While we are focusing our attention on the individuals and companies that compose our current customer base, it is important not to discard information regarding nonrespondents to our solicitations. A key to effectively determining the factors distinguishing between positive and negative respondents is comparing and contrasting the two groups. It is possible that characteristics of the nonrespondent universe may be valuable in eliminating low-potential groups from subsequent tests. It may also be that there is a missing link in the sales process, which can be gleaned by actively and creatively assessing the decision pattern of the nay sayers.

There are two methods of generating information about nonrespondents. One is to analyze these names against the database as a whole and look for demographic and psychographic criteria which may serve to identify this segment. The other is to ask questions of the nonrespondents to determine their reasons. This may be accomplished through market research or, if outbound telemarketing is being employed, by following up a "no" answer with a polite request for a reason.

The Special Role of Telemarketing

The use of telemarketing in building the database warrants special attention. Unlike other mass-marketing media, telemarketing provides a two-way communications path. This is advantageous to the customer because it allows him or her to ask questions about particular aspects of the offer which may be unclear or which are especially significant to that individual's distinctive requirements. The two-way path is also advantageous to the database-oriented marketer because the screening questions which can be asked of prospects enhance the value of each name for future marketing efforts.

In an inbound telemarketing order-taking contact, the amount of probing must be limited to avoid turning the convenience of 800-number ordering into the inconvenience of responding to a survey. However, if the caller is new to your company, you can compile a basic profile over the telephone. If the caller is an established customer, the telemarketing representative can update the information in the customer database and ask about related areas of interest to gain information that may be useful for future offers.

Simple cross selling is often attempted on an incoming call. However, we can go beyond this request for an immediate order to determine additional areas of purchase authority or interest. The caller ordering records, for example, might be interested in seeing a catalog of videotapes as well. The person who calls for further information about home equity loans might be a prospect for a credit card, or for a credit-card loss-protection plan. A well-thought-out question or two can provide qualified leads.

Outbound telemarketing can provide even more information. A cooperative respondent will generally be willing to answer a series of questions about interests and needs. In addition, negative responses to an offer made through outbound telemarketing can be probed for greater depth of information. A negative response to a direct-mail solicitation is like hitting a brick wall: there is no indication of why this response occurred, or even whether the marketing message was received at all. On the telephone, though, the communicator can determine what aspect of the offer led to a "no" answer. Price and product features can be evaluated in light of these responses and acted upon to make future offers more attractive.

Whether the response is positive or negative, additional prospects may be uncovered through this process. This is particularly true in a business-to-business contact, where personnel and job responsibilities are constantly shifting. If the call is being made to a company in which you do not know the name of the individual with purchase authority, that information can be gathered during the course of the call and added to the file for future mailings and calls. You may also be able to request references to other individuals within the company who might be interested in hearing about your offer.

The Connection between Database and Market Research

Database creation and analysis and market-research methodology share a common goal—to produce an increasingly precise portrait of the companies and individuals who constitute the marketplace. What do they need to hear to make an informed purchase decision, and how can that message be delivered to them most economically and effectively? Each of these disciplines adds its own distinctive elements to this picture.

According to Ray Greenhill of Oxxford Information Technology, Ltd.,

> Database analysis and market research go hand in glove together. Database is good for identifying areas in which additional research is necessary. In traditional external databases you never have enough information to identify *why* something works or *why* it exists. You use database analysis to determine the ways in which groups of individuals or individual companies are broken up into segments. To understand *why* this segmentation holds true, to uncover the motivations underlying the behavior, we turn to market research. We use external databases and analysis of these databases to identify the areas we want to explore with market research.
>
> Traditionally, say 20 years ago, much market research effort went into determining the size of the market for a product. Today you don't have to do that, because the external databases in most cases will allow you to get a reasonable estimate of market size, based on the generic areas in which you're operating. The question that is most significant to market researchers in a program that combines database analysis with research is to learn what characteristics are most important to consumers in those products.

To illustrate the combined information-producing capabilities of market research and database analysis, we turn to John Wilczak—formerly corporate marketing director at Ipco Corporation and now president of Harvard Consulting, a Los Angeles-based marketing and business-strategy consulting firm—who successfully employed the two disciplines to overturn preconceived notions about product positioning and provide an accurate basis for management decision-making.

A Case in Point

Ipco—Blending Market Research and Data Analysis

John Wilczak, *Harvard Consulting*

Ipco Corporation is the parent company of several companies in the health field, including Sterling Dental Centers, a retailer of dental services.

Sterling Dental Centers is Ipco's venture into the retail dental-service market. The "retailing" of dental services and the concept of "chains" of dental-service providers resulted largely from the FTC's 1977 ruling permitting professionals to engage in advertising in order to promote a more market-oriented environment. A number of entrants to this marketplace have been long on public relations and puffery, but short on management expertise and systems, the result being a fallout of get-rich-quick franchise operators.

Ipco's approach to the business has been cautious. Seven dental centers have been opened to date in the Washington, D.C., area, with other openings planned. A major concern and focus of management attention has been the ability to continue to generate sufficient new-patient demand (traffic) for its dental center services. Further, the mix of new-patient-services demand is also important to the overall revenue and profitability picture of the business.

Sterling has been testing the role of integrated direct marketing in generating traffic.

When we initially began to explore the various opportunities to market this business, some fairly basic questions arose:

- What is the product or service we offer?
- Who are our customers?
- How do they perceive us as compared with other practitioners or competitors?
- What unique benefits do the dental centers offer?
- Are our location-selection processes and communications strategies consistent with the desires of the marketplace?
- How have we positioned the business?

Market Research

Posing these questions led to a market-research project designed to add greater depth to our understanding of the customer base for Sterling Dental services.

The methodology for this research was a controlled, two-part, self-administered questionnaire. The first part was given to patients before their examinations. It included questions about their initial interest in Sterling Dental and a variety of other questions about demographics, appointment preferences, and reading and listening habits. The second part was given to patients after their examination, asking about their experience at the dental center.

The study was conducted among Sterling Dental patients both new and existing. No other prequalification existed for the participation (i.e., age, sex, etc.). A minimum of 100 patients from each of the six centers completed questionnaires. A total of 928 patients participated. Detailed instructions and procedures for the research implementation were developed to facilitate this project.

The executive summary of this consumer research included some interesting findings:

Patient Profile

- Significantly more females than males.

58 percent female   42 percent male

Yet this percentage of males was much *higher* than originally expected.

- Household incomes ranging from $15,000 to $50,000 and over:

$15,000–$29,000   36 percent
$30,000–$50,000 and over   36 percent

- 70 percent of patients came from homes with 2 to 4 people (and we were achieving significant penetration within those homes).
- A significant number of individuals chose Sterling Dental because of proximity to their jobs as opposed to their homes.

A problem arose as a result of the findings of the research. Management had previously decided that the business was to be positioned generally to appeal to downscale nonusers of dental services. Yet the research suggested that Sterling's current patient base was more upscale and had used other dental services in the recent past.

Fortunately, the database-analysis tools available to direct marketers today allowed us to go several steps further in this research process. After reviewing a number of different vendor product services, we contracted Donnelley Marketing Information Services to perform a geodemographic analysis of our total patient record file.

We needed to prove to management that the questionnaire information was entirely accurate. To achieve this, we decided to undertake an independent database analysis of our current patient files. By comparing and contrasting the results of our questionnaire research with the analysis of established customer characteristics, we would arrive at a more precise, cross-referenced picture of the Sterling Dental marketplace.

This enhanced customer knowledge would provide the basis for customer segmentation and outside list selection for direct marketing purposes, as well as criteria for evaluating and selecting future sites. In addition, the output would provide solid management information for reevaluation of the product-service positioning and direction for the creative efforts.

Donnelley's Clusterplus system features 47 distinctively different American lifestyle clusters, which are coded S01 (highest) through S47 (lowest), to reflect their relative standing on the socioeconomic scale. These clusters can then be further broken down based on household characteristics, offering a more refined segmentation analysis.

Thus we began to assemble the information needed to match our patient records, as kept at the branch level, with Donnelley's Clusterplus household file. The resulting patient profiles were used in conducting a market-penetration analysis within defined geographic areas around each branch, or dental center. The specific geographical area is referred to in the Clusterplus system as a *cell of demand*. Penetration of the cell of demand is your market share. The market share you don't have is your opportunity.

Using the results of the Clusterplus system, we tested numerous variables in order to increase both market share and response rate within the captured market share.

While the development of these analyses could have been relatively simple because the dental centers had computerized many of their internal functions, we initially ran into a roadblock. The computer systems Sterling Dental had installed were simply incompatible with Donnelley's system. They learned a hard lesson: when it comes to developing customer databases, one would be well advised to seek the services of a professional *before* embarking on the project.

In order to get around this unexpected roadblock, we worked closely with the vendor of the Sterling systems to print out hardcopy of the more than 20,000 patient records. The hardcopy was then sent to a service company which provided optical character reading and the formatted tapes necessary to perform the Clusterplus analyses.

When the analyses were completed, Donnelley provided us with a series of reports and subsequent management meetings which allowed us to review and discuss in detail the findings, conclusions, and recommendations of this work.

Target Markets

The Clusterplus analyses evaluated each individual cluster with respect to the key attribute we selected: the relative penetration of Sterling Dental patients within the Donnelley household file. Then the household-level analysis was performed by examining hundreds of possible subsegments within each cluster and choosing the ones that produced the finest selectivity.

The top-ranked cluster can be profiled as working couples with average education, who are homeowners, earn above-average incomes, and reside in homes built in the 1950s. In contrast, the clusters with the largest number of Sterling Dental patients shared the common characteristics of younger mobile professionals who are often single (yuppies and baby boomers).

Thus while the *greatest penetration* of Sterling Dental customers was in the "typical" American family, the *greatest concentration* of patients was in younger, baby-boomer types. This finding is consistent with the original survey research and provides vindication for the sampling techniques employed.

The three top-ranked clusters can generally be described as having above-average income and professional job status—a very different target audience from the group originally targeted by the business (downscale nonusers of dental services). Suffice it to say, the lowest penetration levels occurred in the downscale clusters of the socioeconomic continuum.

The household-level analyses offered even greater selectivity. By testing hundreds of variables against the cluster household findings, we found that several variables offered significant improvement in selectivity. They included:

- Estimated household income
- Male title on the address
- Single-family dwelling unit
- Moderate length of residence

An immediate result of this work was a lengthy discussion about who our typical patient really was. One thought came immediately to mind: Our largest concentration of patients consisted of baby-boomer types, yet no positioning strategy had ever been developed to reach these people.Without the in-depth customer-base knowledge provided by the combination of market research and database analysis, our fledgling integrated direct-marketing efforts would have been targeted in an entirely inappropriate direction.

Technology plus Analysis
Equals Profitability

The growing quality and importance of database marketing are rooted in heightened capabilities on both the technological and the analytical front. Computers offer us growing power to compile facts and figures. To comprehend the meaning of this abundant data, the analytical experts continue to refine their ability to synthesize demographic and psychological data to uncover significant patterns and models, making response to marketing stimuli increasingly predictable.

On the computer side of the coin, these developments include:

Increased Mass-Storage Capabilities. Size alone need not be a significant limiting factor for databases at this time, thanks to the growth of technological capabilities and the concurrent drop in the price of undertaking a particular task. The raw size of the file is a concern not only because of a growing population but also, and more importantly, because of the increasing number of factors we want to record about each individual in the database. Whereas name and address might once have constituted a complete record of an individual for marketing purposes, we now look for telephone numbers; recency, frequency, and size of prior purchases; and potentially, additional demographic and psychographic data to be used in scientifically segmenting the list.

Improved Reporting. Feeding enormous amounts of information into a computer is clearly useless if the information cannot be extracted from the database in a timely and efficient manner. Our ability to produce reports promptly, taking into account increasingly complex combinations of factors, has progressed rapidly and continues to move ahead.

One significant development in this area is the ability to efficiently cross-check files against one another. What began with simple weeding out of duplicate names between lists has grown into a powerful ability to identify significant relationships between a thoroughly analyzed, "known" list and a second list of individuals whose key marketing characteristics are unknown. In this way, in-house lists gain enormously in value through sophisticated analysis of their correlation to "known" commercial lists. We will explore this concept more thoroughly later in this chapter.

Decentralization of Computer Power. The growth of personal computers (PCs) has had an impact upon many areas of direct marketing, from the telemarketing representative receiving in-depth product information through a personal computer on his or her desk to the clerk in the warehouse logging a running inventory on a PC as each shipment is processed.

Equally important for the future is the ongoing networking of personal computers. Enabling individual PC users to share a common pool of data allows the telemarketing representative to tap into up-to-the-minute product-availability information, for example, accurately reflecting what happened at the warehouse just moments ago. On-line information can be valuable not only in streamlining the internal workings of a marketing operation but as a customer benefit as well. For instance, Federal Express invested millions in an extraordinarily precise computerized package-handling system. This system gave the company better internal control of business as well as the ability to answer telephone inquiries about the whereabouts of a package within minutes. This unique benefit became a key advertising point in a highly competitive market.

The significance of networked PCs to the database function is an enhanced two-way flow of information. Data can be pulled out of the files at remote locations as needed. The inventory-control example above is one demonstration of this capability. Another is the customer-service representative who can instantly access up-to-the-minute records.

Equally important are the diverse sources of information that can conveniently feed into the database. Each contact between your customer and your company can be tracked in a unified, coordinated database across department lines, and this information can then be used to good advantage.

For example, if the customer-service department enters records of product problems into a computer database, the direct marketing department can tap into this source of information and look for the opportunities represented by the reported problems. Perhaps a service contract could be offered? Maybe the equipment being used is inadequate for the volume of work being done, and a larger unit should berecommended? At the very least, extra steps should be undertaken to ensure that a current customer is not lost because of service problems. And at the same time, customer-service information can point out potential product improvements for R&D attention.

To sum up, the technological developments of the recent past have enabled development of a rich marketing-information resource, shar ing data between relevant departments and making it accessible to everyone with a need to know.

This does not mean, though, that American business has been quick to take advantage of this opportunity to use the wealth of available customer data for marketing purposes. As Ray Greenhill of Oxxford Information Technology Ltd. explains,

> In most companies today, data processing is not oriented toward a marketing structure but toward the general operation of the business. In many businesses with large, established data processing operations, such as airline reservation systems, banks, and insurance companies, the information system *is* the operation of the business. However, a major change has occurred in the past 5 years with the advent of the personal computer. We now see more of an orientation toward taking the raw information and having the manager use a PC with appropriate software to organize and analyze it to provide information in a form suitable for making management decisions.

The Ins and Outs of IDM Database

We rely on two interrelated database resources:

- In-house files
- Outside lists

As is so often the case, the first step is to look inward at the information available within your company. This information is often dispersed through many departments. Sales records may exist in different product areas, while payment history is locked away in accounting files, and customer-service records are filed somewhere else. Additional fragmentation may take place when different transactions are handled through different channels. For example, initial equipment sales may belong to one area, while ongoing supplies and service transactions are recorded elsewhere.

Our first goal in organizing a marketing-oriented database, then, is to compile all relevant data in a comprehensive information resource. As Ray Greenhill suggests,

> The data that relates to potential customers is external to the company's operations, and should be maintained by the marketing department. However, information about current customers should be available centrally so that it can be tapped by each of the various marketing and service groups

who need it. If I am in the marketing department of a company, I would like to be able to call up on my computer screen at any time what the profitability of customers is, and segment those customers to find the characteristics that made one customer profitable and another customer not. That same information is relevant to the manufacturing or financial department of the company, and all should have access to a unified, up-to-date information resource.

The depth of customer information kept on file will, of course, vary from company to company. As an example, though, Figure 6.1 is an overview of requirements for a direct marketing database designed to serve the needs of a client pursuing an IDM strategy in the financial services industry.

The internal information you gather is important in a number of ways. It is axiomatic that your current customers are your best prospects. By evaluating the descriptions of your customers contained in the records of their past transactions with your company, you can determine their buying patterns, their general areas of interest, and their value as customers. By assessing this information, you can efficiently target your contacts by areas of product interest and chronological periods of peak activity. You can also assess the level of direct marketing expense justified by the profit potential inherent in the customer's past buying activity, and increase or decrease your marketing expenses accordingly.

Organizing your internal information resources is also the key to utilizing the substantial external resources now available. What began as simply the "list business" has blossomed into a source of detailed information about individuals and businesses, organized in databases offering in-depth demographic and psychographic profiles. Research companies like SRI International and Lifestyle Selector continue to refine psychographic techniques that sort and classify the population according to their values and lifestyles. From a theoretical basis in psychology they have gathered empirical data to demonstrate the ways in which these value and lifestyle differentiations successfully predict purchase behavior, product usage, media usage, and activity patterns.

This resource can be used in two ways:

1. By comparing known customers against commercially available lists, we can determine the categories which are currently proving profitable. This may indicate additional areas of opportunity for our in-house list.

2. By determining the profile of current customers, we gain a means of pinpointing high-potential prospects for market expansion through testing of outside list segments.

I. DEMOGRAPHICS

Name_____   Address (home)_____

Telephone number: Home (owned or rented)_____
       Home_____   If owned, morgtage (yes or no)_____
       Business_____

Name of spouse_____   Date of birth (husband)_____
                                        (wife)_____

Employer_____

Title_____   Children (yes or no)_____

Business address_____   If yes, age range_____

II. FINANCIAL INFORMATION

Salary_____   Other household salaries_____

Other income_____

Social Security Number:

Husband_____   Assets_____

    Wife_____   Tax ID number_____

    Children_____

Investment profile and activity_____

III. MARKETING INFORMATION

A. *Product*
    Specific product or products offered_____
    Media mix_____
    Date_____
    Response via what medium_____
    Specific product offer (i.e., rate, premium, free trial, etc.)_____
    Product or products selected_____
    Response to cross sell or add-on_____
    Source of name_____
    who is decision maker (product-specific)_____
    Best time to contact by phone_____
    If requested literature:_____
      What product or products?_____
      Follow-up date_____

B. *Payment Preferences*
    Credit card or cards; specify_____
    Check_____
    Bill me_____
    Automatic check deduction_____
    Automatic savings deduction_____
    ATM_____

IV. CUSTOMER RELATIONSHIP
    What product or service relationship does the person have with the
    company?_____
    What product or service relationship did the person have with the
    company in the past?_____

Figure 6.1. Questionnaire: information on customers.

A Case in Point

Christie's Successful List Segmentation

An example of successful list segmentation involves Christie's, the fine-art auction house. The program was conducted entirely through a lavishly designed direct-mail package, as befits the top-of-the-line image of Christie's. As a result, the cost per contact was high relative to average mail costs, so stringent requirements for productivity per contact were similar to those involved in a multimedia campaign.

As an alternative to their traditional marketing of art catalog subscriptions, a membership club called *The Christie's Society* was created. The society satisfied the needs of over 40 individual categories of art interests and included eight art-related benefits, such as subscription to the catalogs.

Two mail packages were developed, but the expense of the mailing required a highly selected mailing list. To achieve this goal, the Christie's existing customer list was analyzed across 8 demographic and 48 psychographic criteria. Then the list was matched against outside databases, for which the demographics and psychographics were known. Based on statistically valid levels of correlation between names found on the customer list and the outside lists, Christie's could develop a very clear demographic and psychographic profile of their customer base. This profile was based on statistically significant name matches against a coded file, not just extrapolations based on zip codes, as is often done. This allowed effective pinpointing of segments which held the greatest promise for the mailings.

The strategy worked extraordinarily well. Not only did the response rate increase by 66 percent, but the average order size jumped by 83 percent. Christie's received a bronze Echo Award, one of the Direct Marketing Association's annual awards for outstanding campaigns, for this innovative program.

New Directions in Database Analysis

The increasing quantity of relevant marketing data, combined with shifts in the American economy from manufacturing to service industries, has led to the development of nontraditional data analysis techniques. Raymond M. Greenhill and Clifford J. Brundage of Oxxford Information Technology Ltd., two of the most astute database experts practicing today, have prepared the following discussion of both traditional database techniques and the newer strategies being employed to meet the more sophisticated challenges of IDM today.

Words from the Wise

Raymond M. Greenhill and Clifford J. Brundage on Database Techniques Old and New

Raymond M. Greenhill & Clifford J. Brundage,   *Oxxford Information Technology Ltd.*

It is axiomatic that a decision is only as good as the information upon which it is based. The vehicle for capturing and structuring information, for converting it into plans and action, is the company database.

The primary impediment to effective communication with the marketplace is the organizational structure of most corporations. This structure consists of discrete functions, activities, and departments at staff level, and dispersed offices, distributors, and sales representatives at field level; thus a coordinated message is rarely delivered to the customer or prospect. Compounding the organizational roadblocks are the divisions within functions, in which advertising, direct mail, telemarketing sales, and service often report to different managers, all of whom have a singular idea of the preeminence of their own departments.

In this environment, databases serve as a common language—an integrating force to allocate resources toward common direct marketing goals and objectives.

Traditional Approaches to Direct Marketing Databases

The traditional approach to building an external database is to purchase broad lists qualified only by a minimum number of selectors or variables. These variables usually include:

- Standard Industry Classification (SIC) code
- Size (number of employees and sales)
- Geographic area
- Executive title of prospect
- Telephone number

There are several reasons for the wide adoption of this broad-based approach:

- The mind-set of most advertising people is more concerned about the initial cost of acquisition (e.g., cost per thousand) than the value per name, since these people rarely are held accountable for the final results produced.
- List selection is usually relegated to subordinates who generally lack knowledge of the range of data available from a variety of sources.
- There is a widespread lack of knowledge about the analytical techniques that can effectively increase the profitability of databases.

The information contained in the database is one side of the coin; the other is the analysis of this data to identify the more desirable prospective customers. There are three generic approaches to traditional data analysis:

1. *Segmentation approaches.*   These statistical techniques attempt to group the "markets" into candidates with common characteristics. This serves to pinpoint opportunities and reduce waste. Segmentation approaches include *factor analysis* and *cluster analysis*, both of which attempt to group data together to find the most relevant variables, and *discriminant analysis*, which determines how individual cases should be classified once you have identified the significant variables.

2. *Regression.*   This is a statistical technique that analyzes a firm's own database to build models which, when compared with outside data, will predict the performance of the outside list. For example, you might analyze your business-to-business sales history and determine the level of purchases produced based on a set of information about the customer: industry segment, inventory policies, and so on. When you then plug information about prospect companies into this model, you arrive at a specific sales projection for each prospect.

3. *Subjective models use "expert judgment" to select characteristics felt to be important in qualifying potential customers.*   This is the human model: an individual says, "Based on my experience, I've determined that these factors are important."

These traditional approaches are *not* particularly applicable outside manufacturing industries. They are based on the premise that generally, given an SIC code and the size of a business in the manufacturing sector, you know fairly accurately the volume of goods and services that the company will consume.

However, we require more significant discriminators when analyzing the purchasing potential of companies in the following areas:

- General service providers
- Producers of goods with higher "value added," requiring very specific segments of the marketplace (e.g. fashion jewelry, large-scale computers, etc.)
- Financial services, including bank lending, leasing, brokerage or investment services, and real estate
- Technologically based products

In these instances the purchasing patterns of the companies are more closely linked to the *way the business is managed* than to the line of business pursued. You can have two firms in the same line of business of the same size, one that's pursuing an aggressive growth strategy and another that's on the decline. Using traditional marketing techniques, it would appear that these two companies were equally viable prospects, since they are in the same SIC code and size category. Clearly, more in-depth information, along with a more incisive means of analyzing this data, is required to distinguish between high-potential and low-potential prospects in this environment.

Sources of Information

A wealth of information is available about businesses today which goes beyond the simple demographic characteristics of size, location, and industry segment to provide the basis for determining the *consumption patterns* of the prospects.

These information resources include the following:

Aggregate Data. This is the general economic and industry data that tracks broad trends in employment, durable good sales, industrial output, and so on. It is typically available from government, trade associations, and private firms.

In using this data, we move from the broad overall econometric picture to greater specificity by industrial segment and geographical region.

Detailed Specific Data. Here we move from the overall industry analysis to information about a particular company. This level of information comprises a wide variety of data available about specific companies from commercial databases, and includes:

- Company size
- Company age
- Number of employees
- Specific purchases of goods and services
- Use of financial services (leasing, secured lending, exporters, importers, etc.)

Using Positional Proxies

Often the piece of information we want about a particular company is not available as such from commercial databases. For example, there will not be a listing in the database which specifies that a company is pursuing an aggressive price-cutting strategy. However, we can define proxies: available data which indicates the strategy being pursued. What's happening to the company's gross margin vis-à-vis its competitors? What's happening to its growth rate? Its output per employee? By selecting the appropriate positional proxies, we can determine the underlying information which is creating the conditions we *can* measure.

Modern Analytical Techniques

Some new approaches are required to effectively analyze this wealth of data and turn it into information for direct marketing decision making. Some of the most significant approaches are outlined below.

Life Cycle of Company. This approach measures the particular stage of a company's development against its own growth pattern, or the growth patterns of competitors, or the growth patterns of the industry. Typically in an early stage of development, the company will be growing substantially faster than industry averages. Because it's growing faster, it is generally run relatively inefficiently, and it is generally not in a profitable position. As it reaches the maturing stages of the business cycle, it becomes a net-cash generator.

We arrive at this analysis by taking the ages and sizes of businesses and comparing them with a set of models developed over time. We look at the age of a business, the rate of growth of the industry, and the geographic location of the business, and we say that a company that has been operating for A years and has achieved B size in C industry located in D geographic region should have achieved E level of sales. If the actual figures are higher than expected, the company is a growth firm. If lower, then the company is probably a maturing firm.

This form of analysis is particularly helpful in determining a company's marketing potential for financial services and products.

Management Strategy Pursued.   This approach involves measurement of the risk assumption of the company. If you have access to the financial statement of the company, you can observe how fast management has caused the company to grow in relation to its industry. What sort of decisions have been made in respect to pricing against competitors? What is the capital structure of the company? For example, if the company is carrying a lot of debt in relation to assets, it means management has assumed a risk-taking strategy, running the business for growth purposes.

This analysis is especially pertinent for marketers of financial services, communications products and services, and other high-technology products.

Asset Structure.   Analysis of asset structure is related to management strategy. By determining the debt level of a company, we can determine how much financing will be needed, and how much will be available through traditional channels. This serves as an indicator of potential for new capital investment, real estate, etc.

Input-Output Analysis.   Input-output (I/O) analysis assumes that, given a particular level of output, a company is likely to use certain levels of input. This information is generally available from the U.S. government, which maintains information on consumption of goods and services against dollar output for particular industries.

Forecasted Growth.   This is a comparison of company performance with industry growth patterns. This analysis is significant in assessing a company's financial requirements, employment needs, and consumption of a variety of services.

Comparative Norm Performance.   This measure determines the "winners" and "losers" over the foreseeable future. If a business is a particular size and age, has a certain level of assets, and so forth, how does it compare with its peer group? The selection of peer groups for comparison can be segmented in any relevant fashion. For example, the company being analyzed could be compared with others growing at the same rate per year, regardless of the industry segment. On the other hand, industry segment could be the criterion selected.

The winner in this case may not be the company with top current performance but rather the company demonstrating dramatic improvement against the industry norm, or its own past performance.

Parent or Subsidiary Relationship.   This analysis of the management structure of a company can be quite revealing in judging potential for certain services. Take telecommunications, for example. A company involved in a parent or subsidiary relationship will have more complex business interactions, and will therefore need more sophisticated communications services. Travel needs are also likely to be higher than for an independent company.

Differing Approaches to Model Construction

Traditional statistical analysis methodologies, such as regression analysis or discriminant analysis, attempt to build a single model for the desired interrelationship of data variables. The problem that arises is missing information; if *all* the data is not available for a potential customer, the model cannot be used to predict that customer's performance. This limits the number of variables that can be included in your model. In the real world, not many databases have complete information on every firm.

The alternative approach is pattern recognition. This statistical technique builds a series of models based on the degree to which a given prospect fits a *specific pattern of elements* (including the availability or nonavailability of data). This technique is very useful because it produces models that can be applied easily to a variety of different external databases, which may contain a greater or lesser number of the pertinent variables.

Pattern recognition allows us to analyze a very large number of variables and determine the patterns produced through this analysis which provide relevant predictive models. We then store these patterns and use them to assess the purchasing potential of the names sourced through external lists, determining which individuals are worth contacting and through what means in our marketing program.

Traditional statistical techniques, on the other hand, frequently will not let us use a large number of variables. As the number of variables increases, the analysis starts to break down, and the computer time required to perform the analysis becomes too intensive.

Oxxford Information Technology's database of models represents a significant resource for pattern recognition. It is a highly specialized database in which past patterns of consumption or demand are maintained. At present the Oxxford database includes over 1000 detailed models on over 40 major products and product groups.

This resource can be used in three ways:

- To determine in advance the potential outcome or yield of a specific list for a specific application, given elements present in the database
- To determine the relative cost of data acquisition and needs for more in-depth evaluation of cost
- To identify the best prospects from an external database, along with the specific probability that they will become qualified leads

The following case history in the financial services industry illustrates the relationship between a well-structured internal database and the available external data sources. The use of pattern-recognition techniques to provide an in-depth analysis of prospect viability from a variety of list sources is particularly noteworthy.

A Case in Point

Federated Financial Services

Raymond M. Greenhill and Clifford J. Brundage, *Oxxford Information Technology Ltd.*

Joe Thomas, senior vice president of marketing for the Federated Financial Services Company, was given the assignment to develop a database to identify qualified prospects for the Small Business Financial Services Group of the company.

The Strategy

The small-business universe (which includes businesses with annual sales between $500,000 and $5 million) represents an opportunity for selling both financial and investment services. The assets and wealth of these businesses are the equity and worth of their owners. Consequently, they are a prospect for both interest-income and fee-based services, such as unsecured loans, secured borrowing, and equipment financing, along with insurance, securities, and financial consulting (e.g., taxes, M&A, etc.).

The Problem

According to market "counts" there were over 300,000 small businesses in Federated's marketplace. Given only 20 account executives, how could they pick the pearls from among the oysters?

The Approach

Joe Thomas analyzed Federated's current customer base of 20,000 business accounts by:

1. Geography, or territory.
2. Type of firm (service, manufacturing, wholesale, retail, etc.).

3. Size of firm by sales, number of employees, and net worth (where available).

4. Services purchased by product (e.g., insurance, investment, loans), dollar amount, and frequency. (This information was available through input-output analysis data.)

5. A profitability formula, used for each account, which determined actual profit produced over the life of the account after subtracting costs of goods, account servicing, and other expenses.

Using this information, which was available for over 75 percent of his customers, Thomas contracted with a consulting firm that specializes in modeling and segmentation techniques for financial services.

It was recommended that additional external databases be acquired to add the following data elements:

1. Financial and operating norms and ratios by industry, size, and geography

2. Projected growth forecasts by line of business and size of firm

3. Financial risk analysis by industry sector

When a pattern-recognition technique, as opposed to traditional methods of segmentation, was used, Federated's customers produced a unique profile: Of the 20,000 (with pattern recognition all customers were included, even those with incomplete or missing data elements) analyzed, 6000 were identified as heavy users of both financial and investment services. They fit the following pattern:

1. These were companies that had been in business over 3 years but less than 10 years. They were in the emerging growth stage.

2. The line of business was relatively unimportant, but service firms were predominant.

3. Financially, these firms were usually highly leveraged (in terms of total debt as related to total equity), reflecting the need for working capital to support growth.

4. Cash flow, especially among service companies, was generally above industry norms. This explained the investment of these firms in money-market funds, certificates of deposit (CDs), etc.

5. The highest industry risks were manufacturing, retail, and several other categories.

With this information, Joe Thomas was able to construct a set of criteria—weighting each one by importance—for use in searching a number of private databases, directories, list compilers, trade associations, and specialized publications.

Of the 300,000 companies in the universe, 46,000 met Federated's specifications. Thomas then called in his manager of direct marketing and telemarketing, and designed the following plan:

1. Rerun the acquired prospects and segment them into three groups.

Group A, comprising 15,000 firms whose "profit potential" pattern warranted *only* a direct marketing solicitation. The message would be directed to those products and services that firms in group A had a high propensity to consume: money-market funds, Keoghs, and partner life insurance.

Group B, comprising 22,000 firms whose purchase characteristics and risk profile warranted direct marketing and a telemarketing callback. The pattern of these firms indicated greater use of financial services. A direct-mail piece was designed to emphasize how Federated could support growth firms in need of working capital.

Group C, representing the 9000 firms of highest potential for both financial and investment services. This select group received a mailing geared to these high-level prospects, including a special offer of a Federated "Blue Chip" Business Card. This card enabled prospects to establish a credit line and to access a range of investment services. Telemarketing was used to set up appointments for the account executives.

All groups were loaded onto a minicomputer, coded, and tracked from the lead to conversion stage. Further analysis fed the results of both respondents and nonrespondents into the system, along with sales and associated costs by group, firm, territory, and account executive. Finally, a program calculated the "true" value of each customer (i.e., the contribution per customer for all sales—broken down by product mix—over the expected life of the account.

The Result:

Without adding account executives (only making existing ones more productive), Joe Thomas, with his integrated marketing approach,

- Attracted 10 percent new customers, whose average value was $55,000.
- Improved product mix by selling higher-profit investment services, adding 25 percent to profit margins.
- Reduced cost per customer acquisition by 40 percent.
- Acquired more "experiences" to include in the database to improve and refine ongoing analysis.

Conclusion

In the passage from the era of "lists" to the age of "databases," it is all too easy for information management to be handed over to the data processing professionals to do with as they may. An astute direct-marketing manager will not get bogged down in the details of *how* the computer churns out the desired information, but will rather guide the in-house and external professionals by setting goals for the project and monitoring the attainment of these goals.

From this perspective, database management is not a technical issue but a strategic one. Information which exists within a company must be organized to fulfill marketing needs, a structure distinctly different from the prerequisites imposed by the accounting department or operational units. The manager must coordinate the information about current customers acquired throughout the organization into a central, powerful database resource. And external resources must be evaluated and brought to bear, when appropriate, to improve marketing efficiencies and expand market penetration.

It is also worthwhile to reaffirm the importance of linking market research to database development, particularly as it has an impact upon introduction of new products or services. Your database is a scientifically organized chronicle of past activity. To the degree that your present needs mirror this historic picture, the database stands as a self-contained resource. However, as you move into new areas, market research becomes the tool which isolates the distinguishing factors determining prospective buying behavior, and the database in turn becomes a universe from which appropriate prospects can be gleaned. This presupposes that the distinguishing factors uncovered by market research are contained within your database. If you are aware of the areas of expansion contained in your business plan, then you can stress the likely key factors in building the database resource. And even if opportunity arises in unexpected directions, your current database can be matched against outside sources to enrich and enhance the customer profile it provides, enabling you to profit from the established relationship you enjoy with your current customers.

Finally, Brundage and Greenhill offer the following caveats regarding database creation and management:

The art of database building is to selectively blend internal customer data with relevant elements from external sources, keeping in mind the following principles:

1. All data is expensive to collect, maintain, and update. Each "field" must pay its own way. The burden should fall on the user to cost-justify their existence.

2. Data should be constantly reviewed—to purge, to update, or to enrich.

3. Unless the databases can be related to specific project results and profit performance, they become overhead and cannot be cost-justified.

7
Toward an IDM Future

Earlier in this book, we stressed that integrated direct marketing does not rely on unfamiliar and untested media, but rather on sophisticated, coordinated use of proven marketing channels. At the same time, though, IDM is definitely a means for maximizing results of changes in direct marketing resulting from new techniques and new technologies.

IDM is the product of an expanding direct marketing universe. This expansion has occurred in two ways:

- Inbound and outbound telemarketing have brought instantaneous interactivity to direct marketing. The effect of this person-to-person link goes beyond the telephone itself. By opening up a convenient response channel, telemarketing has fueled the growth of catalogs, direct-response print advertising, and direct-response television.

- The role of direct marketing has expanded. Once a *direct-response campaign* was defined as a marketing effort which resulted in the placement of an order through the mail. Now direct marketing also includes functions which produce purchases at the field sales-force or retail level. Two applications which have brought about a redefinition of the term *direct response* are (1) screening and qualifying leads for sales-force follow-up and (2) building traffic at the retail level through personally targeted promotions to high-potential prospects.

- The central concepts behind IDM are optimizing the information flow required to make an informed purchase decision and improving the interactivity between prospect and marketer. Any new development of direct marketing technology or technique will simply add to our capabilities in achieving these two goals. As a philosophy, IDM provides the perspective for employing the direct marketing means at our disposal for maximum profitability. As new media arise, they become additional channels to be incorporated into the media mix, according to the principles we have described. As new techniques for analyzing and segmenting the marketplace become available, they add greater sophistication to the practice of IDM techniques.

This chapter will explore the new developments currently underway, or immediately on the horizon, which hold significant promise for integrated direct marketers in the years to come.

The Significance of Home Shopping Channels

The phenomenal growth of televised shopping programs and networks is a textbook example of the promise of integrated direct marketing on the consumer level.

Available in the form of home shopping shows distributed as syndicated programming, such as the 1-hour Cable Value Network presentations, or 24-hour separate channels, such as the industry leader Home Shopping Network, and carried on cable systems or UHF broadcast stations, home shopping programming takes advantage of the modern consumer's demand for convenience. By delivering product information via television and accepting orders through an 800 number, home shopping creates a tight loop between the viewer or shopper and the product purchase.

The "program" content of the home shopping channels is lively and pleasant, but there is no question that what the viewer is watching is essentially a long string of direct-response advertisements. The merchandise offered is always marked down from higher prices and often represents good value, but price alone is not enough to account for the extraordinary volume of business being done through these channels. Experts have projected up to $250 million in sales for home shopping programs in 1986, with predictions of over $3 billion in sales by the year 1990. Home Shopping Network alone claimed to have made sales to 1 million people by early 1987, at which time it reached 31 million homes nationwide.

Not surprisingly, Home Shopping Network is looking beyond merchandise sales at this writing. In January 1987 it agreed to acquire

Baltimore Federal Financial, paving the way for offers of financial services over the air. The company was reportedly considering expanding its direct-mail activities in conjunction with this move.

Perhaps the ultimate ratification of the home shopping concept took place in November 1986, when Sears, Roebuck and Co. gave QVC network exclusive rights to present Sears products in a home shopping program.

Home shopping is happening in a big way today. Like the mail-order-catalog boom that preceded it, this broadcast development demonstrates that people still enjoy shopping, but increasingly prefer convenience versus driving to a crowded shopping center or mall. Shopping through the television-telephone connection is a utility, with the offers flowing like water from a faucet when you turn your television dial. It is the integration of television and telephone that makes it work. And we will be very surprised if the home shopping companies do not rapidly expand their promotional activities into mail and outbound telemarketing, in order to make the most of the extraordinary wealth of proven buyers generated through television.

Additional Video Marketing Channels

Television is undeniably the central information channel in American life. The medium is no longer the sole domain of three monolithic networks, though. Cable television now reaches nearly 50 percent of American homes, and with cable comes an increasing number of programming choices. As independent stations gain a growing share of the audience, the number of direct-response possibilities increases as well. A higher degree of targeting is possible as programming becomes more specialized. At the same time, the cost of advertising on television comes down as the audience becomes more segmented, opening the way for profitable promotion of products and services which could not be efficiently marketed via "broadcasting," but are prime targets for "narrowcasting."

The other major force fragmenting the television audience is the videocassette recorder (VCR). By the end of 1986 there were 25 million households in the United States with VCRs. With that level of market penetration, it was inevitable that marketing uses would be found for this new technology. And they have been found. For example:

- Numerous real estate firms across the country are producing taped tours of homes available for sale, giving prospective buyers shop-at-home convenience with a depth of information far greater than a photograph and a description on paper.

- While it has not appeared nationally on store shelves to date, Pacific Arts Video has announced plans for the first videocassette magazine, to be priced at under $4 and to contain both programming and commercials.

- The first commercially made videocassette to include a commercial message appeared in early 1987. The tape release of *Top Gun*, the hit movie, starts out with a 60-second commercial for Diet Pepsi.

- There is widespread interest in creating videocassette "catalogs" to be distributed through rental outlets, with 800 numbers for ordering merchandise. *Channels* magazine reports that the first national release came in late 1986 from a company selling lingerie. The 17-minute tape was distributed to over 3000 video stores. Company president Peter Granoff reportedly explained, "We started with lingerie because so many people are embarrassed to go into stores and buy it." If this release is successful, more fashion-oriented video catalogs are planned.

Television in all its forms represents an important direction for expansion of the IDM concept. It is a proven marketing channel, and the current high level of direct-response activity in this area should be self-reinforcing. It seems logical to assume that a satisfied customer of a home shopping program will be inclined to respond positively to other broadcast direct marketing solicitations, although it is too soon to offer statistical proof to back up this assumption.

Marketing via Computer

The computer is already a central aspect of integrated direct marketing, which relies on computer technology for list selection and processing, and for the tracking and analysis of results. There is another side to the personal computer from a marketing standpoint: the computer as a communications medium. For a discussion of the potential of this aspect of the silicon revolution we turn to Steve Morgenstern, president of Morningstar Communications, a New York marketing communications company. In addition to his marketing activities, Steve writes about computers for several magazines, and serves as consultant for private companies and government agencies on the state of home computing in America.

Words from the Wise

Steve Morgenstern on Computers as a Communications Medium

Steve Morgenstern, *President, Morningstar Communications*

If you needed to find a single word to describe the rise of personal computers in American life, it would have to be *impatience*. Swept along by excitement and the profit hunger of hundreds of high-tech companies, the question heard throughout the land is "Why doesn't everyone already use a personal computer?" Even a glance at the chronology involved reveals how ludicrous this attitude is. Personal computing had barely begun 10 years ago. The original Apple II hit the market in 1977—the IBM PC not until 1981—and at that point a bare-bones system with 64K memory and one disk drive, with no monitor or operating system, cost over $2000.

We have traveled extraordinarily far extraordinarily fast in the mass computerization of America. Software is now plentiful, hardware is more powerful and less expensive, and computer usage in both business and home settings continues to increase. Without dwelling on the matter, continued growth is inevitable. Typewriters can't compare with word processors in price or performance. Electronic spreadsheets are as important as sharpened pencils in the business world. In the home, the ability to accomplish financial tasks, educate children and adults, help with schoolwork, and entertain the family are increasingly compelling reasons to buy a computer system, as the price of a useful configuration falls to the level of a color television set or a decent-quality stereo system.

While every direct marketer now uses computers in day-to-day business operations, the use of the computer as a marketing medium has barely been exploited. There are fascinating experiments underway, though, and technological improvements waiting to be implemented. Let's look at a few current undertakings and future trends.

An Interactive Information Resource

A computer diskette can hold a wealth of information and present it in an interactive format, complete with graphics and question-and-answer activities.

The automobile companies have begun using this means to provide information about new cars. Both Ford Motor Company and the Buick Division of General Motors have produced programs; the Ford version is called a *Disk Drive Test Drive*. Such programs are sent free of charge to consumers who respond to ads in computer publications. Since computer ownership is a decidedly upscale demographic characteristic, the audience receiving these free diskettes is prescreened and prequalified. And by aligning itself with the computer user, each company makes a distinct between-the-lines statement about its own commitment to high technology.

The programs combine attractive graphics with the ability to choose the part of the presentation you want to view from easy-to-use menus. In effect consumers create their own sales presentations, selecting those areas of particular interest and reviewing sections repeatedly if desired. Technical specifications are available to those interested in the figures, and suitably persuasive ad copy is available for those who want a more general sell. The interactive format provides some of the question-and-answer advantages of telemarketing, but places the process entirely in the hands of the user.

CD-ROM

A diskette is a powerful mass-information storage medium, but it pales in comparison with the compact disk with read-only memory (CD-ROM), an up-and-coming medium for storing computer data.

CD-ROM employs the same format as the CDs now being used to provide digital-quality music for stereo systems. Instead of filling the disk with music, though, the CD-ROM stores information, which can then be read into a computer using a special-purpose CD player.

The quantity of data that fits on a CD-ROM is staggering. A single CD-ROM disk can store 550 megabytes of data—the equivalent of 1500 floppy disks, or 250,000 pages of typewritten text!

For a taste of the possibilities, consider a program recently introduced by Microsoft Corporation. The CD-ROM program called *Microsoft Bookshelf* combines a complete dictionary, a thesaurus, *The World Almanac, Bartlett's Familiar Quotations*, and a national ZIP-code directory on one CD-ROM disk—and all that fills up slightly less than half the capacity of the disk.

An additional advantage of CD-ROM is the relative sturdiness of the medium as compared with floppy disks. CD-ROMs are immune to traditional disk-crashing accidents, magnetic fields, dust, and the like.

At this writing the price of CD-ROM technology is still too high for home usage (over $1000), though there are already intriguing applications in the business environment. Donnelly Marketing Information Services now offers on CD-ROM a database containing demographic data for a quarter of a million neighborhoods in the United States. Honda is experimenting with automobile-parts catalogs on CD-ROM, and McGraw-Hill has combined its scientific encyclopedia and its scientific dictionary on CD-ROM

The technology bears careful watching by direct marketers. CD-ROM is like the interactive floppy disks described above in that it allows presentation of a large quantity of information to a prospective customer—and delivery according to personal preference, with sound and graphics included for dramatic effect. This could be the ultimate catalog format, presenting the equivalent of a store full of merchandise with absolutely complete descriptions available at the stroke of a key, and an indexing system to take the consumer directly to items of interest.

Videotext

A computer sitting lonely on the desktop is an effective means of delivering certain kinds of information. Attach it to a modem, though, and you have a powerful link to computer systems down the block or around the globe.

A modem is a relatively inexpensive device (costing as little as $100) which connects the computer to a telephone line, allowing data to be sent and received. This interactive connection allows personal computers to be linked to one another, or to large mainframes with a wealth of information stored in their databanks.

The widespread use of modems has led to the creation of a new interactive communications medium called *videotext*. Videotext services include home banking systems, which allow users to conduct financial transactions from their desktops, and informational services such as CompuServe and the Source, which provide reference information, make transactions such as travel reservations and home shopping, and allow social interaction with other users.

The growth of videotext systems has been relatively slow and, in many cases, painful. Knight-Ridder, Inc., and the Times Mirror Company each sank tens of millions of dollars into developing systems which simply could not attract enough subscribers to be profitable, and have since folded. Still, there are over a million videotext subscribers nationwide as of 1987, and that figure is growing annually at a healthy rate.

Major players in the current videotext scene include IBM and Sears, Roebuck, with their Trintex joint venture and AT&T, Chemical Bank, and Time, Inc., with the Covidea system. Where the videotext pioneers emphasized information services, the new generation is stressing transactional services, including shopping, as a means to achieve profitability.

Several strategies are involved in making videotext more accessible and more appealing to home users.

One such strategy is lowering the price of using the systems. Videotext users pay a per-minute fee for the time they are connected to the service, in addition to their regular telephone charges, and these costs can add up rapidly. By shifting the emphasis from information access to profitable sales transactions, the connect-time charges can be lowered, making system access more frequent and less burdensome.

Covidea is trying to reach out to those who feel they don't want or need a personal computer by providing a dedicated terminal for use strictly as a telecommunications device. As Francis J. Heffron, chairman and CEO of Covidea, explains it, "The consumer cost is under $100—a price comparable to that of a quality telephone." In fact, the terminal has been offered at under $50 in promotional programs to bank customers who can use it to hook up to Covidea bank-by-telephone services and access additional services as well.

Another development on the immediate horizon is the incorporation of computer graphics in the on-screen presentation. In the past, videotext systems have essentially been limited to transmitting words and figures, largely because many different computers with incompatible graphics standards will be connected with the same central mainframe computer system. A set of standards for sending computer graphics called *North American Presentation Level Protocol Syntax* (NAPLPS) has been developed, though, which overcomes this lack of compatibility. Trintex will employ this system to deliver high-resolution graphic images to its subscribers.

The technological development which could truly revolutionize computer communications, however, is Project Victoria, a system currently being tested by Pacific Bell. Project Victoria uses digital technology and existing telephone lines but increases the number of signals which can be carried simultaneously. With this system a single telephone line can handle two voice conversations and five data transmissions at once. At present, if a modem-equipped computer is on the line, the telephone is tied up. Project Victoria would change all that, opening the way to a rich, interactive information interchange to any home with a telephone.

Shopping by computer is already a reality, with services such as CompuStore offered through CompuServe and the Source. With the development of graphics-oriented systems and less expensive access, the computer could become a major channel of distribution. The computer connection provides complete product information, in a format as browsable as a catalog and absolutely up to date. Placing an order is a simple matter of answering questions that come up on your computer screen. And of course, all the purchase information produced in the transaction is easily captured and used to develop detailed marketing lists for future solicitation.

Improvements in IDM Tecniques

The basic skills and resources employed in developing integrated direct marketing campaigns are continually advancing. The following are just a few of the significant changes occurring as this book is being written.

Database Developments

"I've been in the mailing list business for 20 years and I've seen a lot more happen in the last few months than I've seen in the last 20 years."

The speaker is David W. Florence, chairman of Direct Media, Inc., addressing the Direct Marketing Association's 69th Annual Conference in 1986. He put his finger on a trend which shows no sign of letting up in the immediate future—the escalating pace of developments in the "list" business, which could more accurately be described today as the *database business*.

All the changes are incremental; there is no revolutionary discovery which is rewriting the rules of prospect selection. However, taken together, these developments do require a major rethinking of IDM opportunities, and should provide possibilities for profitable programs as the cost of information decreases.

Some of the changes taking place are discussed below.

New Sources of Data. Companies and institutions which traditionally have kept their lists to themselves are now offering this information to the direct marketing community. Citicorp is the first major financial institution to allow commercial access to its credit-card customer file for direct mailings. AT&T has also joined the fray with lists of recent service connections to identify new residents. Even the U.S. Postal Service reportedly plans to enter the list business, with its own list of address changes.

In addition to expanding the variety of available data, these new vendors bring greater competition to the marketplace, and there are indications that the price of accessing outside lists will come down as a result.

Greater Depth of Information. Direct marketers who want to use modern database-analysis techniques to define and refine their prospect selection require an increasingly detailed file on each name on the list. The list compilers are responding, combining information from several sources to produce an enriched list. For instance, a consumer list may now include information on favorite charities, income, product ownership or usage, investments, home ownership, and more, according to DMA experts.

The Citicorp list mentioned above, for example, will include more than the pertinent credit-card information. CCX Network, Inc., will "enhance" the list, adding information about age, income, family size, hobby interests, etc.

The Perils of Invasion of Privacy. All this information access is wonderful from the marketer's perspective, but the more sophisticated the database resource becomes, the greater the potential for governmental action in safeguarding the privacy of individual citizens. The privacy issue is a complex one, worthy of long and serious discussion. For our purposes here, it is enough to raise the red flag and preach watchfulness and restraint. Ask yourself, how much does the prospect *want* me to know about him or her? How much do *I* want a marketer to know about *me*?

As long as the information in our database resources is used for the purposes of increasing the relevance of our direct marketing offers, there should be little resistance on the part of the public. But imagine receiving a direct-mail letter saying something like this:

> Mr. Jones, your daughter Elizabeth is 13 years old now, and you will need extra money to send her to college. Yet you have less than $5000 in savings, your credit rating is only fair, and you make less than $40,000 a year. How do you plan to pay for your daughter's education? Acme Mutual Funds has the answer....

Chilling? Absolutely. In horrendous taste? Indisputably. Yet the very fact that this kind of information is available may lead some marketers to cross that line of good taste and discretion, and we all must be wary of this possibility.

The Direct Marketing Association established its Mail Preference Service in 1971, enabling those who do not want to receive direct mailings to have their names removed from commercial lists. A similar program for those who take offense at telemarketing solicitation began in 1985. Still, most people in the general public have never heard of these options, and there is undeniably a segment of the population that takes offense at receiving direct-response offers. As direct marketing continues to grow, and particularly as we apply IDM techniques to concentrate and intensify our contact with the most promising prospects, we must be extremely sensitive to this segment, or risk outside regulation.

Joan Throckmorton, president of Joan Throckmorton, Inc., summed up the problem nicely in an article for *Direct Marketing* magazine:[1]

> The growing computer information network that helps direct marketers be personal and caring and highly service-oriented can also become a weapon to be used against them if it is abused. Be careful how, and to what extent, you use personal data. (You want to make friends but don't be impudent. It's still a customer/business relationship. You're not one of the family.)

Direct-Marketing Creative Treatments Moving Upscale

The movement toward offering more expensive products and services through direct marketing, combined with the integration of direct response into established channels of distribution, has led to a continuing improvement in the quality of direct-response media. This is evidenced by higher production values overall and a new emphasis on the role of graphics in direct marketing media.

Advertising Age ran an interesting article on the topic in October 1986. A few comments from industry experts quoted in that article:

> New non-traditional users of direct marketing such as Bristol-Myers and other package goods advertisers are moving direct marketing closer to the elegance of general advertising.[2]

> Clients are applying the same aesthetics to direct marketing as they are to package goods advertising.[3]

> I think the blurring of the lines between advertising and direct marketing is great. I want to know who drew the lines and what's the benefit of drawing them?[4]

We would suggest that the lines were drawn along marketing specialty divisions, as opposed to perceived distinction on the part of the

---

[1]"Whither Direct Marketing?" *Direct Marketing*, October 1986, pp.80-86.

[2]Emily Soell, president, executive creative director, Rapp & Collins.

[3]Bill Butler, executive vice president, creative director, Wunderman, Ricotta & Klein.

[4]Jim Punkre, Caples award winner for DM creativity, president, Brainstorms.

public. Direct marketing draws on areas of expertise which are foreign to general advertising—concerns such as fulfillment, and customer service, and database management, and the production of mailing packages. This situation led to the development of a separate and distinct group of companies which are capable of handling these concerns. From the end user's perspective, though, the impression made by an image ad on television combines with the psychological response to a mailing or a telephone call from the same advertiser. Hence, the number of companies employing direct marketing distribution in addition to their advertising activities continues to grow. This inevitably will lead us to a new level of marketing consciousness—integrated marketing.

Integrated Marketing: The Ultimate Goal

This book has been written to address the conditions which exist today. We have focused our attention on enhancing the impact of diverse direct marketing channels to achieve maximum response with the greatest economic efficiency. While we have stressed the importance of designing creative materials which are consistent with the established tone and philosophy of a company's general advertising activities, we recognize the fact that, in today's business world, direct marketing is a specialty unto itself, a separate division which is only tangentially integrated with general advertising.

We don't think this artificial distinction should last much longer. As IDM becomes an increasingly important channel of distribution in both business-to-business and consumer marketing, the need to maximize response will inevitably lead to general advertising which is strategically integrated with direct response.

Direct marketing will not replace advertising. The two disciplines serve different functions in the marketing process. However, the two must increasingly be used in a complementary manner. This can only occur when senior management makes the commitment to business planning which incorporates the broad spectrum of marketing activities from the start, and encourages the development of unified messages and delivery systems. That goal is integrated marketing, the next logical step. Those who grasp the lessons of IDM, and work now to expand their capabilities in its implementation, will be well positioned for this next development.

8

Making It Work— A Management Checklist

To provide an organized framework for exploring and implementing integrated direct marketing techniques, we have prepared the following step-by-step checklist. These steps are roughly chronological, although the actual process will vary depending on the nature of your company, your marketing goals, and the current level of direct marketing expertise and involvement.

1. Develop your personal knowledge of direct marketing as a whole, and the IDM philosophy and methodology in particular.

2. Determine the core elements of strategic planning as they relate to your company. These questions include:

   - Who are we as a company?
   - Where are we?
   - What future do we want for our company?
   - How are we going to achieve these goals?

3. Explore the present and future impact of direct marketing on your industry:

   - Does direct marketing by competitors represent a significant threat to your market share?
   - Does direct marketing represent a new opportunity for your company's growth by opening up a new channel of distribution?

4. Identify the leading direct marketers in your product category, customer base, or both, and analyze how they are presently utilizing direct marketing techniques:

- What competitive advantages (lower price, ease of purchase, etc.) are the leading direct marketers focusing on in your product category?

5. Consider the areas in which integrated direct marketing can improve your present business operations:

- Will IDM improve profitability?
- Pricing?
- Customer-service levels?
- Customers' access to or control of the sales process?

6. Select the individual who will serve as IDM manager. Consider the following prerequisites:

- Direct marketing experience
- Years with the company
- Entrepreneurial inclination
- Diplomatic skills

7. Consider hiring a consultant to assist in any or all of the following areas:

- Exploring potential areas for IDM deployment
- Developing marketing action plan
- Developing in-house resources
- Recommending outside vendor resources
- Creating and monitoring management communications systems
- Evaluating program results and recommending further action

8. Determine the level of market research required for effective decision making.

- What pertinent research findings already exist?
- What are the goals of your market-research activities? To provide basic direction? To determine specific creative approaches? To test the effectiveness of current efforts?

9. Develop a clear, detailed statement of direct marketing strategy. It should include the six "winning" factors identified by the Michael Allen Co.:

- Market focus
- Competitive advantage
- Integrated business equation

- Actionable, functional programs
- Resource concentration
- Aggressive implementation

10. Consider conflicts which may arise if direct marketing is employed as a separate distribution channel (as opposed to a means of supporting sales force or retail sales), and take steps to eliminate or minimize these conflicts.

11. Determine which products or services are best suited for promotion through integrated direct marketing. For each potential choice, consider the following:

   - What is the purpose of this product or service? How is it used? How does it work?
   - What are the benefits of this product or service? What problems does it solve? Does it save money? Time? Lives?
   - Who is the target audience? Who is in each target segment? Who is the end user? Who is the decision maker?
   - How much does the product or service cost? To what degree is price an issue?
   - How does it compare with competitive products?

12. Develop alternative offers that can be made to profitably market the product or service. Which of these offers is most compelling?

   - What type of guarantee will be offered?
   - What methods of payment are acceptable?
   - What payment terms can be offered?

13. Prepare a strategic IDM proposal including:

   - Statement of purpose
   - Summary of strategic considerations
   - Outline of steps required before and during implementation
   - Anticipated revenues
   - Budget estimate

14. Analyze the trade-offs entailed in utilizing outside direct marketing suppliers versus developing in-house capabilities:

   - Does the IDM plan effectively utilize available external and internal direct marketing experts and experience?

15. Determine the time frame for the IDM effort:

   - What are the near-term goals?
   - What are the long-term goals?

16. Obtain senior management's approval for the strategic proposal and agreement on the criteria which will be used for assessing success or failure of the enterprise.

17. Investigate the ways your company can best integrate direct marketing techniques and capabilities into the strategic marketing plan.

18. Calculate the value of a customer over time.

19. Develop the marketing action plan, working in conjunction with all affected departments. These may include, but are not limited to, the following:

    - Senior management
    - Sales and marketing departments
    - Finance
    - Legal
    - Data processing
    - Personnel
    - Customer service
    - Fulfillment

20. Develop database resources to precisely target marketing efforts:

    - Organize and analyze in-house customer files, and use the data to prepare a profile of purchaser performance.
    - Secure outside lists based on internal database-analysis and market-research data.
    - Implement a centralized information resource accessible to all relevant personnel.
    - Design systems for sharing data between marketing-media resources, adding up-to-date results from each to the central file.

21. Develop a media mix that will maximize response and minimize expense per order:

    - What are the intermediate goals that must be attained before a positive purchase decision can be achieved, and which media can best meet these individual requirements?
    - How can the interrelationships between media be structured to maximize their synergistic impact? In creative approach? In timing (i.e., response compression)?

22. Compile a "competitor file" of media and promotional materials used by your competitors. Learn from them.

23. Examine previous promotional materials:
    - Were they successful?
    - What were the reasons for their success or failure?
    - What elements can be picked up from existing promotional materials to create recognition and continuity in the minds of the target audience?

24. Create the consistent, focal statement of benefits that will be used throughout the media mix:
    - What are the "hot buttons" that will produce response?
    - What words and phrases does the customer use to describe your product or service?

25. Develop copy and graphics that integrate and coordinate across the media mix:
    - What is the total information required to make an informed purchase decision, and which media is best suited to carry each part of this message?
    - Are there testimonials available? Comparative test results against the competition?
    - Is the use of an endorser appropriate?
    - Should there be a premium offer?

26. Implement the program on a test basis.

27. Analyze results.

28. Fine-tune program elements, and retest with a larger universe.

29. Roll out the program to a wider prospect list if testing indicates profitability from a larger audience.

30. Review and assess the IDM capabilities developed in the course of creating and implementing the initial program, and look for additional areas where this expertise can be brought to bear.

Software for Direct Marketers

John Stevenson

Senior Vice President, Database Marketing,
Krupp/Taylor USA—Experts in Direct Marketing

I. Guidelines for Selection, Purchase, and Maintenance of Your Systems and Applications Software

Given the bewildering supply of software (and the "user-friendly" ideal which is still only rarely achieved), it is easy to make wrong choices. Software is rarely inexpensive and almost never returnable. Just breaking the seal of a microsystem package is typically a $200 to $2000 proposition, and it is tragic if the answer to one's needs proves not to be inside.

Therefore, experts approach the subject of computer purchase with a simple but powerful rule:

1. First, clearly determine your *needs* or end purpose.

2. Next, locate the software, or choice of software, that meets the need. (And be honest about any failure to do so, or near misses.)

3. Only then—and last—buy the hardware which is able to run that software.

Software selection is the crux of the matter.

The General Categories of Software

The computer is only a box in which to run software. Without a program it is useless and passive.

There are two kinds of software. *Operating-system* software runs the machinery and may add to it certain special functions. Some minimal amount of this may be built into the machine, but most is on disks (or tapes), which are read into the computer as needed. Operating-system software allows manipulation of the system's resources (files and input-output devices) without the need, generally, for a user to understand how they are all structured; and it provides "languages" and utilities which permit the user to create or rewrite programs, for new functions.

Applications software, as implied by its name, provides the user with specific, useful end products for the computing process.

Choosing a System, Rationally

In real life—whether or not all the issues are resolved—more computers are going to be acquired. Here is a pragmatic, workable approach to testing the validity of the investment and carrying it through.

A. Cost-Benefit Equation. Any computer acquisition should have a reason. There will be times when valid reasons exist in the absence of a quantifiable way to support them, but such times are actually rare. Most installations can be a result of steely-eyed business planning, and of course they should be.

Good management usually will require a rationale based on productivity and profit. The burden is on the would-be system buyer and user, to be able to respond with a businesslike cost-benefit statement. This drill is also essential, not only to satisfy management's questions but as an excellent way to sort out the array of choices in the buying decision as well.

In an orderly progression, the steps we would suggest, to arrive at a valid cost-performance ratio, are these:

1. *Determine the operation the computer will be used for.* We encountered this primary rule earlier. Now we are interested in attaching a number.

2. *Determine what the anticipated savings will be upon obtaining a system appropriate to the need.* This number, usually expressed as a yearly figure, should include such considerations as *human time* and *error reduction,* as well as application-dependent figures such as *better reaction time,* say, in media buying or inventory control.

3. *(a) Calculate the return on investment; (b) determine the amount that can be accommodated in a budget, to pay for the machine each year.* As a rule of thumb, item b should range between 40 and 70 percent of item a. This allowable cost must include not only the *amortization or lease expense* of the system but also the *costs of media, disks, and supplies; software updates; consulting assistance; etc.* And also, one must quantify and put a price tag on the *additional people time, at future wages,* which the system will require, during the learning phases as well as for ongoing operation. Another factor entering the calculation is the system's *salvage value* at replacement time. Again, as a rule of thumb, a system can be expected to be replaced in about 3 years (not because it is worn out, but from obsolescence).

4. *The numbers can then be modified for certain corporate intangibles.* Such as "public-relations value of computerization." This is the black-magic area.

If done carefully, the combination of true price (as calculated above) and the measures of performance (not forgetting hardware and software support, or lack of same) will reduce the number of choices to a manageable few candidates and provide justification for the outright investment, at the same time.

B. The Decision-Making Process. The next line of reasoning attempts to reduce that narrowed-down number of cost-effective alternatives to one choice, for the final buying decision. Below are the key elements of that process.

1. *The staff person or persons who will actually use the system should be involved in the selection process.* This need not be for technical reasons, but to give the end user a chance to try out the machine and get a true "feel" for it. This process helps in selection, according to the subtle—but ultimately valid—differences in comfort, accessibility, "friendliness," and so on, and it also involves the end user in the success of the procurement and installation process.

2. *Relate the systems to the peripherals carefully in terms of functions, variety, costs, compatibility, etc.* Some systems provide for many choices. Others are so idiosyncratic that these "back-end" limitations are a reason for eliminating them from consideration.

3. *Consider the flexibility of the system and its position in the mainstream.* Some systems are orphans. Some are not. Some obsolesce soon. All the rest, later. A system's flexibility and longevity are functions of its maker, its design components and bus structure, the type of microprocessor and chips inside, the type of operating system used, the fi-

nancial health and track record of the maker, the maker's reputation for quality control and support, and of course, the enthusiasm of the user as well. Is there software for the computer? Is there enough? Is there more and more?

4. *Weigh the reputation of the maker and seller; avoid the first editions of anything.*   This is common sense, balanced by experience: whenever possible, the wise give the luckless time to find and fix the "bugs," before buying.

5. *Emphasize support and recourse, and be sure they exist.*   In this area, the dealer is at least as important as (or more important than) the manufacturer. Warranties should be included and validated. Help for the inevitable glitches and questions should always be available by telephone, and in person, and at the buyer's site if necessary. The buyer should expect notices of updates and upgrades. If the machinery is expensive or needed for critical tasks, service contracts should be considered, as well.

6. *Consider the working environment.*   Are there special problems (dust, heat, cold)? If possible, a computer should be on its own grounded circuit, with its own circuit breaker. Some installations will require power-conditioning equipment, such as surge protectors or standby power supplies. The machinery must be well ventilated. Static electricity is a common problem; it can cause data losses and even destroy microchips. Computers also generate radio interference, which occasionally can be troublesome to other equipment nearby. These limitations can affect the buying decision, as well as how or where the equipment is used (or whether it can be used at all).

Selection of Software

As emphasized earlier, software is the single most potent factor in the choice of hardware. Therefore, the selection process should be given the greatest care possible—all the more, since there are so many choices to be made.

The following considerations are offered to help the business planner make informed and judicious software choices:

1. *Analyze your present needs.*   Computer programs often have a great deal of flexibility, but each has its strong and weak points, and each is best for specific tasks. A program can actually be "too powerful" for a particular need—cumbersome and cluttered with unnecessary features, hard to learn, hard to use.

2. *Analyze your future needs.*   Needs tend to grow rapidly, and to fill and exceed available hardware and software capabilities. (For example,

if you need to maintain a file of 2300 customers today, a program that can handle 4000 is probably too small.)

3. *Analyze your equipment in relation to the program.* Will the program work properly on your personal computer as it is presently configured? Or will you have to add more memory, or a color graphics board, or a new coprocessor chip? Can the program be copied, or will it always have to be run on the original disk?

4. *Analyze your particular environment.* Will one person or many people use the program? If employees will use the software, consider the rate of turnover. Will audit trails or password protection be necessary for sensitive data?

5. *Analyze the program's features.* What does the software do, and what does it not do? Which of these abilities are necessary for your needs, which would be nice, and which would get in the way?

6. *Analyze the program's ease of use.* Does it need special installation, or customizing for your situation? Or can you just load it and start running it immediately? How difficult is the program to learn and use?

7. *Examine the documentation closely and critically.* This will be the primary source of information that orients, trains, and supports the user. It should help in gaining an understanding of the program, not just teach it by rote. The better programs include a tutorial that cover the sorts of tasks for which they will be used. The documentation should provide complete and efficient assistance whenever a question arises; this means a good table of contents and a good index.

8. *Find out about available support.* The word *support* has two meanings—one before you buy, and another after. Training (and the degree of it) can be important: but who will do it? And will the dealer answer questions as they arise? For how long? Is there an 800-number technical-support number for the manufacturer? If so, test it. Can you get through? Are the technical-support personnel really helpful when you reach them? Find out also about future support for the program—not only in its present form but also for updates. If bugs are found or new enhancements added, what will the new version cost you?

9. *Analyze software reviews.* Reviewers are reasonably objective and experienced (although their needs and perspectives may not be the same as the buyer's).

10. *Try it.* Whatever the program, feed it enough data to test it adequately, preferably using some of your own work.

Following the above steps reasonably well should help you to narrow your choices to two or three programs for a given application. Then some thinking about price, presentation, etc., will produce the final decision.

II. A Directory of Direct Marketing Systems and Applications

Listed below are some direct-marketing systems and software that are currently available. New commercial packages are rapidly coming on the market, and so this listing cannot be all-inclusive (nor is it an endorsement).

A. Systems

1. Advertising Management
   Data Directions, Inc.
   1705 Analog
   Richardson, TX 75081
   (214) 637-1767

   An integrated system (Xenix) for advertising-agency media and billing functions.

2. Arclist
   Arc Tangent, Inc.
   923 Olive Street, P.O. Box 2009
   Santa Barbara, CA 93120
   Cathy Wolfe, (805) 965-7277

   A list-management system for IBM-PC/XT/AT and compatibles with multiple output formats. Carrier-route, zip + 4, bulk-rate sorting, bag tags, etc. Dupe identification, merge-purge, nth-name selection.

3. Broker/Owner Orders Management
   D-J Associates, Inc.
   P.O. Box 2048
   Ridgefield, CT 06877
   Richard Josephs, (203) 431-8777

   Order entry, analysis, invoicing, and accounting system for list brokerages and list management.

4. The Controller—Mail Order Inventory Tracking System
   Sigma/Micro Corporation

1238 North Pennsylvania
Indianapolis, IN 46250
Al Langsenkamp, (317) 631-0907
An integrated system (UNIX 7300) for up to 99 multicompany oper-
ations, utilizing the same or separate inventories.

5. The Correspondent: Direct Sales Lead Tracking System
   Selkirk Associates, Inc.
   338 Newberry Street
   Boston, MA 02115
   Martin Kane

Personalized direct-mail correspondence, list management and tracking for customer relations, lead generation, telemarketing.

6. Direct Marketing Work Station
   Insight Marketing Systems, Inc.
   401 Commonwealth Avenue
   Boston, MA 02215
   Paul DuBois, (617) 353-1757

A hardware-installed system which supports direct-marketing campaigns, lead tracking, market segmentation, and list maintenance for up
to 150,000 names. Links with MDR and CCX on-line inquiry and list
order-entry systems.

7. Fastfax
   LCS Industries, Inc.
   120 Brighton Road
   Clifton, NJ 07012
   (201) 778-5588

A list- and database-fulfillment ordering system, in an on-line environment. Generates demographic counts, profiles, and segment selections.

8. Future Tech II—Telephone Order Entry Module
   Lesifco, Inc.
   100 Fifth Avenue
   Waltham, MA 02154
   Jackie Massan, (617) 893-2270

An order-input system, for entries while the customer is on the line.
The program can suggest substitutes for out-of-stock items or recommend complementary products.

9. Infomark Laser PC System—Demographic Analysis
   National Decision Systems
   539 Esconitas Boulevard, Box 9007

Encinitas, CA 92024
Rich Farrell, (619) 942-7000

Optical laser-disk storage system incorporating six databases, including geodemographic segmentation, shopping center data, and color mapping. Analyzes and reports demographic and marketing information for any U.S. location.

10. Mail Order Pro
Professional Publications, Inc.
P.O. Box 199
San Carlos, CA 94070
(415) 593-9119

Mail-order fulfillment and inventory control. On-line entry, with everything related to the customer automatically adjusted.

11. Marketfax
LCS Industries, Inc.
120 Brighton Road
Clifton, NJ 07012
(201) 778-5588

A PC-based sales-support system. Allows data management at the branch-office level, or integrates with the main database; assigns leads to the sales force and tracks the subsequent contacts.

12. Marketmanager—Lead Generation and Tracking System
CCX Network, Inc.
301 Industrial Boulevard
Conway, AR 72032
Carolyn Nankervis, (501) 329-6836

Integrated software for managing coupon, telemarketing, or sales-force leads. Generates contact calendars and maintains and categorizes customer records.

13. Marketmanager Plus—Database Management for Larger Files
CCX Network, Inc.
Accepts converted data from mainframe into a PC database.

14. MOME—Mail Order Management System
International Software Technology, Inc.
1112 Seventh Avenue
Monroe, WI 53566
John Grochola, (608) 328-8870

Support for customer order entry and fulfillment, with functions in processing, inventory control, packing and shipping, and list management.

15. MORE
     Persoft, Inc.
     600 West Cummings Park
     Woburn, MA 01801
     Bill Small, (617) 935-0095

Mainframe application; large house-file analysis and targeting software, for selecting best customers and prospects. Employs name-by-name scoring and ranking which uses all available data.

16. MORE/2
     Persoft, Inc.
     Bill Small, (617) 935-0095

A modification of the MORE application, licensed to selected service bureaus on a royalty fee.

17. Name Base
     ExecuComp Inc.
     620 South Belmont Avenue
     Indianapolis, IN 46221
     (317) 639-2289

Mail-order entry, inventory control, and fulfillment management.

18. PC Mail Order System for Small Companies
     Professional Business Solutions, Inc.
     4719 West 69th Terrace
     Shawnee Mission, KS 66208
     Dan Adler, (913) 677-1024

A single order entry automatically controls all other functions: sales journals, pick-pack tickets, inventory control, master customer-list maintenance, and source code analysis.

19. People Trak—Membership and Donor Management
     Noesis Computing Company
     615 Third Street
     San Francisco, CA 94107
     Bob Walters, (415) 495-7440

A member and donor database management system. Profiles and tracks donor information, interests, transactions. Produces direct-mail letters and mailing labels.

20. R:BASE 5000
     MicroRIM, Inc.
     1750 112th Street, N.E.
     Bellevue, WA 98004
     (206) 453-6017

Relational database-management system which can handle up to 40 files and 100 billion records.

21. Response
    CoLinear Systems, Inc.
    P.O. Box 11562
    Atlanta, GA 30355
    Lloyd Merriam, (404) 433-3217

A database-management system for mail order, telemarketing, demographic analysis, order history archiving, and prospect management.

22. Spectrum—Market Segmentation and Targeting
    Claritas Corporation
    201 North Union Street
    Alexandria, VA 22314
    Patricia O'Brien, (703) 683-8300

Links the user to a proprietary system of geodemographic market segmentation and targeting by neighborhood type, for profiling, graphics, and direct-response analysis.

23. Statmap
    Rand McNally Infomap
    P.O. Box 7600
    Chicago, IL 60680
    Jeff Carter, (800) 332-RAND

Map-making software for visualizing U.S. demographic and census statistics.

24. The Target-Zip Demographic Retrieval System
    CACI, Inc.
    310 Madison Avenue, Suite 1804
    New York, NY 10017
    Alan Michaels, (212) 370-0440

Current and 5-year demographic forecasts for characteristics, providing purchase-potential indices for selected product and service categories. Aggregates to best-customer zip codes.

25. Telemarketing Online
    Whelan Associates Incorporated
    P.O. Box 650
    Spring House, PA 19477
    (215) 643-7470

Real-time telephone sales and marketing system. Provides multiple windows of information for the operator. Adapts to existing data processing systems.

26. Datatrak Direct Marketing System
    Travis DataTrak, Inc.
    Riverside Office Park, Suite 201
    Weston, MA 02193
    (617) 891-6365

Prospect profiling, lead processing and sales follow-up reporting, prospect targeting, promotion analysis, and letter preparation.

27. Quick Order Processor
    Nashbar Associates, Inc.
    4111 Simon Road
    Youngstown, OH 44512
    Howard Jesko, (216) 542-2828

A multiuser hardware and software system for mail order, which handles order entry, inventory control, credit-card processing, shipping, on-line customer service, mailing-list management, back orders, and reports.

B. Templates and Vertical Software

28. Basic Campaign Budget Planner
    Passavant & Quick, Inc.
    193 Main Street, P.O. Box 1206
    Middletown, CT 06457
    (804) 361-1270

A Lotus template which allows for up to 45 front-end and back-end planning assumptions. Each automatically recalculates profit and loss (P&L) for a complete campaign, and up to four scenarios can be compared side by side.

29. The Direct Mail Planner—Subscription or Product Direct Marketing
    Lighthouse Software, Inc.
    575 Madison Avenue, Suite 1006
    New York, NY 10022
    Don Nicholas, (212) 605-0286

A Lotus template which generates list plans based on history of cost and availability, against goals of campaign net orders and P&Ls. Provides revised performance reports and budgets from each set of assumptions; also bid requests, list orders, and specifications.

30. Direct Mail Test Assistant
    SPSS, Inc.
    444 North Michigan Avenue

Chicago, IL 60611   ♠
(312) 329-3500

Applies regression analysis to predict response rates, cost per response, and profit per thousand mailed. Evaluation of risk and return for alternative strategies.

31. Fastpak—Mailing List System for Small House Lists
    DHA Systems, Inc.
    832 Jury Street
    San Jose, CA 95112

Simple, inexpensive, yet powerful list-management capability. Names can be keyed and sorted by attributes. The program generates personalized fill-ins for letters, and performs mail-merge functions.

32. Financial Model for a New Continuity Venture
    Canova & Company
    7704 Alstaff Road
    McLean, VA 22102
    (703) 893-1410

Captures the key financial factors of a business to generate a 5-year P&L balance sheet, cash flow and return on investment (ROI) reports, and sensitivity analyses with individual P&Ls.

33. Postman
    Mom's Software
    P.O. Box 19418
    Portland, OR 97219-0418
    (503) 244-9173

Translates mailing-package weight into appropriate postage, and shows data for alternative carriers.

34. Pubsight—Magazine Circulation, Earned
    Income and Cash Receipts Forecasting
    Historical Times, Inc.
    P.O. Box 8200
    Harrisburg, PA 17105
    David McCoy, (717) 657-9555

Handles over 20 different circulation sources, each with up to three offers, using standard and nonstandard source production. Generates ABC circulation; analyzes magazine start-ups and acquisitions.

35. The Publishing Model—Magazine/Newsletter Publishing
    Lighthouse Software, Inc.
    575 Madison Avenue, Suite 1006

New York, NY 10022
Don Nicholas, (212) 605-0286

A Lotus template which captures circulation print orders; ad revenues and earned income; and expenses for promotion, fulfillment, production, and overhead. Reports cash flow and P&Ls, with print order and paid circulation.

Bibliography

Books

Baier, Martin: *Elements of Direct Marketing*, McGraw-Hill, New York, 1985.

Caples, John: *Tested Advertising Methods*, Prentice-Hall, Englewood Cliffs, N.J., 1974.

Cohen, William A.: *Building a Mail Order Business: A Complete Manual for Success*, John Wiley & Sons, New York, 1985.

Direct Marketing Creative Guild: *Direct Marketing Design: The Graphics of Direct Mail and Direct Response Marketing*, PBC International, Glen Cove, N.Y., 1985.

Gosden, Freeman F.: *Direct Marketing Success*, John Wiley & Sons, New York, 1985.

Gottlieb, Richard: *Directory of Mail Order Catalogs*, Grey House Publishing, Sharon, Pa., 1984.

Harper, C. R.: *Mailing List Strategies*, McGraw-Hill, New York, 1986.

Hill, Lawson Traphagen: *How to Build a Multi-Million Dollar Mail Order Business by Someone Who Did*, Prentice-Hall, Englewood Cliffs, N.J., 1984.

Hodgson, Richard B.: *Direct Mail and Mail Order Handbook*, Dartnell, Chicago, 1980.

Hoge, Cecil B.: *Mail Order Know How*, Ten Speed Press, Berkeley, Ca., 1982.

Kobs, Jim: *Profitable Direct Marketing*, Crain Books, Chicago, 1979.

Lewis, Hershell Gordon: *Direct Mail Copy that Sells*, Prentice-Hall, Englewood Cliffs, N.J., 1984.

Muldoon, Katie: *Catalog Marketing: The Complete Guide to Profitability in the Catalog Business*, R. R. Bowker, New York, 1984.

Nash, Edward: *Direct Marketing: Strategy, Planning, Execution*, McGraw-Hill, New York, 1982.

——— : *The Direct Marketing Handbook*, McGraw-Hill, New York, 1984.

Ogilvy, David: *Ogilvy on Advertising*, Crown Publishers, New York, 1985.

Posch, Robert J.: *Direct Marketers' Legal Advisor*, McGraw-Hill, New York, 1982.

Rapp, Stan, and Tom Collins: *Maximarketing*, McGraw-Hill, New York, 1987.

Ries, Al, and Jack Trout: *Marketing Warfare*, McGraw-Hill, New York, 1983.

——— and ——— : *Positioning: The Battle for Your Mind*, McGraw-Hill, New York, 1980.

Roman, Murray: *Telemarketing Campaigns that Work*, McGraw-Hill, New York, 1983.

——— : *Telephone Marketing: How to Build Your Business by Telephone*, McGraw-Hill, New York, 1976.

Simon, Julian L.: *How to Start and Operate a Mail-Order Business*, McGraw-Hill, New York, 1980.

Stern, Edward: *The Direct Marketing Market Place*, Hilary House Publishing, Hewlett, N.Y., 1986.

Stone, Bob, and John Wyman: *Successful Telemarketing*, National Textbook, Chicago, 1986.

Stone, Robert: *Successful Direct Marketing Methods*, Crain Books, Chicago, 1984.
Throckmorton, Joan: *Winning Direct Response Advertising*, Prentice-Hall, Englewood Cliffs, N.J., 1986.
Witek, John: *Response Television: Combat Advertising of the 1980s*, Crain Books, Chicago, 1981.

Periodicals

Advertising Age, Crain Communications, 740 North Rush Street, Chicago, IL 60611. Weekly, $57 per year.
AdWeek's Marketing Week, A/S/M/ Communication, Inc., 49 East 21st Street, New York, NY 10010. Published 64 times a year, $50.
Catalog Age, 6 River Bend, P.O. Box 4949, Stamford, CT 06907. Monthly, unpaid.
Direct Marketing Magazine, 224 Seventh Street, Garden City, NY 11530. Monthly, $42 per year.
DM News, 19 West 21st Street, New York, NY 10010. Semimonthly, unpaid.
Marketing & Media Decisions, 1140 Avenue of the Americas, New York, NY 10036. Monthly, $45 per year.
Sales & Marketing Management, 633 Third Avenue, New York, NY 10017. Monthly, $36 per year.
Telemarketing, 17 Park Street, Norwalk, CT 06851. Monthly, $49 per year.

Index

ABOUT THE AUTHOR

Ernan Roman is president of the New York–based Ernan Roman Direct Marketing Corporation, a consulting firm specializing in integrated direct marketing campaigns.

His clients include Citibank, IBM, Christie's Art Auctioneers, Xerox, New York Telephone, Avis, Johnson & Johnson, and the Metropolitan Museum of Art.

An active member of the Direct Marketing Association (DMA), in 1979, Mr. Roman won the first Marketing Leader Award ever given by the DMA for a telemarketing campaign. In 1985 he earned the prestigious DMA Echo Award for outstanding consumer direct mail.

Mr. Roman's articles have appeared in numerous direct marketing publications, and he is among the contributors to *The Direct Marketing Handbook.* He has lectured at direct marketing seminars around the world and has taught marketing seminars for the American Management Association.